RODEHEAVER BOYS RANCH
STATEMENT OF FAITH

We believe that whatever the Bible says is true –
which means that we believe in the inspiration of both
the Old and New Testaments.
We believe that man was created by the direct act of God
and in the image of God. We believe that Adam and Eve,
in yielding to the temptation of Satan, became fallen creatures.
We believe that all men are born in sin.
We believe in the Incarnation, the Virgin Birth,
and Deity of our Lord and Savior, Jesus Christ.
We believe in His vicarious substitution in atonement
for the sins of mankind by the shedding of His Blood on the Cross.
We believe in the resurrection of His Body from the tomb,
His Ascension to Heaven, and that He is now our Advocate.
We believe that He is personally coming again.
We believe in His power to save men from sin.
We believe in the necessity of the New Birth, and that
this New Birth is through the regeneration by the Holy Spirit.
We believe that salvation is by grace through faith
in the atoning Blood of our Lord and Savior, Jesus Christ.
We believe that His creed is a sufficient basis for Christian fellowship,
and that all born-again men and women who sincerely
accept this creed can, and should, live together in peace,
and that it is their Christian duty to promote harmony
among the members of the Body of Christ, to be good stewards of the
material blessings with which they are provided,
and also to work together to get the Gospel
to as many people in the shortest time possible.

OUR MISSION

Rodeheaver Boys Ranch provides a

wholesome home environment with

religious, educational and vocational

training for at-risk boys.

These boys have no home of their own

because of parental death, desertion,

divorce, disability or dysfunction.

Rodeheaver Boys Ranch provides these

deserving young men a second chance

in life and an opportunity to build a

strong foundation for the future.

Rodeheaver Boys Ranch has been

carrying out this mission since 1950.

RODEHEAVER BOYS RANCH

"It is better to build boys than to mend men."

Founded 1950

Written by Susan D. Brandenburg

Edited by Lois Johnson

Published by Susan the Scribe, Inc.
www.susanthescribe.vp.web

ISBN: 978-0-9990882-9-6

Publication Design by Philip Barnes
Riverducks Design
riverducksdesign@gmail.com
Photography & Archival Scanning by
Philip Barnes & Susan D. Brandenburg

Rodeheaver Boys Ranch, Inc.
380 Boys Ranch Road
Palatka, Florida, USA 32177
(386) 328-1281
rodeheaverboys@gmail.com
www.rbr.org

Table of Contents

Acknowledgements: i

Introduction: The Man and His Vision iii

Chapter One: Celebrating 70 Years of Building Boys 1

Chapter Two: After Rody 7

Chapter Three: The Early Years – Biggers Chapel 47

Chapter Four: Loaves and Fishes................................... 71

Chapter Five: Welcome Home, Mr. and Mrs. Johnson 85

Chapter Six: Y2K ... And All Is Well................................... 111

Chapter Seven: A New Decade & A Firm Foundation................ 153

Chapter Eight: Tribute to Timothy Officer 187

Chapter Nine: Moving On – 2015-2019 203

Chapter Ten: 2020 – Forging Ahead Into the Future 239

Acknowledgements:

It is with deep gratitude that I pay tribute to those people who helped to make this book possible:

- Philip Barnes, Graphic Designer whose vast expertise and artistry transformed a manuscript of words and photos into this beautiful book.
- Lois Johnson, wife of retired Executive Director Ken Johnson, whose expertise in English combined with her memories of 23 years of Ranch Life, enabled her to edit this book.
- Lynn Moll, executive assistant to Ranch Trustee Carlton Spence, who contributed her editing expertise to this book.
- Sara Josephson, long-time executive assistant at Rodeheaver Boys Ranch, who contributed her editing expertise to this book.
- Andrea Jackson, graphic designer and companion to Ruby Spence, who contributed her editing expertise to this book.

As a professional biographer, one of the great honors and joys of my life has been chronicling the history of Rodeheaver Boys Ranch in two books – the first published in 2013 and the second in this 70th Anniversary year of 2020. As a member of the Rodeheaver Boys Ranch family for more than a decade, I have had the privilege of knowing the Board, Staff and Boys well and, through them, deepening my personal relationship with my Lord Jesus Christ. God has blessed me with the gift of words and allowed me to use this precious gift to write the stories of His people.

This book is a tribute to His power and glory.

Susan D. Brandenburg

Susan the Scribe, Biographer

INTRODUCTION:
THE MAN AND HIS VISION

In the late 1940s, Homer Rodeheaver rode horseback over a piece of prime, pristine acreage along the sparkling St. Johns River. He envisioned boys – many boys – living, hunting, fishing, learning, thriving and loving God on that beautiful unspoiled land destined to be called Rodeheaver Boys Ranch.

Homer Alvan Rodeheaver was born on October 4, 1880 in Hocking County, Ohio. He became one of the world's most beloved American pioneers of sacred music, evangelism and philanthropy.

Homer grew up in the Cumberland Mountains of Newcomb, near the town of Jellico, Tennessee. His father, Thurman, ran a furniture manufacturing company and sawmill. His family attended the Methodist Church and there, at an early age, Homer (or "Rody" as friends and family often called him) learned to play several musical instruments including the trombone, which was to become a golden, melodic symbol of his talent and tenacity. There was an innate leadership ability in Homer Rodeheaver that was enriched by his homespun sense of humor, worshipful spirit and compassionate heart.

Homer's mother, Fanny, died when he was just eight years old, instilling in him a lifelong empathy for other young boys who had also experienced the loss of a parent.

INTRODUCTION: THE MAN AND HIS VISION

Unlike many of the boys who have come to Rodeheaver Boys Ranch over the past 70 years, though, Homer was blessed with a father whose strong faith in Jesus Christ kept his sons on the straight path and his family together.

At age nine, little Rody got his first job, hitching a rickety sled to his father's blind old horse and hauling groceries from the railroad station to his uncle's store for ten cents a load. The gift of entrepreneurship was just one more of God's blessings bestowed on him and he used that blessing to turn money into good works for the rest of his life. While still a teenager working in his father's sawmill hauling lumber, Homer heard the spirituals of negro laborers on the railroad track and saw the power of music. "They sang at work and at play, with a special peculiar tempo for every mood," he said. "They could make themselves happy or sad, simply by changing the rhythm of their songs; they could make labor slow or fast, easy or hard." The power of music to enrich the human spirit was in him. He wanted to share it with the world.

In 1898, Homer was working his way through Ohio Wesleyan University as a music student when he heard the call to go to the Spanish-American War and help his fellow man. He served in Cuba with the Tennessee Fourth Regiment, soothing the souls of fellow soldiers by playing his trombone. During World War I, he served with the Y.M.C.A., encouraging troops with hymns and gospel songs. There was a difference between hymns and gospel songs, Rody insisted, "Gospel songs are addressed to the people; hymns to God."

Homer Rodeheaver was song leader for Dr. W. E. Biederwolf in Winona Lake, Indiana when he caught the eye and ear of famed evangelist Billy Sunday, who hired the young musician in 1910. For the next two decades, Sunday and Rodeheaver won souls for Christ throughout the country with sermon and song. They were the most famous revival team of

Homer Rodeheaver and Billy Sunday

the early 20th Century, leading millions of people to the Lord Jesus Christ. Later, Homer Rodeheaver immortalized their dramatic ministry by writing a book entitled *Twenty Years with Billy Sunday.*

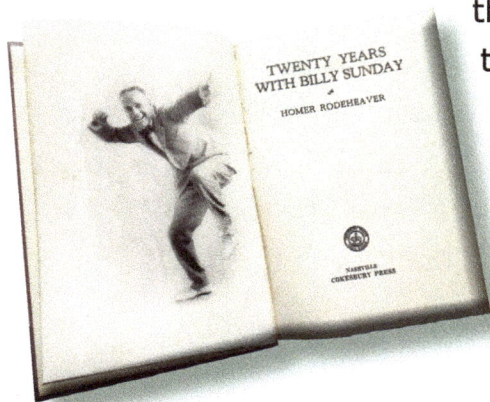

A man who always went the extra mile, Homer joined his brothers in founding The Rodeheaver Publishers of Sacred Music in Chicago, originally as a means to provide Billy Sunday's campaigns with sheet music. The Chicago company expanded so rapidly that by 1912, they had opened an eastern headquarter in Philadelphia and by 1938, merged with Hall-Mack Publishing Company of Philadelphia to become Rodeheaver Hall-Mack Publishers of Sacred Music. A Los Angeles branch was also opened later, with the symbol of the firm being a rainbow arched over a line of musical notes from Homer Rodeheaver's theme song, "Every Cloud Will Wear a Rainbow if Your Heart Keeps Right."

By the mid-1920s, Homer's home, Rainbow Point on Winona Lake, Indiana, became known the world-over as a welcoming place of fun and fellowship. Guests visited Homer Rodeheaver from around the world, and he entertained them royally whether they were statesmen, celebrities, taxi drivers or under-privileged children. He provided a slide that extended out from the sundeck into the lake below. Many guests enjoyed hilarious fun sliding on it until humorist Will Rogers wrote about it and so many visitors came that it had to be removed for fear the entire house would collapse under their weight.

Homer also owned the Westminster Hotel in Winona Lake, which eventually housed his publishing company. Each summer, he would direct his annual Sacred Music Festival at the huge Billy Sunday Tabernacle, training hundreds of choir directors, evangelistic song leaders, soloists, instrumentalists and others in the religious music field.

An avid sportsman, Homer "Rody" Rodeheaver loved to play tennis and golf, hunt, fish and ride horseback. He was instrumental in forming the Tennessee Walking Horse Association at Shelbyville, Tennessee, and later owned and raced quarter horses in Florida.

A man who believed in happy Christianity, Homer Rodeheaver's hearty laugh was nearly as famous as his singing voice. He had the unique ability to move folks from laughter to prayer to serious thought to song and, as such, his songs of salvation and his practical, often hilarious, object lessons were all wrapped up in Christian living. Homer had a penchant for breaking out into song whenever the spirit moved him and when he met John D. Rockefeller on the golf course, the two men stopped golfing long enough to join in singing, "I'll Go Where You Want Me to Go, Dear Lord."

Homer Rodeheaver was admired for many qualities such as his unflagging enthusiasm, good will, energy, sense of humor and hospitality, and especially his ability to encourage thousands of people to raise their voices in song. He was the man chiefly responsible for starting the American custom of Easter Sunrise Services. Christian holidays were especially dear to him, and he is known to have captured the spirit of St. Nicholas for the Union Mission Christmas Party in Washington D.C., and, accompanied by the U.S. Navy Band, led 1600 children in song while Mrs. Eleanor Roosevelt distributed gifts. He followed that Christmas tradition for nine years.

Excerpts from Homer's 1949 collection of jokes and humorous stories entitled "F'r Instance," are highlighted in the introduction to this history of Rodeheaver Boys Ranch, a fitting tribute to the man, his heart, his humor and his most ambitious dream of helping needy boys in a warm, healthy Christian environment.

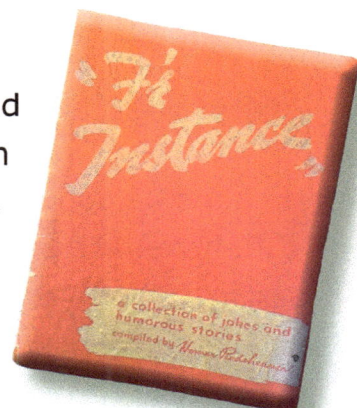

As Homer became prosperous enough to put his dream into action, there were several close friends who helped him along the way. These friends, he fondly called "Pardners," and the late Bruce Howe of Winona Lake, Indiana was one of the most devoted "Pardners" to Homer and to the boys.

At age 19, Bruce Howe applied for a job with Homer Rodeheaver. "The entire job interview consisted of three questions," Howe later remembered. "Do you smoke?

It's been said of Columbus that when he started out, he didn't know where he was going; when he got there, he didn't know where he was; and when he came back, he didn't know where he had been. Homer Rodeheaver, "F'r Instance"

Bruce Howe

Do you drink? Do you plan to?" His firm "No, sir!" earned him a job at $17.50 a week, and a dear friend in Homer Rodeheaver. When World War II came along, Howe went into the Army and "Mr. Homer" went to the train station to see him off. He gave Howe two New Testaments – one old and one new. In the new one, he wrote, "I know you'll be a good soldier. I'm counting on it." Howe took those two Bibles with him into the Battle of the Bulge, earning five battle stars at Omaha Beach.

In 1945, "Mr. Homer" took Bruce Howe to Florida on a hunting, fishing and golfing trip. They stayed in Homer's Rainbow Ranch in Palatka, Florida. Howe, an honorary board member of Rodeheaver Boys Ranch until his death at age 95 in 2015, remembered a day in 1947 when he and "Mr. Homer" were riding horseback to their favorite fishing spot on the Ranch – Horse Landing on the St. Johns River. Pausing for their horses to drink, Homer turned in his saddle and gestured expansively toward that picturesque, valuable parcel of land bordering the river. "Bruce," he said, "This would be a good place for the boys' ranch." It is the exact location of Rodeheaver Boys Ranch today.

Rodeheaver's Rainbow Ranch was the focal point of his dream to establish a sanctuary for homeless, wayward boys – boys like the ones he had seen on the streets of cities across the land where he had played his golden trombone. He had been purchasing tracts of land in and around what was once the sawmill town of Rodman, near Palatka, Florida. With his eventual goal being to set aside a portion of the land for a boys' ranch, he established a huge and profitable cattle, timber and sawmill operation which was headquartered in the old Rodman farmhouse. He partnered with Harry Westbury, the former Putnam County agricultural agent who had helped him locate a great deal of the acreage. Harry and his wife, Mickey Westbury, moved into the Rodman farmhouse and ran Rainbow Ranch for several years while Homer was on the sawdust trail of evangelism. Over the years, at Homer's urging, the Westbury's took in several homeless boys, exchanging their hard work for food and shelter, and giving them an extra boost toward finishing school.

Homer cemented his plan after a visit to Father Flanagan, Founder of Boys Town in Nebraska and came back to Florida in 1949 to share his vision with Harry Westbury and a select group of influential people that he hoped would support him going forward. Sitting around the kitchen table at the old Rodman farmhouse, Homer outlined his plan for a boys' ranch. With the support of several "Pardners," including the late Tommy Clay of Palatka who was there at that first meeting and remained a lifelong partner of the Ranch, the property was deeded and a choice 320 acre piece of land overlooking historic Horse Landing

The original Rainbow Ranch House

on the St. Johns River became the first site of Rainbow Ranch for Boys. The site quickly expanded to 790 acres and Homer Rodeheaver began to actively recruit "Pardners" for his beloved boys ranch at every revival and wherever he roamed.

Dick Westbury, Harry and Mickey Westbury's nephew, recalled moving to Rodeheaver's Rainbow Ranch house in 1950 and meeting "Mr. Rody." He recalls that, "George Burke, the first Ranch boy, stayed in my bedroom at the old farmhouse for a while." After Westbury got to know Mr. Rodeheaver, he was invited to spend the summers of his college years in Winona Lake, Indiana, working as a bell hop at the Westminster Hotel. "Mr. Rody was a wonderful man," remembered Dick. "... I knew he was concerned about my progress in education and he always took the time to be friendly."

Later, in 1965, Dick Westbury wrote an article that ran in *Daytona Beach News Journal's All Florida Magazine* with the headline, "Thirty Boys Are the Top Hands at Rodeheaver Ranch Where Today's Youngsters Are Helped to Better Manhood Tomorrow." Westbury quoted Bishop Arthur J. Moore of Atlanta, Georgia, who said, "Here is a vibrant Christian service station dedicated to needy boys. Its ideals and aims are the same to which Rody dedicated his entire life."

> *LENDING EAR*
> *Magistrate:*
> *"I understand that you overheard the quarrel between the defendant and his wife?"*
> *Witness:*
> *"Yes, sir."*
> *Magistrate:*
> *"Tell me, if you can, what he seemed to be doing."*
> *Witness:*
> *"He seemed to be doing the listening!"*
> *Homer Rodeheaver,*
> *"F'r Instance"*

The last paragraph of Westbury's 1965 article followed a heart-felt plea for much-needed day-to-day funding, noting that Rodeheaver Boys Ranch was "wholly a non-profit organization ... supported entirely by voluntary contributions, adding to the contribution left by Homer Rodeheaver. Estimated annual cost per boy for housing, clothing, food and other services is $1,500.00." While Rodeheaver Boys Ranch remains a wholly non-profit organization supported entirely by voluntary contributions, the annual cost of raising a boy in 2020 has risen to more than 10 times that amount today and, sadly, the struggle for day-to-day funding continues.

But in June of 1950, after the land had been cleared with great purpose and hope by Homer Rodeheaver and several of his "Pardners," the State of Florida granted a charter to the new non-profit charitable organization, and Rainbow Ranch for Boys was recognized by the Internal Revenue Service. The first officers were Homer Rodeheaver, President, Jim Thomas (Homer's brother-in-law), Vice-President, Harry Westbury (Rodeheaver's Ranch Manager), Treasurer, and Harry F. Edwards (Chief Probation Counselor of the Juvenile Court in Orlando), Secretary.

George Burke the 1st Ranch boy

George Burke, the first Ranch Boy, was living at the old Rodman farmhouse with Harry and Mickey Westbury until a ranch building could be constructed. Homer Rodeheaver's vision had become a reality.

The first Annual Meeting of the board was held on January 23, 1951, at the old Rainbow Ranch farmhouse, attracting only fourteen people. That year, volunteer carpenters using lumber from the Rainbow Ranch sawmill, electricians and plumbers built the first cottage on the present site. It was a small wooden building with four rooms for the boys; it was named Biggers Hall in honor of Mrs. Helen Biggers, a donor. George Burke was joined there by two more boys, Barry Morrison and Clyde McKendree. The first cottage parents, Mr. and Mrs. Bob Catledge, were hired.

At the second Annual Meeting of the board in January of 1952, the Ranch's name was officially changed from Rainbow to Rodeheaver Boys' Ranch and the first license ever given by the State of Florida to a Boys Ranch was presented to Homer Rodeheaver by O. Marshall Dutton of the State Welfare Board. The group also participated in the dedication of Phillips Cottage, a new concrete block structure that had been built by the boys and volunteers, using funds donated by Ellis L. Phillips, an official with Con-Edison Electric in New York.

Yes, through the positive publicity generated by Homer Rodeheaver at every opportunity everywhere he traveled, word was getting out about the boys ranch in Florida.

While the Ranch was occupied by boys and cottages were being built, it was still located in an untamed wilderness, ten miles out of Palatka on a road that was nearly impossible to navigate when it rained. Cottage parents found living out there a challenge. The Catledges soon left, to be replaced by Dr. and Mrs. L. I. Jemison, then, in 1952, Mr. and Mrs. Lee Fisher.

The June 1953 edition of *Trucking Magazine* ran a four-page spread on the Ranch entitled "Wild Colts Make Fine Horses," calling it a "new deal" for neglected and underprivileged boys. Lee Fisher and his wife, Betty, were called "Uncle Lee and Aunt Betty," by writer Leigh Culley. When the article in *Trucking Magazine* came out, encouraging readers to become involved and to help Mr. Rodeheaver in supporting the Ranch, there were 24 boys there and applications for many more. "One has only to visit the Boys Ranch – and the gates are always open –

to see the wonder that is being worked," she wrote. "The fellows of the Ranch are making inspiring progress, becoming good citizens, good Christians, good young Americans." Happily, in 2020, the fellows of the Ranch continue to make inspiring progress in those three areas, and Grace still comes before Grits and Gravy in the Rodeheaver Boys Ranch Dining Hall.

**Grace before Grits and Gravy at mealtime on the Florida Ranch
where there's no such thing as an unwanted or neglected boy**

Barry Patrick Walsh (listed in our Rodeheaver history as Barry Morrison) remembers when *Trucking Magazine* staff was visiting the Ranch in 1953 and took the "Grace before Grits and Gravy" photograph at the dining table. He is the boy in the plaid shirt bowing his head in prayer.

INTRODUCTION: THE MAN AND HIS VISION

Barry was the second boy to come to live at Rodeheaver Boys Ranch back in December of 1950. His mother had married a man named Bill Morrison in Daytona and she enrolled Barry in school under the name Morrison, thinking he was going to adopt her son, but that didn't happen. Barry got his social security number early under the name of Morrison when he was working in Daytona at the bus station; he came to the Ranch under that name, but many years later, at age 46, he took back his father's name of Walsh.

Barry was 12 years old when he came to the Ranch. "I was an incorrigible kid," he remembers. "Got kicked out of school, ran away from home; my step-father would take me out to the yard and cut switches off the tree and wail the heck out of me for leaving a light on in my room. My mother took me to the Ranch right before Christmas. I was a bedwetter and scared to death the boys would make fun of me. I was praying all the way here like a little 12-year old prays - and I never wet the bed again."

The boys lived in a small wooden house on the Ranch, at first, with an older couple who were friends of Homer Rodeheaver – retired missionaries – and then Lee and Betty Fisher came. The boys called them Uncle Lee and Aunt Betty. While the Fishers were there, Barry remembers that Billy Graham came to visit and donated a boat. "We had dinner and Billy Graham sat across the table from me and his wife, Ruth Graham, sat at my right side. That was a privilege," recalls Barry. "Uncle Lee would ghost-write with Billy Graham and he was with him for thirty years or better. That was before television and every Sunday afternoon, we would have to listen to Billy Graham on the radio because Uncle Lee had written some of those sermons with him."

Remembering Homer Rodeheaver as a "happy gentleman," Barry was blessed to be invited to travel with Homer Rodeheaver. "We traveled in a couple of wooden-trimmed station wagons. He would drive. When we went to church on Sundays, he and his sister Ruth would have me sit between them. That time really stood out for me."

"There is a picture of him and me on the dock," he recalls. "I'd caught a big bream for him and it made the front cover of his newsletter." Barry also remembers Tommy Clay and his wife, Lorene Clay, coming out to the Ranch regularly, bringing horses and cows and visiting the boys.

"It's Better to Build Boys than to Mend Men"

Barry Morrison Walsh
2nd Boy 1951 - 1957

On the St. John's River

"Mr. Homer," as Barry calls him, loved to take the boys fishing.

"Back in those days, the horses would be in the corral and the field and I'd just go up to the horse, grab a handful of mane, jump on and ride. There was one horse, "Outlaw," a brown and white quarter horse, who was real mean. He started bucking and kicking with his hind legs. They finally had to find a home for him."

Barry used to be in charge of the chickens – caring for 500 "layers" at a time, using some of the eggs and chickens for their own use, and selling eggs at different stores in town. The boys also spent a great deal of time learning carpentry and construction by building houses on the Ranch, including Phillips Cottage and Westbury Cottage. The last time Barry visited the Ranch, he was astounded at the beauty of the houses that had been rebuilt and refurbished since those days so long ago.

The Ranch boys went to public school and were driven in an old school bus by the oldest Ranch boy, Clyde McKendree, who was about 16 to 18 years old when he became, as Barry calls him, "The youngest school bus driver in the state." "We tormented the heck out of Clyde," Barry says, "Sometimes he'd stop the bus and walk back and beat on us. It was 15 miles from school to the boys ranch – six miles of paved road and the other nine miles dirt road."

"There was so much Christian influence there at the Ranch. All of the cottage parents that came in were Christian and God was always part of my life," Barry says. "I was at the Ranch until I was about 18 and went in the Army in 1957." Barry got his GED while in the Army and says he went to the University of "Hard Knocks and Tough Breaks" until he hit on his goal of becoming a dog trainer. "I've always loved dogs and I was working for the Santa Fe Railroad driving a truck when I read an inspirational book by Og Mandino called *The Greatest Salesman in the World* that encouraged me to venture out on my goal. I did, and I was blessed to

LADY, if you'll give us a nickel, my little brother will imitate a hen." "What will he do," asked the lady, "cackle like a hen?" "Naw," replied the boy in disgust, "he wouldn't do a cheap imitation like that. He'll eat a woim." Homer Rodeheaver, "F'r Instance"

make a living." With their base in Ormond Beach, Barry's company, All Breed Dog Training, had locations in Orlando, Tampa, Clearwater, Ft. Lauderdale and Miami. He and his late wife, Iris Walsh, worked together for 45 years before she passed away. A devout Christian, Barry prayed for a good woman to be with him in his retirement and once again, the Lord answered his prayer. He and Faye Walsh, his second wife, met at a local restaurant when they were both doing their morning devotionals.

Faye and Barry Walsh

Barry and Faye have visited the Ranch several times over the last few years, and he eagerly awaits the publication of this 70th Anniversary edition about the place that helped to make him the good man he is today.

In late 1953, Mr. and Mrs. Fred Borg became the director-cottage parents and two more staffers, Mr. and Mrs. J. P. Love were hired as cottage parents. A new dining room was built in 1954 and the ranch boys began raising chickens and selling eggs. During the summer of 1955, the boys cut several thousand feet of pulp wood using an old-fashioned two-man crosscut saw. After that, a barbecue was held to raise money for a power saw.

Homer Rodeheaver's music company, The Rodeheaver Company, published a song booklet with the sheet music a song, "Building Boys," dedicated to Rodeheaver Boys Ranch by the Brocks, Virgil P. and Blanche Kerr Brock, with arrangement by W. Roland Felts. Today, the yellowed music booklet, with collages of early Ranch photos on the front and back cover, is on display at the Ranch Museum.

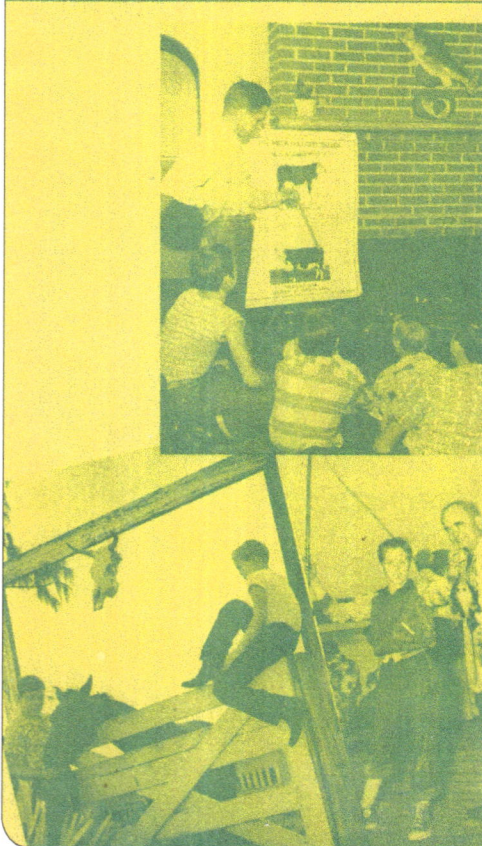

Get in - to the sad - dle ride the range in style;

Throw the las - so firm - ly, rope the things worth while.

Build - ing boys not mend - ing men, That's the

Rod - e - heav - er Boys' Ranch plan._____ plan._____

In March of 1955, members of the Kappa Sigma Fraternity at the University of Florida in Gainesville made their annual trip to Rodeheaver Boys Ranch, having voted to change "Hell" Week into "Help" Week.

In Homer Rodeheaver's *Ranch Rambler* of July 1955, he wrote that the Kappa Sigs had come every year since 1951 prepared to spend a weekend in painting, scrubbing, fence building, etc., and this year was no exception:

Headed by Jack Allabene from Jacksonville, this year's pledge master, seventy Kappa Sigs arrived at the Boys' Ranch early Saturday morning, March 26th, fortified for work and determined to further the original transition plan.

This time they were organized into work details and accomplished the following: removed all of the rotten dock material and made it ready for repair; cleaned about two acres of land which is now ready for planting; piled and burned brush and stumps which made several more acres available; and one of the main things about the whole project, cutting of timber which will be used in the new cottage. All of these projects represent a great deal of hard work and many blistered hands. This is a wonderful group of young men.

We offer the interesting pictures, taken by Richard McLemore, Fraternity photographer, as undeniable proof of their hard work and endeavors on the following page.

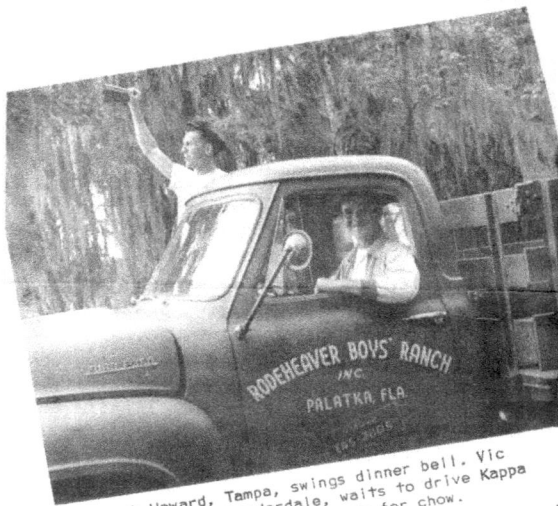

Jack Howard, Tampa, swings dinner bell. Vic Sortino, Ft. Lauderdale, waits to drive Kappa Sigs back to the ranch house for chow.

Ronnie Reyer (left) and George Burke of Rodeheaver Boys' Ranch show the Kappa Sigs how it's done.

Nothing like a cold drink on a hot day.

Fred Borg, superintendent of the Rodeheaver Boys' Ranch (left), and pledge master, Jack Allabene, smilingly agree that it was worth the effort.

As he so often did in his writings, Homer Rodeheaver took the time to thank each of the Kappa Sigs for the good work they had done. He valued all of his "Pardners." This was one of the last Ranch Record newsletters written by Homer Rodeheaver in 1955.

Kappa Sigma officers from the University of Florida who participated in "Help Week" at the Rodeheaver Boys' Ranch included the officers: Fred Bell, President, Titusville, Florida; Jim Keathley, Vice President, Miami; Bridger Kirton, Treasurer, Boynton Beach; Jack Allabene, Pledge Master, Jacksonville; Newt Colee, Secretary of St. Augustine.

Fraternity members were: Chick Wright, Ft. Lauderdale; Dick Marshall, Havertown, Pa.; Loren Axtell, Jacksonville, Bruce Anderson, Ft. Lauderdale; Eliot Kerlin, Orlando, Ronnie Masters, St. Augustine; Steve Estill, West Palm Beach; Richard McLemore, Macon, Ga.; Sonny Bloodworth, Ft. Walton,; Bill Broadfoot, Clewiston; Bob Medlin, Orlando; Charlie Mitchell, Jacksonville; Jack Morgan, Tampa; Gordon Boucher, Ft. Lauderdale; Arnie Steinmetz, Ft. Lauderdale; Jack Bierley, West Palm Beach; Garner Lindelow, St. Petersburg; Lamar Davis, Tampa; Vince Sortino, Ft. Lauderdale; Jack Howard, Tampa; Bill Weathers, Cocoa; Joe Shuttleworth, Ocala; Chan Creighton, Tampa; John Yancey, Ocala; Bob Chalom, Boynton Beach; Donn Hickman, St. Petersburg; Ed Williams, Ft. Pierce; Ledge DeWees, Miami; Henry Rioux, Atlanta, Ga.; Jim Allen, Daytona Beach; Bill Bailey, Maysville, Ky.; Jack Burns, Miami; Bob Carnahan, Bradenton; Jim Catlin, Miami; Russ Christman, Miami; Jan Dazey, Danville, Ill.; Don Dewallot, Delray Beach; Wayne Gaskins, Orlando; Bart Hanson, Sarasota; Keith Hall, Tampa; Ronnie Hasselman, Daytona Beach; Bob Heidenreich, Ft. Lauderdale; Bill Hennessey, Ft. Lauderdale; Gary Holdrum, Homestead; John Houston, Tampa; John Lund, St. Petersburg; Gene Krielow, Jacksonville; Russ Maxcy, Miami; Melton Morrison, Lake City; Charlie Mullins, Bartow; Jim Padags, Ft. Lauderdale; Starling Perkins, Miami; Burns Rutty, British West Indies; Dick Strypkowski, Miami; Frank Usina, St. Augustine; John Walter, Lake Worth; Horace Walters, West Palm Beach; Lloyd Watkins, Jacksonville; Jack Whittaker, Rodney, Ont., Canada; Jim Zinn, St. Petersburg.

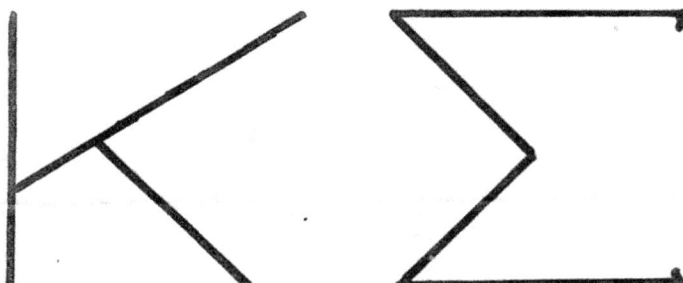

ΚΣ

I would like to take this opportunity to publicly express my personal appreciation both for myself and on behalf of the Boys' Ranch for the help of this fine Kappa Sigma Fraternity of the University of Florida. Kappa Sigma, in this project, for the Boys' Ranch found so much more fun and self-satisfaction from "Help Week" instead of "Hell Week" that we would like to heartily recommend it to other fraternities.

Homer Rodeheaver

INTRODUCTION: THE MAN AND HIS VISION

The Borgs and the Loves left the Ranch in September 1955 and Mr. and Mrs. E. F. Hafling arrived in October 1955. It was a time of transition, as the boys kept coming and the cottage parents kept leaving. The trustee board members and volunteers often spent the night with the boys in those transitional times.

It was on December 18, 1955, at his home in Winona Lake, Indiana, that the big heart of Homer Rodeheaver stopped beating. Bruce Howe, who was later Winona Lake's Fire Chief, remembered Homer Rodeheaver's sister, Ruth Thomas, meeting him at the door on a Sunday morning with the words, "I think we've lost Rody." Howe desperately tried to perform cardio-pulmonary resuscitation (CPR) on him, but it was too late. The world had lost a great man.

And, while the world mourned the death of the revered song leader, evangelist and philanthropist, the young boys at Rodeheaver Boys Ranch personally felt the stark absence of their vibrant "Mr. Rody" who visited regularly and brought Christmas and Christian values to them annually.

Together, a group of dedicated board members, including Tommy Clay and Walt Pellicer of Palatka, continued the Ranch work, filling in when needed. In April of 1956, a newly completed cottage was named The Homer Rodeheaver Cottage and dedicated to the founder. And life went on. Those years were difficult ones as the Ranch struggled to recover from the loss of Homer Rodeheaver's heart for the boys and his constant, enthusiastic support. While there were some who doubted the Ranch would survive without its founder, it has been proven time and time again that God's hand was guiding Homer Rodeheaver to provide a sanctuary for His lost boys, and to God be the glory. His lost boys continue to be nurtured at Rodeheaver Boys Ranch.

Today, celebrating seventy years of growth, the Ranch that Homer Rodeheaver and his "Pardners" carved out of the wilderness continues, with God's blessing, to build boys and grow good men.

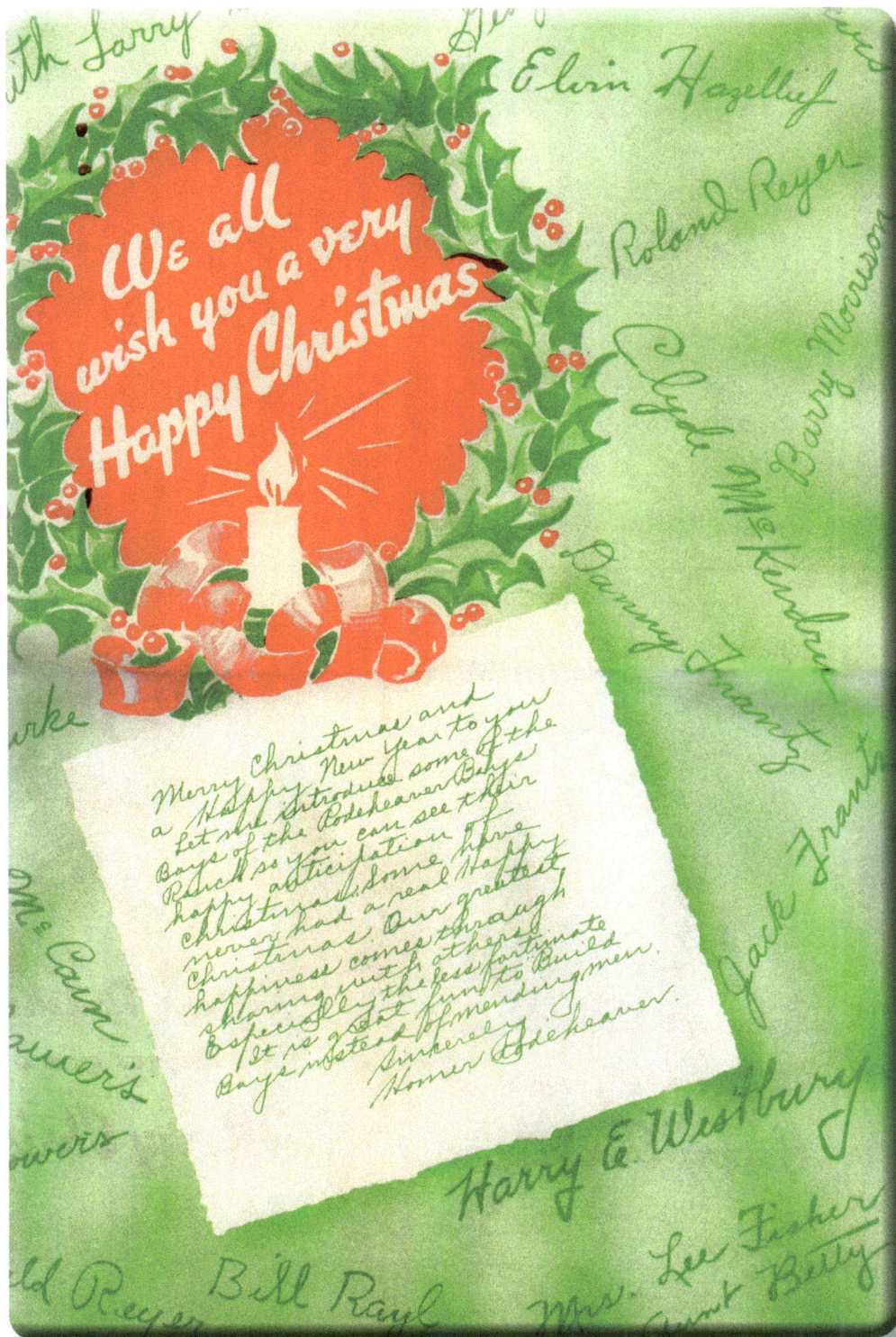

Part of one of the earliest Rodeheaver Boys Ranch Christmas cards

CHAPTER ONE:
CELEBRATING 70 YEARS OF BUILDING BOYS

Homer Rodeheaver's vision of a Boy's Ranch in Palatka, Florida became a reality in 1950 when the State of Florida granted the new non-profit organization a charter. Today, in 2020, Rodeheaver Boys Ranch is fulfilling the vision of that great evangelist, and more!

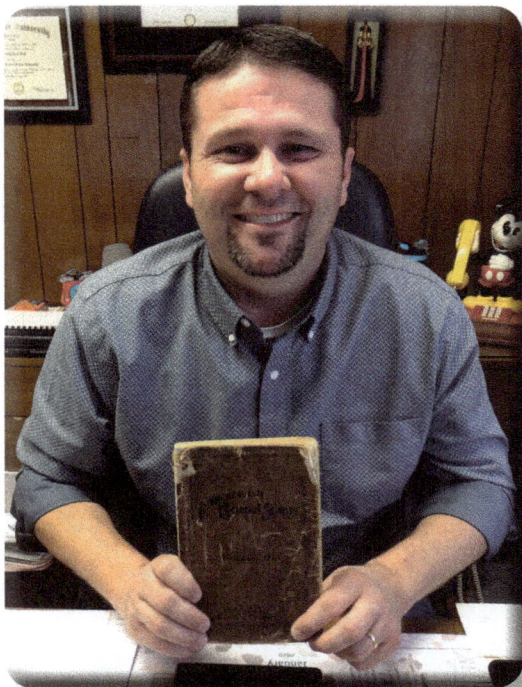

Brad Hall, Executive Director 2020

Florida's oldest Christian Boys Ranch launched 2020 under new, dynamic leadership with Executive Director Bradley Todd (Brad) Hall taking the helm. The former Senior Pastor of First Baptist Church of Palatka, Brad Hall was called to fill the position of former Executive Director, Ken Johnson, who had been at the Ranch for 23 years.

The day that Brad and his wife, Karen, turned onto Boy's Ranch Road and saw the Ranch for the first time, they were filled with the joy of coming home. "We realized our entire lives had prepared us for this Ranch," says Brad. "It was a call that we recognized would forever change our lives, the lives of our family and the lives of many others ... just how many is still part of the story to be written."

After a short season of prayer and introspection, on September 30, 2019, Pastor Brad Hall was elected by the Board of Directors of Rodeheaver Boys Ranch as the new Executive Director. Brad, Karen and their children, Hannah and Micah, took up permanent residence at the Ranch in November of 2019, and become a natural part of Ranch life overnight. Their move was meant to be.

ONE: CELEBRATING 70 YEARS OF BUILDING BOYS

Born February 22, 1978 in Hopkinsville, Kentucky, Brad grew up in rural Christian County, where his boyhood was filled with much of the same abundance enjoyed by Ranch boys of today ... sprawling fields, dense woods, verdant pastures, and farmlands - horses, cows, cats, dogs, pigs and wildlife - vegetable gardens and hayfields. Growing up with an intimate relationship to God and His creation did, indeed, groom Brad to be a knowledgeable role model and leader for God's children at Rodeheaver Boys Ranch.

Much as Homer Rodeheaver felt the call of this beautiful piece of land along the St. Johns River, so did Brad Hall know in his heart that it was where God meant for him to be. The former Executive Director of Rodeheaver Boys Ranch, Ken Johnson, felt that same strong pull back in 1996 when he first laid eyes on the Ranch.

Ken, who served as Vice-President of Faith Bible College in Milton, Florida before taking the top position at Rodeheaver Boys Ranch, had high hopes and goals for the Ranch from the moment he drove beneath the Rodeheaver Arch.

Ken Johnson, Executive Director – 1996 - 2019

He and his wife, Lois Johnson, had brought up their children in Milton, and she was somewhat reluctant to leave their comfortable life for a Boys Ranch out in the wilderness. The day Ken and Lois pulled up to the Executive Director's house, Lois then knew God had led them there. "A group of raggedy young boys were standing in front of the house clutching a home-made sign that read, 'Welcome home, Mr. and Mrs. Johnson,'" remembers Lois, her eyes filling with tears.

Ken Johnson told a reporter, "These boys need the same shot at life with no less opportunity available, just like any other young person starting out. I don't want this to be just an average place. I want this to be the 'crown jewel' of Christian children's homes in the state of Florida. If we accomplish that, then very quickly we can become the 'crown jewel' of Christian children's homes in the United States." Over the twenty-three years that Ken served God as Executive Director of Rodeheaver Boys Ranch, it became the "Crown Jewel" that he had envisioned and so much more.

Today, the Ranch has achieved a stellar reputation throughout the United States as a wonderful home where boys can grow and thrive in Christian love. People across the nation know about it through social media and through the popularity of two Bluegrass Festivals a year at the Ranch. The Bluegrass festivals draw thousands of visitors annually in February and November to share in three days of joyful down-home fellowship, delicious barbecue, and classic country music, mixed with the folksy humor and heart of old-time gospel tunes. Much as our founder, Homer Rodeheaver, recognized the power of music to enrich the human spirit, there is a strong resemblance between the Ranch's Bluegrass festivals and the Christian revivals the famous evangelist led around the country. The melodic circle of love remains unbroken as the faint echo of Homer's hearty laugh can nearly be discerned at each Bluegrass Festival, where hundreds of new "Pardners" are won for the Ranch's mission through the magic of music and Christian fellowship.

> "Anyone who has had a bull by the tail knows 5 or 6 things more than someone who hasn't."
> Ken's Favorite Sayings

Homer Rodeheaver and Ken Johnson, with God's help and the support of dozens of devoted "Pardners" along the way, created today's incredibly beautiful sanctuary for boys; a sanctuary that prompted a powerful man of God like Brad Hall to also make it his life's work.

As the late Paul Harvey said when he came to visit the Ranch, "It is not a long-distance call to God from here, but a local call."

Paul Harvey felt the presence of God at Rodeheaver Boys Ranch, as did Ken Johnson and Brad Hall. This 70th Anniversary Book will tell "The Rest of the Story."

Homer Rodeheaver wishes you a most sincere
Merry Christmas
and invites you to come on inside and sing

Hello, My Friends! On an inside page you will find a lovely new Christmas song with the good wishes of Mr. B. D. Ackley and myself.

Homer Rodeheaver
Luke 2: 11 and 12

One night on a field near Bethlehem, where shepherds watched their flocks, I played the trombone and sang Christmas carols with a group of friends.

Then we followed a bright star which led us across the fields and up a stony path through the village to the Cathedral which covers the stable where Jesus was born.

On the way we passed a home where they were having a wedding celebration. One of the friends from Jerusalem went in and talked to the folks. They invited me in to play the trombone. Two years later a visitor here from Palestine told me that the people of that home were still telling how a heavenly visitor came from the fields of Bethlehem and played a golden horn at their wedding. They were proud of their visitor.

May you invite the real Heavenly Visitor into your home where He will bring melody and harmony and the Peace that passeth all understanding.

Then you too will be proud of your Visitor.

Pages from Homer Rodeheaver's last Christmas card before his death

CHAPTER TWO:
AFTER RODY

For the first five years (1950-1955) Homer Rodeheaver was the smiling face of Rodeheaver Boys Ranch, talking non-stop about the Ranch to anyone who would listen, visiting the boys often and writing generous checks to support the growing needs of the Ranch. Then "Rody" was gone, but the boys were still there. The Ranch had to survive, somehow, and, with God's help, survive it did.

Like his hero, "Mr. Rody," George Burke, the first Ranch boy, grew up to be an avid hunter and fisherman, and like Homer Rodeheaver, Burke mentored many boys in his role as a high school football coach, teaching them about honor, teamwork, good sportsmanship and goal-setting. A coaching legend, a family man, a Sunday School teacher at the First Baptist Church in Stuttgart, George Burke lived his life by the Christian values he learned at Rodeheaver Boys Ranch.

Having come to the Ranch in 1950, George Burke entered 7th grade at Palatka Junior High that year and continued to make the Boys Ranch his home until he graduated from Palatka High School in 1956. He attended Arkansas A & M College and graduated in 1960, majoring in Physical Education and minoring in History. Soon after graduating from college, George began his career of coaching high school football in Arkansas.

In 1987, George Burke returned to visit the Ranch, having accrued a list of honors, and having been repeatedly named Coach of the year in Stuttgart, Arkansas where he coached the high school team. He was also Chairman of the Muscular Dystrophy Campaign, Counselor for Boy's State, Director of Youth Baseball, Coach at Northwestern State University's Football Camp and more.

Burke passed away in 2003 and was inducted into the Arkansas High School Coaches Association/Arkansas Officials Association Hall of Fame. Today, the

**"Mr. Rody" with Ranch boys – Barry (Morrison) Walsh (L),
Clyde McKendree and George Burke on the far right**

George Burke Fieldhouse at Stuttgart Junior High School is a tribute to the man who came to Rodeheaver Boys Ranch as a youngster and grew to be a fine man. George Burke's gratitude for the start he got at the Ranch remained with him all his life. He was the first boy of many who learned to be a man at the Ranch.

After Homer Rodeheaver died in 1955, a small contingent of dedicated board members led by Tommy Clay rallied to run the Ranch, and by the Annual Meeting in January of 1958, an impressive group of supporters came to the Ranch including Homer Rodeheaver's brother-in-law, Jim Thomas, from Winona Lake, Indiana; Mrs. Asa A. Candler from Atlanta, Georgia; and Mr. Clarence Jacobs from Chicago, Illinois. R. C. Beaty came from the University of Florida, Gainesville, Fred Lynch from New Smyrna Beach, D. L. Tullis and Finley Tucker, Jr., traveled from Jacksonville and the local board members from Palatka were Mrs. H. P. Huff, Harry Westbury, L. C. McCall, Marshall Hall, J. H. Millican and Tommy Clay. Dr. Norman Vincent Peale and Rev. Billy Graham willingly lent their names as Honorary Board Members.

The Annual Meeting in 1958 was marked with the confirmation by the board of the appointment of Rev. Walter A. "Skipper" Pierce as Executive Director of the Ranch and Mrs. "Mom" Pierce as assistant executive director. The Pierces were a dedicated couple who earned the love and respect of the boys and remained at the Ranch for several years. Even after Skipper Pierce passed away in 1963, their son, Chuck Pierce stepped in and stayed until 1968.

The Pierce family worked closely with the board, particularly Tommy Clay, who, with his wife Lorene, devoted a great deal of time and energy to the Ranch and continued to do so throughout his life.

In 1958, having seen the need for the boys to have some sort of well-organized summer activities, Clay recommended hiring seventeen-year old Ed Hedstrom as the Ranch's "Summer Recreation Director." A 1958 graduate of Palatka High School, Hedstrom worked at the Ranch every summer thereafter through his graduation from the University of Florida's Law School in 1965. Two years after being admitted to the Florida Bar in 1965, Hedstrom was voted onto the Rodeheaver Boys Ranch Board of Directors. In 2000, Ed Hedstrom was appointed a Circuit Judge by Governor Jeb Bush. He retired from the Bench in 2010 and remains an active member of the Ranch Board of Directors, an honored past president and a trustee of the Rodeheaver Foundation (a separate fundraising organization formed by long-time ranch supporters). Judge Hedstrom, who was nearly the same age as the oldest boys when he began working at the Ranch, always remained close to his friend and mentor, Tommy Clay.

Ed Hedstrom

In 2012, Tommy Clay proudly posed for a photo at the Rodeheaver Boys Ranch Lodge in front of the portrait of Homer Rodeheaver on horseback.

During the years that Skipper Pierce was Executive Director at Rodeheaver Boys Ranch, several improvements were made including the addition of a workshop, a recreation room and improved pasture for horses and cattle. The faithful and ever-present Tommy Clay brought in some of the first ten or fifteen heifers to fill the improved pastures and his "cowgirl" wife, Lorene, brought the cow truck, horses and cow dogs so she could work the cattle right alongside the boys. Wives of the staff and board members regularly helped run the Ranch, working side by side with their husbands for the sake of the boys. That remains the case to this day, as current board members and their wives come out to the Ranch regularly to help with events and provide support to the boys.

Gordon Philbrick, Former Ranch Boy

Saturday, April 4, 1959 is a day that Gordon Philbrick won't forget. That day, he rode with his mother and grandmother to Rodeheaver Boys Ranch where his older brother, Clark, lived. When Gordon saw Clark, he jumped out of the car and ran to him. Out of the corner of his eye, he saw his mother talking to Ranch Director Skipper Pierce. "Gordon," Skipper called to him, "I want you to go with your brother to see the horses." As the boys headed for the corral, Gordon heard his mother's car starting up and turned just in time to see the dust flying as she sped away. "No goodbye. She didn't even say goodbye." Gordon was numb. He stood stock still, watching the car disappear. Then a strong arm encircled his shoulder. "C'mon, let's go see those horses," said Skipper. As they walked, boys began to show up. One by one the boys welcomed Gordon, each of them shaking his hand. "I was 11 years old and I wasn't used to shaking hands, but I liked it. Then Mr. Pierce said, 'You'll find that everybody loves you here.' That was the day I died and went to heaven."

Gordon was a boy who understood about challenges – even in heaven. One day he walked by Skipper's office and saw the big man sitting with his face in his hands. "Skipper, you okay?" he asked. "No, Gord, I'm not okay," was the reply. "Right now, our donations are down and we need food for supper." Within minutes, Skipper, Gordon and Mrs. Batemann, the secretary, were on their knees in prayer. "Skipper taught me to pray. He had bad knees, but he would drop down and pray about everything," Gordon remembers. "That day a $100 check came in the mail, but there were a few times we had nothing but popcorn and ice cream for supper. The Baptist church gave us a 50-pound bag of popping corn. We had no soap to wash dishes, so we had our homemade ice cream on waxed paper. Things got better after we started working with the paper mill. We had regular money coming in then and regular meals, too. Sometimes, we even got new clothes for school."

When Skipper Pierce died of a heart attack in 1963, everyone at the Ranch was devastated. His widow, "Mom" Pierce, and their son, Chuck Pierce, stayed on and ran the Ranch until 1968. At Skipper's funeral, Gordon and his friend, Joe Brewer, stood at the casket for a long time. They were remembering how, when they were little, the big man would open his arms wide and say, 'C'mon boys. Get over here,' and they would run into his arms for a huge, warm hug.

Skipper Pierce

"The Pierces were like family to me," says Gordon. "There was a day I found a big blackberry patch out near the canal and ran in the kitchen to ask Mom Pierce for big coffee cans so I could pick the berries. I saddled up Rainbow (Homer Rodeheaver's prize-winning Tennessee Walker) for Mom and Mary Pat for me, and we rode out to the patch and picked blackberries all day. She made blackberry pies for supper that night and she made one pie especially for me. She kept it back in the kitchen and told me I could go in and cut a piece whenever I wanted – it was my pie."

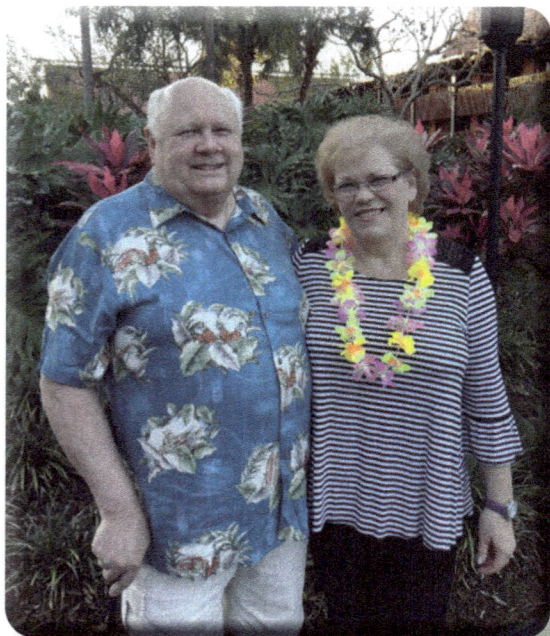

Gordon and Susan Philbrick

After leaving the Ranch in 1968, Gordon went to Vietnam as a Marine. Now retired after working more than thirty years with the Boilermakers Union, Gordon has been happily married to Susan Philbrick for forty-nine years. They are proud parents of Tammie, an attorney, who has given them two grandchildren, Anna and Jake Benosky. "Our grandchildren stay with us almost every weekend," says Gordon. "They know all about my years at the Ranch. It was where I learned to love God and be a responsible man."

Hugs and hard times, popcorn and blackberry pies, prayers and prize horses ... Gordon Philbrick remembers them well and wouldn't trade those memories for anything. Rodeheaver Boys Ranch was home for him. Today, much has changed for the better at the Ranch, but some things remain exactly the same. The Ranch boys need the handshakes, hugs and reassurance that "Everybody loves you here," just as much as Gordon did then, and the Ranch staff still prays for donations to keep the boys fed and clothed.

The Ranch boys began regularly winning blue ribbons at the county fair during the late 1950s for their excellent cattle, poultry and farm products. It was during those early days that some of the most enduring Ranch traditions were established – traditions like raising the finest livestock, preparing the best barbecue and instilling the highest Christian values in the hearts of boys.

"A people that values its privileges above its principles soon loses both." Ken's Favorite Sayings

Ranch boys also learned a great deal about construction due to damage done as the result of Hurricane Donna in September 1960 and a tornado in 1961. They made quick work of repairs to the workshop, boathouse and dock, and even had time to bag live turkeys for a publicity stunt in November, 1960, presenting Governor-elect Farris Bryant with a live Thanksgiving turkey. This was followed the next November by seven Ranch boys presenting seven live Thanksgiving turkeys to the new governor in Tallahassee. The stunt got the attention of Governor Farris Bryant who came to the Annual Meeting at the Ranch in 1964 as guest speaker. Headlines in the Florida Times-Union read: "Bryant Says Florida needs Dedicated Christian People."

Judge Ed Hedstrom looks back at summers in the early 60s at the Ranch with a great deal of nostalgia. "I'd handle the work crews in the morning, play ball with them, go camping and fishing. We swam every afternoon in the river and every Saturday morning, we took the boys into town to the movies. It was our Saturday treat. There were about twenty-five of them – quite a group!"

One special memory for Judge Hedstrom is the all-expense paid trip that the boys and staff took to Washington, D.C. and New York City in the early 60s courtesy of a gasoline distributor from Daytona Beach named Reid Hughes. "We took a train to Washington, D.C., toured the capitol and then went to New York to watch the Yankees play baseball," recalls Hedstrom. "We went into the locker room and met Yogi Berra, Mickey Mantle, Roger Maris, all the greats who were playing back then. It was unforgettable."

Following the construction of the new paved road, thanks to Tommy Clay's persistence, the barbecue fund-raising tradition truly came into its own. Several of the Ranch board members joined Clay's regular "grill-masters," including Fount Rion, Sr., Sheriff Walt Pellicer and Bill Penn.

David Campbell, Former Ranch Boy

October 10, 1963 was a sad day for the Ranch. The Rev. Walter "Skipper" Pierce died of a sudden heart attack. Former Ranch boy David Campbell talked about his memories of the day Skipper Pierce died. David was an 18-year old student at St. Johns River Junior College and was visiting the Pierce's on October 10, 1963. He fell asleep watching television and was awakened by a frantic Mom Pierce, shaking him and saying, "Skip's having a heart attack! Come quick!" At that time, David was the only boy who had a driver's license to take Skipper to the hospital. He remembered Mr. Pierce coming out of the cottage wearing a robe and boxer shorts – struggling down the side-steps to get into the passenger side of the Oldsmobile. "Mom put a pail between his legs and closed the door," said Campbell. "It was a long way on the dirt to get to the main road and he kept saying, 'Hurry, David,' but I was afraid to speed with him in the car. It was against the rules." When they got to State Road 19, Skipper fell against David and he tried to nudge him back, but he was such a heavy-set man. As they pulled up to the emergency entrance, David blew the horn loudly and people

David Campbell and Ranch Boys at the 2020 Fishing Tournament

came running out, but it was too late. Skipper Pierce was dead. Mom Pierce had stayed behind at the Ranch because she was the only adult there that night and wouldn't leave the boys unattended. David remembered Mom Pierce fondly and called Skipper Pierce a big, loving man who was a father figure for all the boys.

An orphan whose life had been institutional until he came to the Ranch, David Campbell learned to love God there, and learned the value of honesty and hard work. He remembered that when Skipper and Mom went to town, "Ed Hedstrom was our babysitter. He could have been in law enforcement because we couldn't get away with a thing when he was there."

David remembers Tommy and Lorene Clay, and all the time they spent with the boys. "Mrs. Clay taught me piano," he said. "I think of her whenever I hear the song, "That Lucky Old Sun Ain't Got Nothing to do But Roll Around Heaven All Day."

At one time, Colonel Harland Sanders of Kentucky Fried Chicken fame visited the Ranch, as did many celebrities over the years. He offered the boys jobs in his franchises and David accepted a job in Palm Beach City at a Kentucky Fried

Chicken place. He soon realized he enjoyed working outdoors more than in and took an apprenticeship position with a construction company, eventually becoming a member of The Carpenter's Union. For the past twenty-five years, David has worked with Hagedorn Construction in Crescent City, building and refurbishing houses. Just prior to the Corona Virus Pandemic of 2020, David attended a Fishing Tournament benefitting Rodeheaver Boys Ranch and met the new Executive Director, Brad Hall. "I made plans then to come out to the Ranch and offer my assistance in any building projects that were underway," said David, "and I still plan to do that when I can. My time at the Boys Ranch stays in my heart as the best time ever."

About three months after the death of Skipper Pierce, his son, Rev. Chuck Pierce, was appointed Executive Director of the Ranch. In order to get much-needed funding, Chuck partnered with Dan Martinez (still quite active on the Rodeheaver Board of Directors and the Rodeheaver Foundation) at the Hudson Pulp and Paper Company (now Georgia Pacific) on a paper pressing and recycling project for the boys. Working under Chuck's direction, the boys collected and pressed the paper into bales for shipment to Jacksonville after school and on weekends. The Hudson Employees Charitable Association became interested in the Ranch and supplied clothing, groceries and Christmas gifts often when funds were short. Kiwanis, Elks and others in the community also chipped in and the Ranch truly became part of life in Palatka.

The Day President Johnson came to the Ranch

Then, on February 27, 1964, the Ranch became part of life in America as U.S. President Lyndon B. Johnson paid a historic visit there to officially launch the Cross Florida Barge Canal (an ill-fated project that never was completed).

With all the activities of the day taking place at Rodeheaver Boys Ranch, much advance preparation occurred, with Secret Service agents, workmen

and special telephone crews working tirelessly to make the place ready for a presidential visit.

Tommy Clay, aided by Bill Penn, Sheriff Walt Pellicer, Fount Rion, Sr., Edgar Johnson, Bill Tilton, Craig Benson, Charles Swain, Buck Walker, J. L. Hooper, Carl Davis, Marshall Hall, Riley Bennett and several others, with Ranch boys taking shifts through the night, barbecued 8,000 pounds of chicken. Lorene Clay and several other wives mixed up 35 gallons of Rodeheaver Boys Ranch Barbecue Sauce and swabbed the nearly cooked chickens with the sauce using brand new dish mops.

When the big day dawned, it was cold, wet and rainy, but there were probably 10,000 people braving the weather to see the President of the United States of America in Palatka, Florida. The March 1964 issue of *Life Magazine* featured a photograph of the boys presenting the gift of a small china bull to

TWO: AFTER RODY

President Johnson. The ceramic bull, created by Mrs. Hubert Maltby, wife of retired Putnam County Agricultural Agent Hubert Maltby, was a symbol of the cattle being raised, along with boys, at the Ranch. The signature in gold of each boy at the Ranch was baked into the bull. Forty years later, in 2004, Bob Mayes of the Palatka Daily news wrote a comprehensive article in remembrance of that special day entitled "LBJ's Rain." An excerpt from that article reads as follows:

"Chosen to give the President the souvenir was 8-year-old Larry Martin. 'I guess they chose me because I was the littlest feller on the ranch," he said earlier this week from Dallas, where he has lived and worked as a welder for the last 18 years. "I must have been well-liked because they had my picture on the cover of the brochure. I had a good nature about me and I was real little – extraordinarily little – and real cute, I guess." Mrs. Pierce remembers that Martin had been given a short speech to memorize and to deliver to President Johnson when he handed him the bull. "It was just two or three lines and they rehearsed it for a couple of weeks," Mrs. Pierce said with a chuckle. "Then when it got time to present it to President Johnson, I guess he got nervous in front of all those people. When he handed the bull to the President, he just froze. Then he looked up at the President and all he could say was, "Here..." More than the weather, more than the crowd, more than the excitement, that's what Larry Martin will remember about the President's visit. "That's exactly the way it happened," he said. "I went back to my room after that and I told myself I couldn't believe I had done that. But the President was real good about it. I think he knew that we were going to give him the bull. He laughed when I froze up. But he did say 'thank you.' I remember that."

The flurry of attention brought by the President's visit soon died down and once again, the Ranch was struggling for donors and name recognition.

Becky Douglas

Mrs. Rebecca Douglas began working part-time in 1965 as the Ranch's laundress and by 1966, she was working full-time. "Miss Becky," as she was fondly called by the boys, was destined to work at the Ranch for three decades. Using antiquated ringer washers, clotheslines and a large gas dryer, she washed, dried and folded hundreds of pairs of jeans and shirts, towels, underwear and socks. She did a "mountain" of laundry for the boys that lived there – laundry that is now done in modern washers and dryers in each individual cottage by the boys and their cottage parents.

Enjoying a new pool!

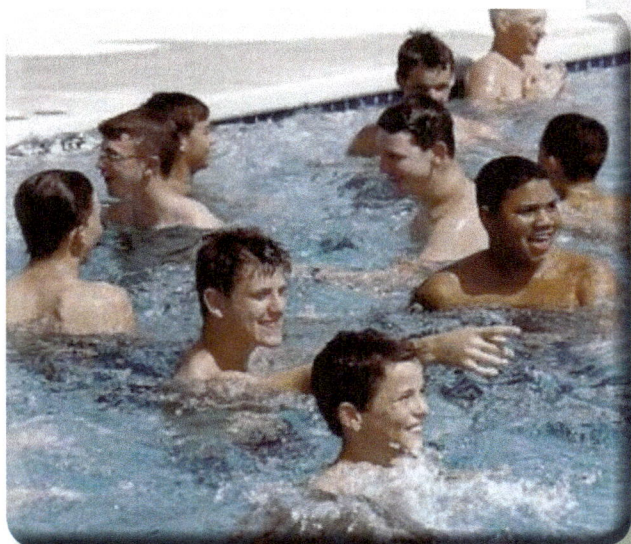

A youthful, laughing Tim Officer.
(Please see Chapter 8)

Much like the transition from old to new in the area of laundry, the boys went from swimming in the river to swimming in a brand new Olympic sized pool in 1968, built and dedicated by Keith Larkin of California in memory of his mother, Mrs. Ruth Larkin of Palatka. Many years later, after the pool had fallen into disrepair due to more pressing needs like food and clothing for the boys, board member Carlton Spence was instrumental in 1997, with the help of several Jacksonville firms (Global Stevedoring, Central Florida Pools and Spas, Jones Turf Grass Farm, Thompson Contractors and Lowman Fence Company), in providing another brand new swimming pool. Supervision of the project was provided by Board of Directors Facilities Chairman Kenny Downs and then by the board's new Facilities Chairman Charles Smith. The pool was dedicated on August 25, 1997, and is still enjoyed by the boys to this day.

After Chuck Pierce resigned as executive director in 1969, the next full-time executive director was Ed MacClellan. Ed had been Assistant Director of the Florida Sheriff's Boys Ranch in Live Oak before being approached about accepting the position at Rodeheaver Boys Ranch. He had served for six years as youth pastor at Highlands Presbyterian Church in Gainesville and his wife Lou Ann had volunteered at Sunland Training Center (a mental health facility in Gainesville, Florida), and had gone on to earn a degree from the University of Florida in Occupational Therapy. Upon visiting the Ranch, both of them felt the calling from God, and on April 1, 1970, Ed and LouAnn MacClellan and their son, Chanse MacClellan, barely 12 months old, moved into Philips Cottage. Their son, Evan MacClellan, was born at the Ranch two years later on June 11, 1971.

"To know what you know and to know what you don't know is what knowing is all about." Ken's Favorite Sayings

Within a year of his arrival, Ed MacClellan had managed to hire new staff and pay off several debts. "God did it," insisted MacClellan. "It was as if we were receiving manna from heaven."

Terry and Jerry Martin, Former Ranch Boys

Terry Martin and Jerry Martin are big men. When they wrapped their strong arms around Ed and LouAnn MacClellan, they enfold them in affectionate bear hugs of major proportions. "Ed and LouAnn are family," said Terry, back in 2013, when the first Ranch Book was written. Jerry agreed. "Ed and LouAnn have been the constants in my life. They helped build the foundation for the dream that Mr. Rodeheaver and his friends had for the Ranch and we owe them our love and honor."

Jerry and his identical twin, Terry, were 7 years old when they came to the

Ranch in 1964. They were destined to be there until 1976. Their dad was gone, their mother had suffered a nervous breakdown; two older brothers were already at the Ranch, and the twins had nowhere else to go. They were "Putnam County poor," which translated back then to the poorest of the poor in that small farming

Terry Martin with Ed and LouAnn MacClellan

community. Terry remembers a first-grade teacher at Campbell Elementary School buying him his first pair of shoes. After they were caught stealing food from Faulkner's Grocery Store, Mr. Faulkner regularly gave the twins food to eat.

Jerry Martin

Two skinny tow-headed blonde boys whose bright blue eyes had seen far too much, Terry and Jerry came to the Ranch at an unfortunate time when leadership, supervision and funds were sorely lacking, but it was still a better place than they'd ever been before. "The Ranch was a big tough, scary place," remembers Terry, "but we were used to being scared. I was afraid of the bigger boys and spent a lot of time hiding in the blackberry patch, but there are some good memories, too. One night I had a stomach-ache and Mrs. Yelvington (cottage mom and cook) gave me Sprite, sat me in her lap and rocked me in a rocking chair until I fell asleep. I was 7 years old and no one had ever done that before. I'll never forget how good it felt."

The twins ate regularly and learned to work hard, obey the rules and get good grades in school (or else!), but they credit Ed and LouAnn MacClellan for giving them the foundation of familial love and faith in God that has helped them survive life's challenges.

TWO: AFTER RODY

"Our best memories of the Ranch begin the day Ed MacClellan came," said Terry. Hired in 1970, Ed MacClellan and his wife, Lou Ann brought stability, order, compassion and a deep faith that God would guide them in making a better life for the boys.

"Ed and Lou Ann opened doors for us that we never could have imagined," said Terry, who developed such skill through working with thoroughbred horses at the Ranch that he earned his living as an equestrian for many years. Noting that the twins had exceptional academic potential, Ed brought them to the attention of a wealthy benefactor and they were the first Ranch boys to graduate from private school. After graduation, the MacClellans took the twins into their own home so that they could attend St. Johns Community College.

"We were given every opportunity," said Jerry, "but we went our own ways and each made our own messes. Life is messy, but I've discovered, thanks to the influence of Ed and LouAnn, that it's how you deal with the mess that tells what kind of a person you are. When you make a big mess, the Lord gives you a bigger mop bucket."

Today, Jerry and Terry Martin are highly skilled electricians working together on mega-projects all over the country. Wherever they go, the twins stay in close contact with the MacClellans, whom they consider to be their surrogate parents. "Ed and LouAnn did everything they could for all the boys," says Jerry. "Please understand that children must know they are loved and valued above all. I cannot remember the days I was hungry or had no clothes or shoes, but every day that I wept over not having a father or mother love me and encourage me is burnt into my memory. Ed and LouAnn arrived and gave us what we needed. They helped make Rodeheaver Boys Ranch what it is today."

Now grown men with families of their own, the twins are in agreement that privately funded Christian children's homes like Rodeheaver Boys Ranch are the only hope for lost, abandoned, neglected, orphaned and abused children. "The state-run, government funded institutions benefit from keeping the kids there.

The longer they stay, the more money they get. That's not the way it is or ever was at Rodeheaver Boys Ranch," said Terry. "The Ranch's goal is to reunite the boys with their families if possible. The people that take care of the boys are there for the boys. And, most importantly, the state does not mandate the mental, physical or spiritual training the boys get at the Ranch ... only God does that."

In 1970, when an electrical storm hit the barn and burned it to the ground, the MacClellans and the boys were convinced that God used the barn fire for good as well. That summer, Jaycees came from Gainesville, Palatka, St. Augustine and Ocala to help the boys rebuild the barn, and ultimately, the Ranch was adopted by the State Jaycee Organization.

Also, during 1970, the L. C. Ringhaver Arch was built, providing an attractive entranceway to the ranch. The new arch was dedicated at the Annual Meeting on January 24, 1971. The late Lambert C. Ringhaver,

according to his son, Randy, Chairman and President of Ring Power, instilled a hard work ethic in his sons, Randy and Lance Ringhaver, insisting that they start at the ground floor before working their way up to management. Giving back to the community was also a basic part of Ringhaver's "ground-up" philosophy, and Ring Power continues to provide large equipment to the Ranch to this day. Randy Ringhaver remains on the board of directors for the Ranch, providing a fine role model for the boys and, often, a potential place of employment.

Bill Green and his wife, Mary Ann Green, with their three children, came to the Ranch in June of 1971 and remained there until 1989. In those years, many improvements were made. Green recalled that Randy Ringhaver loaned the Ranch bulldozers and road graders to clear land and dig landfills. "We couldn't have done it without the borrowed equipment," said Green. "The Ringhavers were great!"

Bill Green

By 1972, the ranch averaged a population of thirty-six to forty boys at all times. At the Annual Meeting, the newly constructed Boeing Cottage was dedicated with a crowd of about five hundred in attendance. Now, with Boeing Cottage open, the wing in the Thomas Administration Building could be converted into a small staff residence as originally planned. Ed and LouAnn had been living in a house trailer adjacent to the construction site where they were building the executive director's house brick by brick after hours. By Christmas 1972, they were able to move into their house and the new Director of Ranch Life, Bill Green, and his family moved into the staff residence at the Thomas Administration Building.

"Half the troubles in life can be traced to saying YES too quickly and not saying NO soon enough."
Ken's Favorite Sayings

Larry St. Amand, Former Ranch Boy

Like so many Ranch Boys, Larry St. Amand was accompanied by siblings when he arrived at the Ranch in 1973. "I was 12 years old when we got there - the oldest of three boys. My two younger brothers stayed at the Ranch longer than I did," he remembers. "What happened was ... our mom decided to go on vacation

Larry St. Amand – 1971 Plymouth "Cuda"

and she just kind of left us at home alone. We'd been there for about a week when my middle brother said something at school and social services came and picked us up because we had no supervision. My grandmother felt guilty because she didn't step up to the plate, but Grandpa was sick. When my mom found out where we were, she came and visited us, but she was never stable enough to get us off the Ranch."

Larry did his best to stay out of trouble and keep his nose clean, but he did not want to be at the Ranch. "Nobody really wants to be there," he says, "but it turned out that the Ranch was good for me in a lot of ways. They teach you right from wrong. They stay on top of you. They teach you a good work ethic and to take responsibility for your own actions."

Today, Larry owns three businesses in Cape Coral, Florida – two mechanic shops and a machine shop. He credits his ability to run a business to his years at the Ranch. "The work I do is hard and it's hard to get good help," he says. "By the time I left the Ranch at 16, I knew about hard work. If the Ranch referred a worker to me, I'd be pretty sure about his dependability. It's just part of being there."

Ed MacClellan was the executive director at the Ranch when the St. Amand brothers arrived and Larry remembers raising thoroughbred horses, working at the barn, and working two summers at a horse farm in Ocala. "The second year I was there, I raised a steer and sold it at the fair. A potato farmer named Mr. Tilton bought my steer and when I thanked him for buying it, he was pretty impressed," recalls Larry. "He took me under his wing for the summer. I learned how a family works together."

Speaking of family, Larry's middle brother, Brett, went to live with a family in Palatka and when his younger brother, Sean, turned 16, Larry took him in. "I remember that I had to prove I had a stable home and a wife and a job before they let me take in my little brother," Larry says. "It turned out Sean didn't want to listen to me, anyway. He's an adventurer and follows the horse business. He got that love of horses from the Ranch, and it's where I learned to fix cars."

Ed MacClellan recalled that Larry St. Amand was the first Ranch boy to buy his own car. "Larry was a good boy," Ed said. "He earned the right to own a car. I'm glad to hear he's done so well in life."

Once in a while, when the Ranch gets a check from a company called Florida Torque Converter in Cape Coral, it's a welcome donation from grateful former Ranch boy Larry St. Amand. "If you don't have that good

upbringing, you're on poor footing when you venture out in the world," says Larry. "Rodeheaver Boys Ranch gave me that upbringing. There was work to be done and we did it."

Tommy Morgan, Former Ranch Boy

Tommy Morgan's life was in turmoil from the time he was two years old. The youngest of Lois Morgan's six children, Tommy Morgan lived near the Civic Center at Ravine Gardens in Palatka where his mother ran a catering business called M & M Catering. She also ran the Candlelight Café, which was where Beef O'Brady's is now in Palatka. When he was just a toddler, their house burned down, and his father left. "Mom did the best she could raising us and working a couple jobs," recalls Tommy, "but it all got to be too much for her. I was nine years old when she took a gun out in the woods and tried to kill herself. The gun jammed and she shot her arm. She was institutionalized and I ended up at Rodeheaver Boys Ranch."

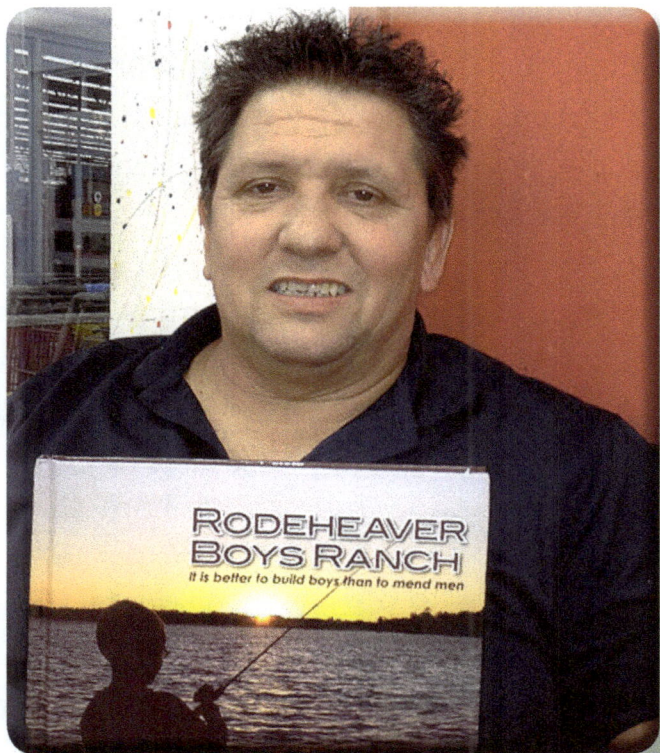

After six years, Tommy's mother recovered. He was in 10th grade when he went to live with her in Dade City, Florida. Soon after they were reunited, his mother fell ill and Tommy quit high school, going to work at Pasco Poultry pulling chickens for $4.50 an hour to keep a roof over their heads. "Mom was too sick to work and couldn't drive, but I learned how to drive in the cow pastures at the Ranch, and how to work hard, too, so we were okay," says Tommy, adding proudly that when his mother regained her health, she took the initiative to go to school and learn to build computer boards for Northern Telecom. She died at age 78, with Tommy by her side.

Looking back on his years at the Ranch, Tommy remembers the good times and the hard times ... traveling with a busload of boys to the mountains of North Carolina in the dead of winter to skim across frozen lakes on makeshift sleds that served as cafeteria trays back at the Ranch; jumping on back of a pickup truck while tagging calves in the cow pasture and getting punched in the jaw by a pine tree ("Dr. Raby wired my broken jaw ... he and Doc Roy Campbell took care of us back then"); catching armadillos to cook for dinner ("tastes just like chicken"); camping out often down by the river and the day he caught his first fish ("I bragged I had the biggest bass around, but it was a mud fish!").

There was a day when Tommy and another boy were racing their horses back to the barn from the barge canal and Tommy's pony, "Little Bit" fell into a ditch and cut her leg. Barn manager Jack Horner showed Tommy how to put purple medicine on Little Bit's leg and wrap it. After that, Tommy got up at 5 a.m. every day to go to the barn and doctor the pony's leg until it healed. Jack Horner was also a man of God, who taught Tommy and other boys how to pray. At the Ranch, they worked hard, prayed hard and played hard.

"'Kill the man with the ball' was our version of football," jokes Tommy, "and we prayed about everything, including our report card. If you got a U on your report card, you had to dig up a Palmetto root with a pickax!"

With strength that comes from knowing God and shouldering heavy responsibility at a young age, Tommy Morgan has become a hardworking family man who is intent on providing for his family. Sometimes he works as many as three jobs a week, including a job at Wal Mart, doing stucco and lathe work, and lawn maintenance, but he provides. Being a role model for his six children is so important to him that he went back to school in 2008 at the age of 44 and earned a high school diploma.

"I wanted to show my kids that an education is important to me and it should be to them," says Tommy. "I learned from my mother never to give up, and I learned from the Ranch to work hard, be kind, and trust in God. I'd like to go back out there and tell the boys how lucky they are to be there. It's the best place in the world for a boy to get his life back on track."

Todd Averett, Former Ranch Boy

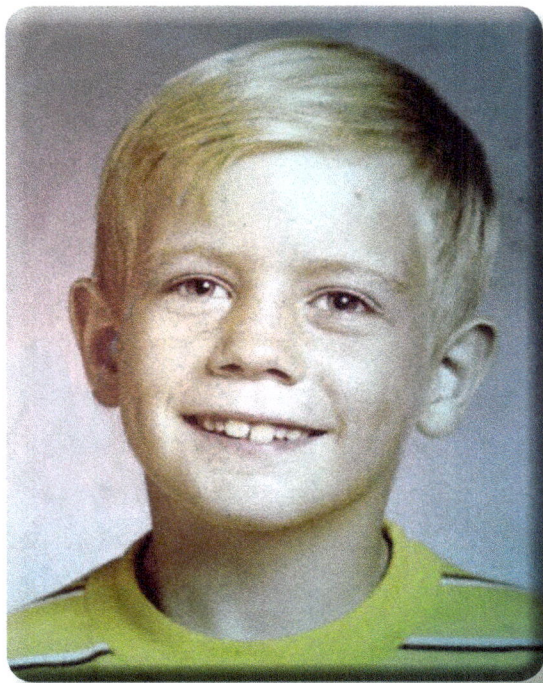

Seven year old Todd Averett

Memory is a remarkable gift from God. At the time that Todd Averett came to the Ranch, Ashley and Melba Jeter worked at the Ranch as cottage parents. Ashley, who is now deceased, would later become the Executive Director of the Ranch, but back in the 70s and 80s, he was exactly where God wanted him to be ... especially for a little boy named Todd Averett.

When he was six years old, life changed forever for Todd Averett and his three brothers.

"Dad shot my mother and then shot himself," Todd says in a calm, gentle voice that belies the terrible confusion and tragic circumstances surrounding his early childhood in Winter Haven, Florida. "Our grandparents tried to take care of us, but we boys were hellions, so they sent my older brothers, Timmy and Ted, and me to Rodeheaver Boys Ranch, and they kept Terry, our little brother."

Upon arriving at the Ranch in 1974, the Averett boys already knew about good morals and manners. They'd been taught respect for adults and were used to attending church every Sunday. Compared to some of the other Ranch boys who'd never been loved or disciplined, the Averett brothers at first seemed to be anything but hellions ... until ... they let their anger out. "We all three had bad tempers," recalls Todd. "We weren't disrespectful of our cottage parents, but we sure did fight among ourselves and the other boys. I had to work hard on my anger. It helped that we had to behave and get good grades or we couldn't play sports. I loved sports, so I learned to control my temper."

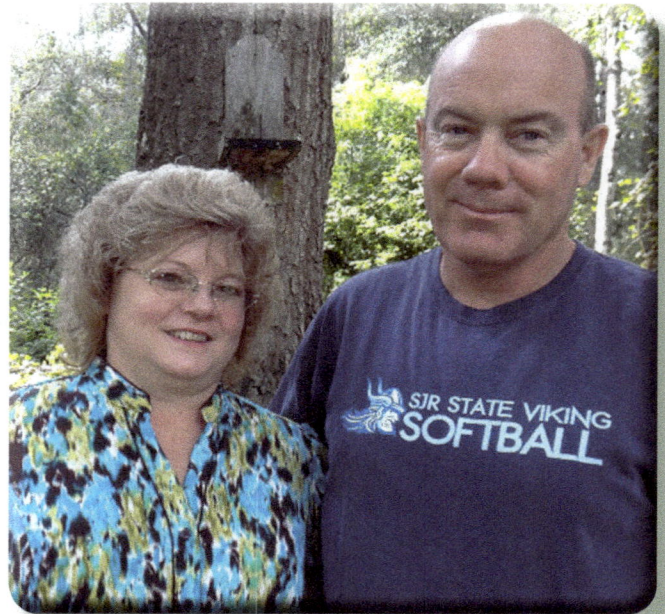

Shelly and Todd Averett, 2013

Ashley and Melba Jeter were Todd's cottage parents and he developed a special bond with them that remains strong to this day. A slow grin plays around Todd's mouth, traveling to his eyes as he remembers a Saturday night long ago. "Let me tell you about a lesson in real compassion that I learned from the Jeters," he says, leaning back and folding his arms. "I was in 9th grade when I went on my first real date. A boy from town named Lamar Cruz came and picked me up in his car and then we picked up the girls. We sat in that car and drank a whole bottle of Canadian Mist. The last thing I remember about that night was staggering into MacDonald's. The next thing I remember is Sheriff Pellicer handing me over to Ashley Jeter early Sunday morning. Ashley took me back to the Ranch and he and Melba didn't say a word. They made me eat a big bowl of cereal with milk. It was terrible. Then we went to church. I knew all through breakfast and church that my butt was in for a big whipping, but it didn't happen. They didn't tell anybody – not even the Ranch Director, Ed MacClellan. In fact, I never told anybody until today. Later, Melba said, "Well, Todd, you learned a lesson," and I said, "Yes, ma'am." That was all. That was compassion."

When they were 12, Todd and fellow Ranch boy, Ricky Gurthie used to go visit a boy named Don Barber and spend time with Don's family on weekends.

Tragically, Don was killed in a tractor accident at 12, and, later, the Barbers took in Ricky Gurthie. In the meantime, Todd's Aunt Sylvia sent for him to come home to Winter Haven for his last two years of high school, but he stayed close to Ricky and the Barbers, and eventually married Shelly Barber. "I consider Ricky my brother-in-law now," says Todd, a strong man who works at the timber mill and has coached girls' softball for many years. Todd and Shelly Averett have been married 31 years and have a son, Dillon, and a daughter, Dawn.

Todd notes that he always tells his story to the girls he's coaching. "Not for sympathy, but as a witness to the power of God," he says. "I tell them there is always someone worse off than they are. I heard stories, sitting on the dock fishing with other guys at Rodeheaver Boys Ranch that made me know I was better off than some. I prayed for them and I prayed for me. The Lord changes things if you let Him. I've been blessed."

Today, Todd looks back at his days at the Ranch and thanks God for the lessons he learned there. "There are some things you never forget," says Todd. "To this day, I can't smell Canadian Mist without getting sick... and, to this day, I'll always remember the compassion of the Jeters. I learned how to be a good parent at Rodeheaver Boys Ranch."

In April of 1974, more than 1000 people gathered to see Hollywood Celebrity Eddie Albert and Florida Governor Reuben Askew dedicate the Brad Robinson Memorial Vocational Building. Brad Robinson, a young boy from Bradenton, Florida, had resided at the Ranch some years earlier and been tragically killed when a tractor overturned on him. His mother chose to remember her son by donating this much-needed vocational building to his memory.

Today, the Brad Robinson Memorial Vocational Building is the site of the VIP (Vehicle Improvement Program), which is one of the biggest fundraisers for the Ranch, as well as a training ground for future automobile, boat and airplane mechanics.

MORE RANCH BOYS REMEMBER ...

Mitchell Johns (1964-1970)

Former Ranch Boy Mitchell Johns & Family
From Left – front row – Grandsons Joshua Jordan Johns and Jace Michael Wilson
2nd Row – Blake Johns, Joshua Johns, Amanda Johns, Kristin Johns & Mitchell Johns
Back Row – Josie Denham (Blake Johns' girlfriend), Daughter Kristen Johns, (behind her – boyfriend Brandon Moore), Wife Fay Johns and Mitchell Johns Sr.

Mitchell Johns remembers a couple of the "Medical Pardners" who treated boys pro bono when he was at the Ranch in the 1960s. Dr. Roy Campbell was one of them and pharmacist, Riley Bennett of Palatka filled Dr. Campbell's prescriptions for the same low fee – zero. "Doc Campbell fixed us up whenever one of us had a broken bone," says Mitchell. "I never broke anything. I was pretty tough."

Remembering when President Johnson came to the Ranch, Mitchell talked about the huge barbecue put on by Tommy Clay and Bill Penn and others. "They were great men," Mitchell said of the board members back then. In

2013, Mitchell Johns was a board member himself, and still close to Tommy Clay. In fact, he lives in Grandin, near the Clay Ranch, and often took the late Tommy Clay to board meetings. As plant manager for Vulcan Materials for more than twenty years, Mitchell left the board because he was spending so much time on the road. Now that he's recently retired, he's hoping to get back out to the Ranch and possibly even become a board member again. "The new leadership out at the Ranch sounds encouraging and I want to do everything I can to help the boys out there become good men."

"The difference between a career and a job is about twenty hours a week."
Ken's Favorite Sayings

Knowing God, learning responsibility, hard work and good manners ... those are just a few of the important lessons that Mitchell attributes to his time at the Ranch. "Some of those were rough lessons that I learned on the work crew while a boy at the Ranch. Sometimes, when I caught myself not making my kids do the right thing, I remember the old days, our work crews and curfews. It was not easy, and some things have changed, but they still teach the boys to work and it's a good place to learn. We need to get more people involved." When Mitchell Johns has gone back to the Ranch, he has always taken the time to talk to as many boys as possible. "I tell them that there's only one person who can hold you back and that's you. If you make up your mind to get somewhere, you can do it."

As a devoted family man who has lived a good life, Mitchell Johns has a great deal of important advice to hand down to his grandsons, and to the boys at the Ranch. "I tell them that the biggest thing in life is integrity. If you can't be trusted, it will go against you the rest of your life. And you must treat people right. We're all equal in God's eyes."

"I was 13 when I came to the Ranch. I went into 7th grade and stayed at the Ranch through high school. I played football and ran track and was President of the FFA. I was determined to succeed, and I did."

"Now, my son comes out to the Ranch and fishes with the boys at their tournament. Last year, they won for the Biggest Fish! I love seeing my family go back and meet the boys and enjoy the Ranch. It's like home to me."

Robert Siemiatkoski (1965-1972)

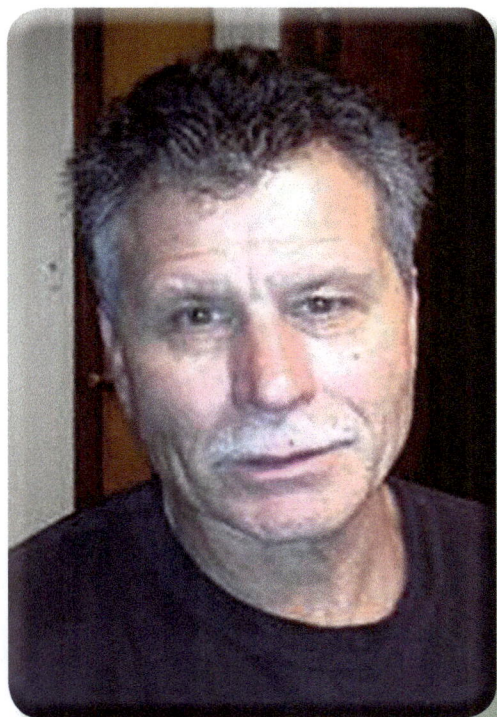

Robert Siemiatkoski was 10 years old in 1965 and had lived in terror for several years. An Italian chef, Robert's step-father beat the Siemiatkoski kids mercilessly when he was angry and often punished them by depriving them of food. "We were so hungry, we ate the dog and cat food he put out for the animals," recalls Robert. "I was deathly scared of him." Neighbors in their Orlando trailer park regularly reported the child abuse to social services. The Siemiatkoski kids were thrown back and forth between the Parental Home for Children and the trailer park, where their step-father waited with his own evil agenda. "My step-dad was teaching us how to steal," Robert remembers. "He'd take us into stores and show us how to put things in our pockets. We were learning the wrong ways of life."

The last time he went to the Parental Home with his siblings, Robert remembers that his mother and step-father picked up their golden-haired boy, Ronnie, and left the other four children there. Soon, Robert was sent to Rodeheaver Boys Ranch. His older brother, Joey, came to the Ranch later, but stayed a short time before joining the Peace Corps. His sister, Theresa, 7, and brother, Christopher, 5, were eventually adopted.

Ronnie (step brother) left front, then Joey, Robert. Theresa and Christopher.

Robert arrived at the Ranch with two chipped front teeth from being slammed against a bed by his step-father. Soon, his teeth were fixed by one of the devoted medical "Pardners," from Gainesville, and his distended, malnourished belly was filled with healthy food, but it took much longer for the fear to subside and the light to return to his haunted eyes.

Today, more than fifty years later, Robert Siemiatkoski is a successful man. He and his wife, Kathy, have three grown children, Jo Leigh, Robbie and Justin, and an adored grandson, Kason. After thirty years with Seminole Electric Company in Palatka, Robert is the Electrical Maintenance Supervisor. Each year, when Seminole Electric Company hosts a special Christmas party for Rodeheaver Boys Ranch, Robert talks with the boys. A strong role model who truly knows what they are feeling, he tells them about his days at the Ranch and encourages them to trust God, listen to their cottage parents, learn the Christian values that are taught there, and concentrate on growing up to be productive men of good moral character.

Over time, Robert has completely lost touch with his older brother, Joey, who eventually joined their mother in Connecticut. Growing up, Robert missed his younger siblings. "I always had a premonition that Theresa was a nurse and Christopher was an attorney," he says. In search of his brother and sister, Robert contacted the Parental Home only to be told they had been adopted and the records were sealed. Twelve years ago, Theresa called the Ranch looking for Robert. When he contacted Theresa in Titusville, Florida, a joyful reunion followed. Theresa is, indeed, a nurse. She remains close to Robert and his family to this day, but unfortunately, they have never been able to find their little brother, Christopher. Robert even contacted former State Representative Kelly Smith to see about having Christopher's adoption records unsealed, but to no avail. The only way to get them unsealed, he was told, would be if it were Robert's deathbed wish to find his brother. "I don't want to have to die to find Christopher," he says. Recently, Robert's pastor suggested that he pursue Ancestry.com's DNA testing, and possibly, if his brother has done it, they may finally have that reunion Robert yearns for.

Talking about his years at the Ranch brought back special memories for Robert. Somewhere on the Ranch there are still two class rings bearing the initials RES … "I lost the first one bailing hay, bought another one and lost it picking corn in our garden down by the river," he remembers. "I couldn't afford a third ring, so I never did have a class ring from Palatka High School."

Robert is still convinced that he and a bunch of other boys saw a UFO while playing football under a full moon in front of Phillips Cottage one night, and he remembers learning to repair cars by working on an old Edsel that they fixed up and then drove around the Ranch. Kathy Siemiatkoski, his wife, says that Robert's eyes sparkle when he talks about the Ranch. She wants to see that sparkle in his eyes when he finds Christopher.

In the meantime, Robert ("SEMO") is a familiar face to the boys at the Ranch, and last year, his son, Robbie, participated in the annual Boys Ranch Fishing Tournament, taking one of the boys out in his boat and bringing in a winning catch. The Ranch is Robert's extended family and he's grateful for the lessons learned there. "If it weren't for the Ranch, I'd probably have landed in jail," he says. "I was headed in that direction when they brought me here."

❧

Robert Manning (1976-1980)

Robert Manning was among the many boys over the years who received medical, spiritual, emotional and practical help at Rodeheaver Boys Ranch. He came to the Ranch in 1976 at age 10, with his 14-year old brother, John. Robert and John had been caught breaking into houses and were out of control when their mother sent them to the Ranch. Single, unemployed and overwhelmed with four children, their mother presented the Ranch to them as a sort of camp where they could go horseback riding, fishing and have fun. They soon found there was much more to it, including chores, strict rules and hard lessons to be learned. For the first few months, Robert was desperately homesick, but he eventually realized that Rodeheaver Boys Ranch saved his life.

"There's no telling what trouble I would have gotten into if I hadn't gone to the Ranch," said Robert when he was interviewed by phone back in 2014. "My brother and I needed discipline and a good foundation and that's what we got." More than that, he learned the core family values that shaped his life. What began as older brothers standing up for younger brothers gradually evolved into a cohesive group of boys that was as close to a family as many of them had ever experienced. "We felt like family," Robert remembered. "What happened to one, happened to all – we had fifty brothers."

Until he came to the Ranch, Robert had been a mediocre student at school. He'd had a hard time focusing on class work and daily routine, but it didn't take

him long to learn that being consistent and paying attention in school equaled achievement and rewards. Robert's first big mentor was cottage parent Ashley Jeter. Consistency was the key with Jeter. "It didn't matter to Mr. Jeter who you were or what you knew – he didn't play favorites and he told the truth … if you do that, this will happen. I respected him for his honesty, but he also engaged with all of us. He played football with us and I loved football. And, he was the study hall teacher so when you had unsatisfactory conduct, he punished you with root field duty." [going out in the cleared field and stacking roots in a pile]

One Saturday, Jeter put Robert in the root field right after breakfast and didn't come back. "I was out there all day, stacking roots and it started to get dark, so I walked back. It was probably a mile from the cottage. Mr. Jeter was rushing out of the cottage to come get me when he saw me walking up. He hugged me hard and said, 'I'm so sorry, Robbie. I forgot you were out there!' He was not above apologizing, and I learned from him that taking ownership of a mistake is not a bad thing."

When Robert was 14 and his brother was 18, they got in touch with their dad in Louisiana and went to see him on summer break. "He had been absent in our lives for seven years, but that summer we built up a pretty good relationship." Robert stayed with his dad and when they moved to Ft. Lauderdale, he started as a freshman on the varsity football team. He and his dad had their rough spots, but by that time, Robert had come into his own at the Ranch and knew who he was.

"I took a lot of things from the Ranch with me, like being neat and organized will help you be more successful in life than being slovenly, and if you apply yourself and work hard, you can do anything." When he graduated from South Plantation High School, Robert went into the Army's 82nd Airborne Special Forces, becoming a Green Beret.

Robert became a Plant Maintenance Network Supervisor with Comcast

Cable, with many direct reports and responsibility for cable service from Brunswick, Georgia to Live Oak, Florida. He is the father of four, and a loyal friend to his brother, John, in Louisiana as well as his Rodeheaver Ranch brothers in Palatka. "I've been back several times over the years and I've always remembered that Mr. Jeter said he'd never ask us to do anything he wasn't willing to do himself. He led by example, and that's how I try to live my life. My time at Rodeheaver Boys Ranch taught me right from wrong and groomed me to be a leader."

Richard Tisdel (1980-83)

I was 14 years old when I went to Rodeheaver Boys Ranch and 17 when I left. I've been a sheet metal worker since I was 18 years old and today I live in Shakopee, Minnesota and run one of the shifts at The Tennant Company in Minneapolis. Luckily, it was termed an essential business during the Covid-19 Virus Pandemic, but even so, we had some people furloughed for a while. My wife, Jodanne, is in a leadership position at her company, too, as a site supervisor at an all-inclusive call center, so we're alright. We work hard and God takes good care of us.

I came from a good family in Jacksonville, Florida but when I was about 12 or 13, I began chasing drugs and alcohol and skipping school. I tried to steal a wallet from a guy near Landon High School and I got caught and put into Juvenile detention. In one of my court appearances before Judge Dorothy Pate, my parents told her they were trying to get me in Rodeheaver Boys Ranch and she let me finish the last of my probation at the Ranch. When I got to the Ranch, my mindset didn't change – I still wanted drugs

and alcohol and still got in trouble. I was suspended from school for a week one time for smoking marijuana and I was working down by the River when Mr. Ted Callahan, our tutor, came and talked with me. I had always known who Christ is, but that day there was a change in my heart. It wasn't an immediate change, though. Mr. Callahan was there every Thursday, giving us a solid foundation. I also had two dear cottage parents, Herb and Joyce Wilson. They were consistent and meted out old school discipline and kind compassion at the same time. They saw me through God's eyes – looked at the potential of who I was as a boy. I was still doing drugs whenever I could, but I stopped getting in trouble after I stole an ink pen from Pic'N Save. The police were kind and Mr. Wilson picked me up at the police station. I never stole again.

I graduated from Palatka High School in 1983 and actually sat in the National Honor Society section, but I still let the drugs and alcohol rule my life for several more years. When I started dating a girl at church and she broke up with me, I harassed her and got into a fight with the cops and got sentenced to prison for 22 months. I was only there for four months, but that was when I really turned around and started putting the lessons I learned at the Ranch to work in my daily life.

I thought about cottage parents, Bud and Sharon Press, and talking to Bud about music while we built wood model airplanes, and talking with Herb Wilson while he was taking apart a small engine – talking man to boy – and I remembered Mr. Bill Green and the MacClellans – how kind Mrs. MacClellan was to me when I was hurting and homesick. I knew I had no excuse for living stupid – I had good parents who cared and good cottage parents and the Ranch gave me everything I needed to live right with God. I loved the horseback riding and fishing. I miss bareback riding. Sunny was a race horse that had been donated to us – he was ornery and skittish but I figured I could handle him. We were at a full gallop when he stopped dead in his tracks at a fence line near the barge canal levy and I went flying over Sunny's head. He raced back to the barn and I got a ride back on a friend's horse. There were some things I couldn't control, but I had to learn that the hard way.

It hasn't been an easy life, but I brought on most of my troubles myself. God was always there waiting for me to follow Him. I love the way He works. My wife and I go to New Hope Baptist Church and we were meeting on Saturdays for Bible study with a retired pastor and his wife, John and Margaret Stange. One day I was telling them about Rodeheaver Boys Ranch and they started smiling at each other. It turned out they were from Wynona Lake, Indiana, where Homer Rodeheaver lived, and they had gone to Mr. Rodeheaver's church. They told a funny story. Back in 1952, while Mr. Rodeheaver was gone on business (probably Boys Ranch business), they were at church with his housekeeper. She told them, "Hey, my boss has a television! Would you like to come and see a Rocky Marciano fight on TV?" The young couple went to Rodeheaver's house and watched the fight on television. Their story and our connection really brought it home to me – how big is God and how small are we? The Stange's had a long ministry in Cheyenne, Wyoming before coming to Minnesota and he has since passed away.

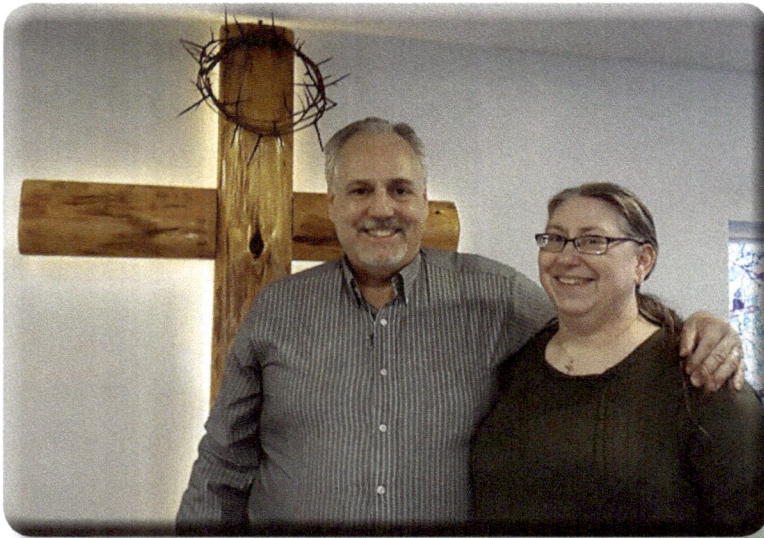
Richard and Jodanne Tisdel

My wife lives out the book of James – visiting orphans and widows – she still visits Mrs. Stange regularly and considers her a mentor. We were reconnected with Homer Rodeheaver through the Stanges all these years later, and I know it was not coincidence. Today, I walk with the Lord and I know we are in His hands. I'm grateful to so many people at the Ranch who gave me such caring attention and showed me God's love no matter how I behaved. God has prospered me more than I could ever have imagined.

Shawn Swigert (1981-1988)

God was in my life all along. I just wasn't listening to Him. It was only a couple of years ago that I finally got my life back on track, and I made a lot of mistakes along the way. Now I've got a good wife, Lori, and my children, Jarred, 17, and Peyton, 12, are kind, caring, loving people – a lot like the people I met at Rodeheaver Boys Ranch nearly five decades ago.

Mom was single and I was searching for a father figure. I was a rough kid and would do anything for attention. I was 8 years old in 1981, and I'd been in a foster home in South Florida when Mom picked me up and told me we were going to Disney World. I woke up at Rodeheaver Boys Ranch and stayed there until 1988. I held a hard grudge against Mom for years, but now I'm grateful to her – in fact, I take care of her. She lives with my family and me.

Back in the 1980s, kids at school were mean to Ranch boys. We were bullied all the time. I was in 4th or 5th grade when this kid used to taunt us with a bag of candy – waving it in front of us. I told the other boys on the way to school, "When he comes today, I'm going to slap that bag of candy out of his hand." When I did, all the kids dove on the candy and I got in trouble – suspended for a week. Herb Wilson told me to grab a pickax and a shovel and took me to the stump of an old oak tree about three feet in diameter that he had cut down with a saw. He said, "When you get that stump out, you're off restriction." I worked on it all that week and then, I worked on it after school and on weekends. Finally, one day Herbie came to me and said, "You've done a good job, but you need help." He hooked up a Ford tractor and pulled that stump out. I didn't realize then what a blessing that was – that stump represented hard work, determination and goal-setting. When I gave it my all,

Herb saved me, just like Jesus has saved me over and over in my life.

I learned how to work the land at the Boys Ranch, how to ride horses and fix engines and build things. Today, I'm a member of the International Brotherhood of Electrical Workers (IBW) and I make a good living, but it took many rocky years of drug and alcohol addiction to get here. I left

Shawn Swigert and Family

the Ranch before I graduated from high school and moved back with my Mom. Judy Watson, the truancy officer at Palatka High School, said, "Shawn, you're not doing this to yourself." She picked me up and took me to St. Johns Community College and I got a GED. I started and quit the IBW apprenticeship trade many times and finally graduated with honors in 2016.

When I look back at the Ranch, everything I learned there has helped me through everything. God is the only reason I'm here and I learned about God at the Ranch. Ted Callahan taught me that with God, everything is possible. He taught me to pray and promised me that God would answer with what I needed, not necessarily what I wanted. Herb Wilson and Bill Green were the father figures I was looking for. Bill Green taught me not to lie. He said, "It never stays one lie - you always have to tell another one to cover up the first one." They both taught me the work ethic and gave me self-worth, but I never thought my Mom would see me successful. I never gave God the glory. Now I pray every day for a 17-year old boy – that he will not make the bad choices I made.

I believe the Ranch is the only thing that taught me the right way to go ... it just took me a while to see the lessons. When God calls me home, I hope they put on my tombstone, "Swag was such a horse's butt when he was a kid, but he turned out to be a good man."

Merry Christmas

and a

Happy New Year

Especially to

YOU

From

The Boys

at

Rodeheaver Boys' Ranch

Because **YOU** Care
Because **YOU** Help
Because **YOU** Have a Big Heart

Only **BECAUSE** of **YOU**

Rodeheaver Boys' Ranch

IS A SUCCESS

•

We Need Your Help

•

MAKE CHECK PAYABLE TO:
RODEHEAVER BOYS' RANCH, INC.
PALATKA, FLORIDA

•

Best of health and

Happiness to You

1960s

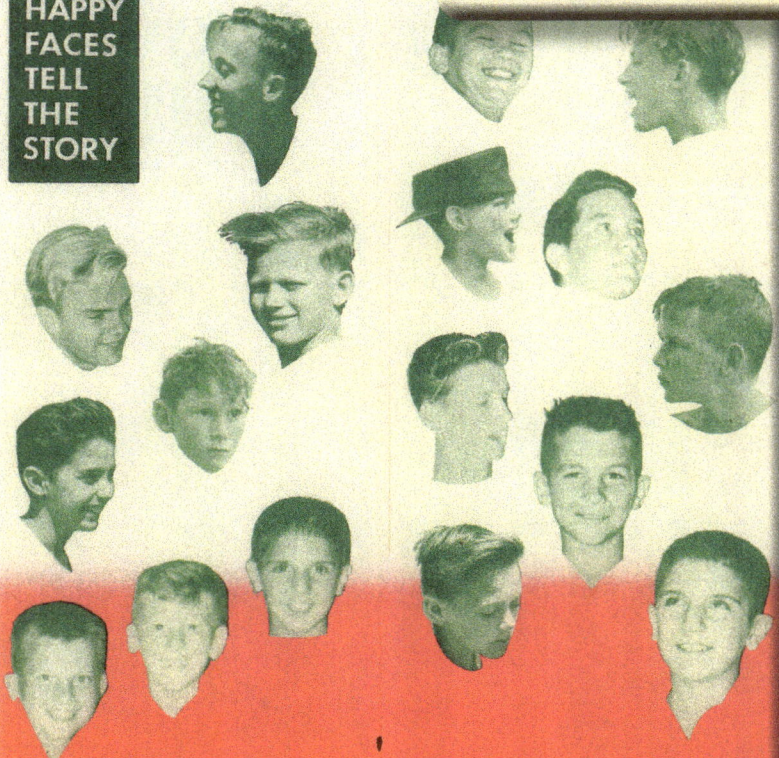

CHAPTER THREE:
THE EARLY YEARS – BIGGERS CHAPEL

In 1975, Rodeheaver Boys Ranch celebrated its Silver Anniversary – twenty-five years of building boys! At the Annual Meeting in April, with the dedication by Secretary of State Bruce Smathers of the newly constructed "Westbury Cottage," it was announced that Homer Rodeheaver's original vision of creating a sanctuary for 50 boys was finally going to be realized.

A listing of the Executive Committee Members from 1950-1975 ran in the Silver Anniversary Program as follows: Homer Rodeheaver, Bruce Howe, Harry Westbury, James E. Thomas, B. C. Pearce, J. H. Millican, Jr., Judge Mattie Farmer, F. H. Rion, Sr., E. M. Hall, Karl Lehman, Rev. Charles Thompson, R. Tommy Clay, Mrs. P. B. Huff, C. D. Middleton, W. M. Thomas, Mrs. Juanita Young, William Penn. L. W. Harrell, Jack Guistwhite, E. W. Pellicer, Dr. Roy Campbell, David Arthurs, W. W. Stuart, Dr. W. W. Weigel, Fred Lynch, Reid Hughes, Edgar Johnson, Robert W. Webb, Irving Weinstein, Harold Watts, Riley Bennett, John H. Trescot, Jr., Craig Benson, J. Jud Chalmers, Ed Hedstrom, W. C. Lewis, Bob Toney, Clayton O'Quinn, Sam S. Browning, III., William Kerr, Randy Avon, Lew Wadsworth, III., Don Hersey, John Aldridge, F. V. Oliver, Bob Kiss, Don Rose, Dr. Clarence Edward, and Gregg Bernard.

When Joe Durkin, Editor of Florida Horse Magazine, suggested to Ed MacClellan that the boys begin raising thoroughbred horses for sale at the Ranch, the boys were all in. For a while, horse raising became an excellent source of funds and provided a future vocation for some of the boys. Horses still play a large role at the Ranch. It was at a horse sale that Ed met George Steinbrenner, owner of the New York Yankees. When Steinbrenner asked Ed what he could do for the boys, Ed replied, "Well, you could play us a benefit baseball game," to which Steinbrenner replied, "Okay."

The Ranch Rambler in the Spring of 1976 read: "Yankees to Play ball at Boys

Ranch ... The New York Yankees will be playing an exhibition baseball game against the University of Florida this spring and all proceeds from ticket sales will go to Rodeheaver Boys Ranch." The exhibition game brought a great deal of state and national attention to the Ranch and resulted in a new baseball field being built. With the national attention came a remembrance from a former Ranch boy, William "Bill" M. Bennett, Director of Development for The Church Divinity School of the Pacific in Berkeley, California. Bill wrote that the new baseball field he'd read about jogged his memory of his time back in 1957, when he came to the Ranch at age 12. "I laid out the first baseball diamond on that spot," he wrote. "Each spring a couple of us would measure out the base lines, stamp down the sand spurs and then stand back and try to figure out ways to level the ground. We tried a number of jury-rigged ideas, but nothing ever worked. I am delighted that you now seem to have a first-class facility."

"If you plant a tree, don't keep pulling it up by the roots to see how it's growing."
Ken's Favorite Sayings

Herb and Joyce Wilson, ages 21 and 19 respectively, became the youngest cottage parents ever hired at the Ranch in 1977. They remained cottage parents for five years and then Herb became Director of Ranch Life for another five years. "My greatest time of life was being there," declared Herb. "The boys come there with no self-esteem and you build them up ... you know you are doing something important."

Bill Green and Herb Wilson loved playing tricks on the boys ... giving them something fun to remember "because," said Green, "many of the boys hadn't had much fun in their lives." One night, Sheriff Walt Pellicer was in on the trick. It was around Halloween and he had a deputy come out and speak to the boys about safety. The deputy casually mentioned that there were two escaped prisoners who had stolen a blue pickup truck and were still at large in the Palatka area. The boys had a Halloween "Spook Walk" lined up by the Sheriff's office the next night and some of the house parents were hiding in trees, wearing sheets and had plenty of scary things planned that the boys expected, but when Bill Green shined his flashlight into the woods on two men wearing striped uniforms, standing next to a blue pickup truck, pandemonium broke

out. "Those boys covered twenty acres of woods in two minutes, screaming and squealing all the way," said Green, chuckling at the memory.

No matter how rough they had it, home was the place the boys talked about the most. It still is. One night a boy stole one of the Ranch vehicles to go home. Ed and LouAnn got a call from the Sheriff's office that a Datsun Pickup had been wrecked south of Salt Springs, near Ocala; the driver was dead. They sped to the scene and discovered the vehicle had been stolen by one of the identical Lamp twins, either Donnie or Ronnie, but they couldn't identify which of them was dead. Bill Green arrived on the scene. He and his wife, Mary Ann, were close to the Lamp twins and there was only one way he could tell them apart: Ronnie Lamp had a separation between his front teeth. Crouching next to the boy lying dead on the ground, Bill asked the officer if he could put his finger in the boy's mouth. The boy was Ronnie. They called the Ranch and a cottage parent found Donnie asleep on the couch. "There were whippoorwills trilling the morning we broke the news to Donnie that his brother, Ronnie, had died," Green recalled. "To this day, Mary Ann cannot hear a whippoorwill without remembering that tragic morning one of the twins tried to go home and didn't make it."

Ed MacClellan, who passed away on February 2, 2020, retired in 1982, after more than a decade at the Ranch. In October of 2019, as he and LouAnn reminisced about their days there, Ed talked of the little homey things they tried to do for the boys. "LouAnn has a sweet, motherly way about her, and that seemed to comfort the boys, most of whom had not had mothering in a long time, or ever," he said. "For instance, they were all supposed to make their beds and straighten their rooms before breakfast, but LouAnn would go behind them after they left for school and tidy things up and straighten their beds again. They knew she'd been there and that she cared for each one of them."

Ed & LouAnn MacClellan

BIGGERS CHAPEL

As the years went on, ground was being broken for new cottages and new structures on a regular basis, but one of the most meaningful groundbreaking ceremonies happened on April 27, 1980, when the construction of The Biggers Spiritual and Educational Center, a chapel and study hall, began. Almost entirely funded by Mrs. Helen Biggers of Tulsa, Oklahoma, the daughter of Mrs. George W. Biggers, a lifelong fan of Homer Rodeheaver, the chapel has become the heart of the Ranch.

Biggers Chapel is a beautiful sanctuary that has been used for Bible study, regular worship, weddings, funerals, and private moments of prayer

and reflection since it was dedicated in 1984, with three distinct areas set up for building boys: 1) For spirituality: the sanctuary with its magnificent stained glass windows and deep wooden pews; 2) the library/classroom (now filled with computers) to reinforce academic endeavors; 3) the arts and crafts area for the enrichment of natural talent and inspiration.

Working together roofing Biggers Chapel

Each of the colorful, elaborately painted glass windows in Biggers Chapel depicts a Biblical scene of either a man or boy. Each was created beautifully and dedicated with love by a supporter of the Ranch. The large central window depicting Jesus, the carpenter, guiding four young boys in fence-building, was dedicated in loving memory to *Rev. and Mrs. Walter Pierce "Skipper and Mom."*

The Nativity
(George and Faye Willey)

The Nativity or Christmas story is about the birth of Jesus Christ, our Lord and Savior. Because there was no room at the Inn in Bethlehem, Mary gave birth to Jesus in a stable and placed Him in a manger (a feeding trough) instead of a crib. Even as an infant, Jesus was King. He might have been born in a fancy, jewel-studded palace, but He came into the world in a rustic place much like our Ranch barn, surrounded by the smell of animals and hay. Surely, this Ranch is a blessed place for good beginnings – just as Jesus began His life in the humble stable.

Matthew 2:1-16

The Loaves and Fishes
(in loving memory of Amy "Mom" Owen by friends)

Grace is still said in the Rodeheaver Boys Ranch dining hall before Grits and Gravy, as we thank our Lord Jesus Christ and his many helpers for the abundance that is shared here every day. Ranch boys never go hungry. Like the Loaves and Fishes, the Beef and Potatoes, Vegetables and Salads, Rolls, Pies, Cakes, and Pastries, just keep coming!
Mark 6:30-44

Abraham Sacrificing his son, Isaac
(In loving memory of Glenn Ward Holmes by Mr. and Mrs. Edwin H. Willis)

Abraham trusted completely in the Lord and was prepared to sacrifice his Isaac, whom he called his "Son of Promise" at God's command. At the last minute, God sent a lamb to be sacrificed in Isaac's place. Trusting in the Lord is not easy, but in the end, Isaac, the "Son of Promise," survived and thrived, just as each of our Boys of Promise will do, once they learn to trust completely in the Lord.

Genesis 22:1-12

Moses in the Bullrushes

(In Loving Memory of H.R. (Skinny) Smith by Bulls-Hit Ranch and Farm Employees and Families)

God had a plan for Moses to grow up and save his people from slavery in Egypt. His mother hid him in the bushes and went away, but he was never alone. He was found, raised well, and delivered his people out of slavery, performing many miracles along the way. God has a plan for each boy who feels abandoned. This story of Moses is a sign that God places boys where they need to be for a reason. God's hand is on this Ranch. There are no abandoned boys here – only boys who are part of God's plan.

Exodus 2:1-10

David and Goliath

(Homer and Julia Ramsey)

David, the shepherd boy, was not afraid of a mortal man. David knew that he had the power of God in him and no one could defeat that power. He killed Goliath with stones from his slingshot and then picked up the Giant's sword and used it to cut off his head. Israel defeated the Philistines because of a boy who had faith and trust in God. When the boys at the Ranch have the power of God in them, they, too, are strong enough to defeat any evil that threatens them.

1 Samuel 17

Joseph's Coat of Many Colors
(Mr. and Mrs. P. P. Pelicer)

Joseph's father favored him over his many older brothers and gave him a special coat of many colors. His brothers were jealous and sold him into slavery, but Joseph was faithful and honest and trusted God, no matter what. He was richly rewarded and forgave his brothers, saving their lives. Joseph's coat of many colors had great significance. He was a Biblical super-hero.

Genesis 37:3

John the Baptist and Jesus
(In loving memory of Ida MacDonald Kane & Mildred Holmes Eakin by John P. Browning, Jr. and Family)

Jesus came from Nazareth in Galilee and was baptized by John in the Jordan River. Just as Jesus was coming up out of the water, He saw heaven being torn open and the Spirit descending on Him like a dove. And a voice came from heaven: "You are my Son, whom I love; with you I am well pleased." At once the Spirit sent Him out into the wilderness, and He was in the wilderness forty days, being tempted by Satan. He was with the wild animals, and angels attended Him. God was well-pleased with Jesus, yet He tested Him. Faithfulness and trust in God will help us pass the daily tests that life puts in our path.

Mark 1:9-13

Shadrach, Meshach and Abednego in the Fiery Furnace

(In loving memory of Mr. and Mrs. Q. I. Roberts, Sr. & Mrs. And Mrs. C. M. Johnson by Mr. and Mrs. Edgar Johnson and Family)

Shadrach, Meshack and Abednego were three men who believed in God and refused to worship a golden idol, even when King Nebuchadnezzar threatened to throw them in a fiery furnace. They trusted God and knew they would be protected from the flames. The King saw a fourth man walk into the furnace ... the fourth was the Angel of God, protecting His own. That Angel of God is here at the Ranch with us as we do God's will.

Daniel 3:16

Daniel in the Lion's Den

(Gift of the Neil Freeman Family)

Daniel refused to worship the King and was thrown into the lion's den. He survived the night in the lion's den because God closed the mouths of the Lions and protected him. God will protect us when we believe in Him and follow His commands.

Daniel 6:10-18

David Fighting the Lion to Save his Sheep

(The Westbury Family, Mickey, Harry & Bill)

David was a shepherd and the safety of his sheep was his responsibility. He killed a lion and a bear to save the lives of his sheep. He did not think he was stronger than either of those ferocious animals – he simply had the spirit of God in him and knew that if he did his job, God would help him. Just as it our job at the Ranch to keep our boys safe from harm, we will trust in God to help us.

Samuel 17:34-36

The Crucifixion

(Given by Stanley, Helen and William S. Weise)

Our Lord Jesus Christ suffered on the cross, was crucified, dead and buried and rose again from the grave so that we could have everlasting life. Jesus died for our sins and set us free to live our lives and worship Him. Jesus loved all of us unconditionally. Because of His sacrifice for us, we must be swift to love one another and see one another as He sees us.

Matthew 27: 32-56

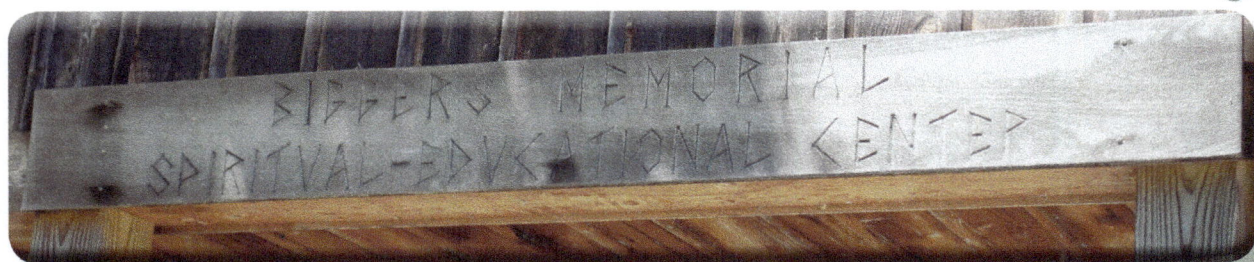

In the narthex of Biggers Chapel is a memorial bench dedicated to the memory of a Ranch boy named Chad Ryan Gosa. Chad and his twin brother, Eric, spent some years at the Ranch as boys and learned much about Christian morals and values. Chad was twenty-four years old when he came to the rescue of a woman being assaulted and was shot dead by her abuser. Chad's mother requested that his ashes be scattered beneath his favorite tree at Rodeheaver Boys Ranch. The plaque on the bench reads:

In Loving Memory of
Chad Ryan Gosa
January 29, 1983 - May 6, 2007
"Be Still and Know that I am God"
Psalm 46:10

In 2018, when Tommy Clay passed away, Judge Ed Hedstrom gave the eulogy at the Memorial Service which was, appropriately, held in the beautiful chapel at Rodeheaver Boys Ranch. The Judge's Eulogy follows:

Today, we celebrate the life of Tommy Clay, a life well lived! Thank you all for being here.

It's appropriate that we're here on the grounds of RBR and in this beautiful Chapel that was completed in 1984. I want to call your attention to the large stained-glass window directly behind me. Tommy and his family donated that in honor of Skipper and Mom Pierce, a former Executive Director and his wife.

If you knew anything about Tommy, you knew he loved this Ranch second only to his family. And I'm sure that sometimes Lorene even questioned that.

Tommy's relationship with Homer Rodeheaver began in 1949. Tommy had just moved to Putnam County with his new bride Lorene, as the newly hired assistant County Agent. In that capacity he met Homer who owned Rainbow Ranch now known as Rodman Plantation, and spent many hours showing him around Putnam County.

That friendship led to Tommy being invited to a meeting at Rainbow Ranch with other local dignitaries where Homer unveiled his plans to establish a boys' home on this property. The plans moved quickly and in June 1950 Rainbow Ranch for Boys was chartered.

At the Annual Meeting in 1952 the name was changed to Rodeheaver Boys Ranch and Homer offered Tommy the position of Executive Director. He declined and was elected to the Board of Directors, thus beginning his 66+ years of service to this Ranch. Mr. Rodeheaver passed away in 1955 and never got to see the fruits of his investment in Tommy Clay.

I really got to know Tommy in high school as a member of the Key Club while attending Kiwanis Club meetings where he was a member.

When I graduated from high school in June 1958 at age 17, Tommy

called me and asked if I wanted to work at the Ranch that summer. "Sure," I said, "What's my job?"

He thought a moment and said: "We'll call you our recreational director. You spend the mornings on work details with the boys and keep them entertained in the afternoon!"

"I can do that," I said.

The second day on the job, a 15-and-a-half-year-old boy twice my size almost beat me up. Tommy's response: "You can't let that happen!"

I thanked him for that WONDERFUL advice!

For the next seven years until I completed my schooling in Gainesville, I worked every summer at the Ranch. Some of the happiest times of my life!

It was during that time that I began to see the real Tommy Clay and the love he had for the Ranch. He did it all. He was as comfortable sitting in any Board Room anywhere taking care of the affairs of the Ranch as he was cleaning out horse stalls or putting up fence at the Ranch. He knew no bounds.

Tommy served on the Ranch Board for 66 years and 11 months, give or take a few days. He was a modest and humble man, never wanting to call attention to himself or receive any accolades for anything. In fact, he was known to try and avoid any such praise.

A good example of that occurred in 2007. The BOD had voted to present him with a "Lifetime Achievement Award," the first and only such award by the Board to this date. It was to be an elegant sit-down dinner at the Ravine Gardens Civic Center. The only problem was that when he got wind of it, there was grave doubt as to whether he would even show up. Lorene and his son Clay were equally skeptical about his appearance. Needless to say, I caught it big time from him. He did show up, a little late, and it turned out to be a very special evening. But I heard about it for months after!

Perhaps Tommy's greatest single accomplishment involved the new paved access road from Highway 19. When the Cross Florida Barge Canal cut off the original access road, the Corp of Engineers had to cut a new dirt road in the present location, but claimed they had no money to pave it. Tommy took it upon himself to travel to Washington DC to talk with then Senator Holland, and the Public Works Committee Chairman, Senator Randolph. When word filtered down that a bill authorizing the paving was probably forthcoming, the Corp of Engineers promptly "found" the money and paved the Road. As usual, Tommy sought no praise or credit.

The Ranch was always famous for its legendary open pit barbeques headed up by Tommy, Walt Pellicer, Bill Penn, Edgar Johnson, and a host of others.

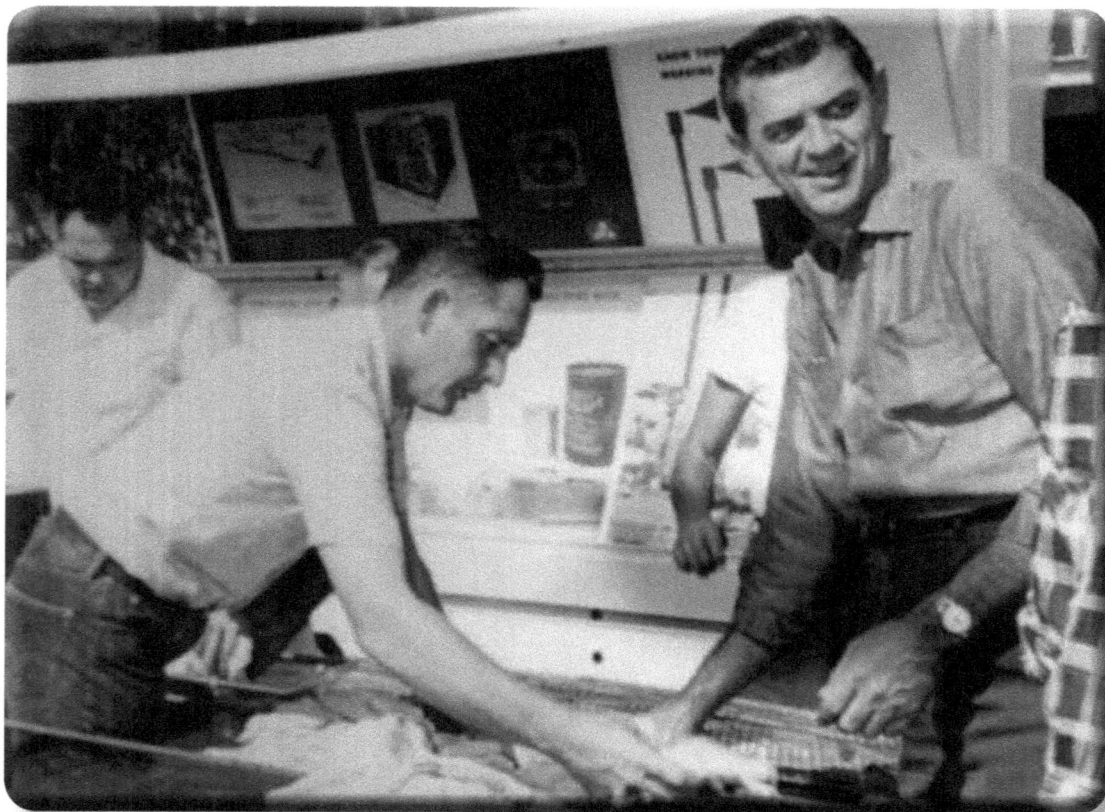

Tommy Clay and Fount Rion, Sr., with Chuck Pierce in the background

The mother of all barbeques occurred on 2-27-1964 when President Lyndon Johnson came to the Ranch to dedicate the Cross Florida Barge Canal.

It was an all-night affair the night before, getting ready to serve what turned out to be some 8600+ meals. Those involved took turns working & resting throughout the night. Tommy frequently joked about having to keep tabs on Edgar to make sure he was working and not sleeping. AND Tommy always lamented the fact that he only charged the Corp of Engineers $.87 per meal served. I loved reminding him of that many times later!

When Bill Penn, Edgar Johnson and Walt Pellicer passed away, it left a void in Tommy that I don't think he ever filled. He really missed those guys.

When Tommy got to the point he couldn't attend the Board meetings on a regular basis and do all the other things he had always done at the Ranch, he felt he should resign from the Board. I promptly told him he couldn't do that.

Why, he asked?

Because you just can't.

That worked for a while, but eventually he began to push me as to exactly why he could not resign. I finally threw a "Hail Mary pass' and said: "Tommy, I'm a lawyer, trust me, you can't resign."

Of course, that went over like a lead balloon.

I finally convinced him that if he did resign it would not be accepted by the Board and he would remain as a director on the Ranch records forever. And, there would be nothing he could do about that. He was satisfied, and the subject never came up again.

In retrospect, he may have been just jerking my chain, but no matter, I always loved bantering with him about anything.

IN CLOSING,
To you, Lorene, I want to say that you have been Tommy's partner, soulmate, wife and supporter in all that Tommy has done in his lifetime. His accomplishments are your accomplishments, his successes are

your successes, and his spot in the history of Rodeheaver Boys Ranch is your spot as well. The Clay name will forever be connected to this Ranch through Tommy and you, through Clay, Jr. who has served on the Board and thru your grandson Chance who is currently serving. And to Tommy, my very special friend, I simply say: May you rest in peace!

MEDICAL "PARDNERS"

Before boys could grow to be strong and successful men, they needed their physical as well as their mental and spiritual bodies in good shape. That was where the medical "Pardners" came in.

Dr. Robert Mitchem

Beverly and Robert Mitchem

Back in 1971, Dr. Robert Mitchem and his wife, Beverly, came to Palatka, where he opened his Optometry practice. It wasn't long before a colleague told him about the boys out at the Ranch and their need of free medical treatment. "I treated the boys – did all the visual exams for them and gave them glasses and whatever they needed over the years. I have a heart for children. Two of my four children were adopted." Beverly Mitchem gave birth to their son, Bobby, and their daughter, Debbie, and they adopted a boy, Jerry, and a girl, Sherry. Sadly, the Mitchem's lost Bobby to leukemia at age 10, and their adopted son, Jerry, had a wild streak that could not be tamed. He is now in prison. "Not every boy can be helped, no matter how hard you try," said Dr. Mitchem, remembering years of heartache, prayer and expensive therapy, all to no avail. "Jerry was more than Beverly and I could handle, but I've seen the way the Ranch has changed the lives of so many boys, and I'm glad we've been part of that." Today, their daughter Sherry is

a music teacher in Orlando – the mother of four children, and the best friend of her sister, Debbie Bacon. Debbie, the wife of Greg Bacon, Vice-President of the Rodeheaver Boys Ranch Board of Directors, lives in Palatka right around the corner from her parents.

Born in Bessemer City, North Carolina, Dr. Robert Mitchem grew up hunting and fishing, but had gotten away from those simple pursuits as he grew his practice in Orlando, Florida. "I saw what was happening with Disney World in Orlando and I knew I needed to be elsewhere," he says, recalling the first day he saw Palatka. "I drove over the bridge and thought Palatka was just about the prettiest little town I'd ever seen. The river was beautiful, and I yearned to go fishing and hunting again." Moving from Orlando to Palatka, the doctor now knows that the true "magic kingdom" is right out at Rodeheaver Boys Ranch, where he is now in charge of setting up hunting trips for Ranch supporters. Dr. Mitchem, a past President of the Rodeheaver Board of Directors and now a lifetime member of the Rodeheaver Foundation, spends a great deal of his time scouting turkey and deer on the Ranch and setting up feeders, helping in every way to make it one of the finest wildlife preserves in the State of Florida.

Dr. Mitchem at a deer stand near one of his feeders

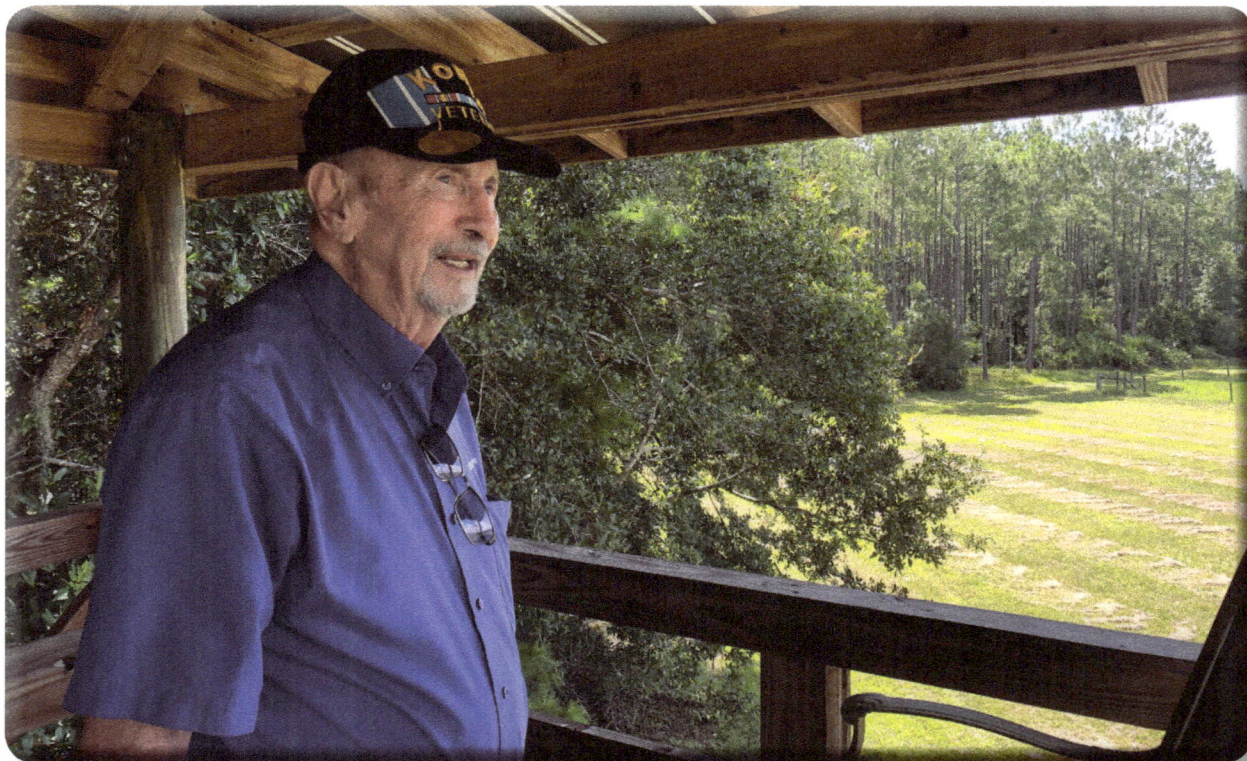

"I feel part of the Ranch," Mitchem says, noting that he had great admiration for the job that Ken Johnson did as Executive Director for 23 years, and he is thrilled that Brad Hall has stepped in now that Ken is retired. "It takes a bold man to run this Ranch," he says, "And both Ken and Brad are bold men of God who are not afraid to do what is necessary." One of the things Dr. Mitchem considers a necessity is getting the word out about the Ranch. "We need to bring people here, put them up in the Lodge, show them why they should support these boys. I'm always asking people to help give these kids a chance at life."

"Success in life should be determined by contributions, not accumulations." Ken's Favorite Sayings

Noting that he and Beverly have been blessed by the Lord, Dr. Mitchem is determined to help make the Ranch a sanctuary for all who live there. "It's a special place for the boys," he says. "I've seen them in the chapel, on the dock and in the woods, praying, studying, fishing and hunting. They are doing their best to give the boys a Christian life – it's all about the boys and God."

Dr. Steve Chapman

Dr. Steve Chapman, a past president of the Florida Association of Orthodontists as well the Rodeheaver Boys Ranch Board of Directors, began treating Ranch boys free of charge back in the early 1980s. "A group of dentists from Gainesville had been helping," he remembers, "but I came into town in 1979 and Dr. Craig Raby (now retired) was an ear, nose and throat physician who told me about the boys ranch and asked me to be on the board. I've been out there ever since, through the tough times and good times." Chapman particularly remembers treating one little boy,

Steve Chapman and family in 2013 at the Bluegrass Festival

about ten years old, who had a big scar across his left cheek. "He was from Ohio and when they found him, his father had chained him to the basement stairs like a dog, fed him twice a day, when he left in the morning and got back at night. They found him with no clothes on. His dad had kept him like that for over a year." To the best of Chapman's memory, the boy stayed at the Ranch until he was 18 and then went in the military. "The boy just craved attention and I was glad to give it to him, as were others at the Ranch. With the background he had, it was amazing that he could grow into a productive adult, but I'm pretty sure he did."

Growing up in Mayfield, Kentucky, Steve was taught the solid Christian values that have guided him throughout his life. "My Dad, George Chapman, died in 1999, and I stood in line for more than three hours at his funeral while people, one after the other, shook my hand and told me how much my father had done for them." With a role model like his father, Chapman is glad that the

Ranch has hired great role models over the past two decades. "Ken Johnson was a great Executive Director and now Brad Hall is following in his footsteps as a fine role model for the boys."

Still keeping healthy, straight teeth in the mouths of Ranch boys, Chapman has a few boys in braces most of the time and is grateful to be able to contribute his services free of charge.

As often as possible, Dr. Chapman invites people to visit the Ranch and have dinner with the boys, especially on Wednesday nights when there is a prayer meeting in the chapel. "If you can attend a chapel service with the boys and come away untouched, there is no heart in you," he says, adding that his heart and soul, like those of executive directors in the past, are fully committed to Rodeheaver Boys Ranch.

Dr. Richard Perallon

An active member of the Rodeheaver Boys Ranch Board of Directors since 1992, Dr. Richard Perallon has been providing free dental service to the Ranch boys for several years. "Steve Chapman brought me out to the Ranch for the first time, and that's all it

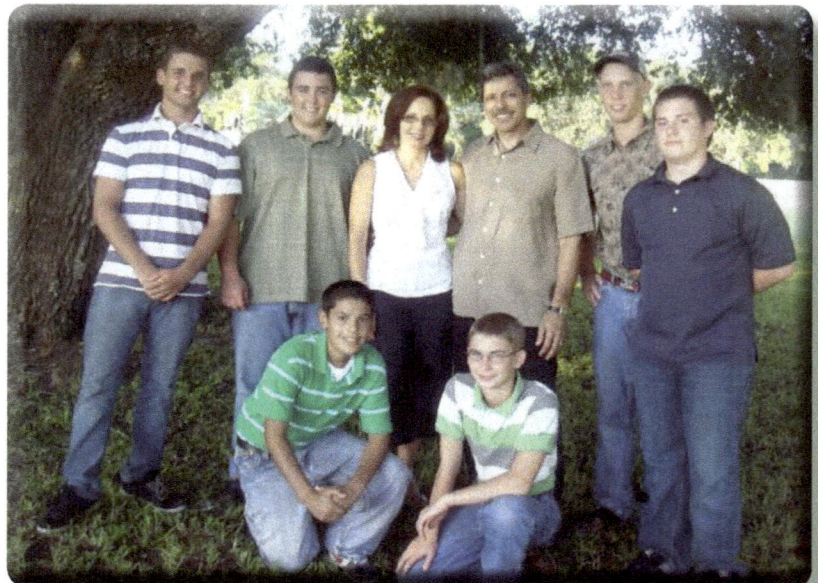

Dr. Richard Perallon and wife, Lisa, with Ranch boys

took," says Dr. Perallon. "It's easy to see how good this place is once you get out here and meet the boys and talk to the staff."

As a past President of the Board of Directors and now a member of the Rodeheaver Foundation, Dr. Perallon talks of the satisfaction he receives from

helping young people learn coping skills with a Christian focus. Over the years, he notes, he's observed a loving family atmosphere in the cottages and deep commitment of the staff to the boys. "I'm in awe of Ken Johnson," Perallon exclaimed in a 2013 interview, talking about Ken's undaunting character, determination and compassion as Executive Director. Today, he is encouraged and confident that the new Executive Director, Brad Hall, is a strong man of God who obviously cares deeply about the Ranch and the boys.

An avid outdoorsman, a devoted family man, successful professional and devout Christian, Richard Perallon is passionate about the Boys Ranch and all of the programs in place to help the boys become healthy mentally, spiritually and physically. "I feel great pleasure in watching them grow and learn," he says. "I can see that they are becoming a part of the solution and no longer part of the problem and that makes me feel good to be involved in their progress. They learn a strong work ethic at the Ranch, and it serves them well for the rest of their lives."

Looking back at the many boys he's treated over the years, Dr. Perallon still gets calls from the Ranch occasionally. A boy has a tooth ache or a broken tooth or some dental issue and needs to be seen. "I try to get him in to the office within a day or two," says Dr. Perallon, "and I've come to expect a well-behaved patient – even more so than most teens. I've seen some boys who had a great deal of tooth destruction due to neglect and I really admire them because they let me do what I need to do – even when a shot is involved and it's not always easy. I've found that the Ranch boys are champions of cooperation. These young men square their shoulders and are prime examples of the level of parenting that goes on at the Ranch. Of course, we usually joke a bit, too, and after I get the job done, I pat them on the back, and they leave with a smile."

Dr. Perallon enjoys going out to the Ranch and racing with the boys and competing in athletic endeavors, but his favorite times of bonding have been when he's been in a tree stand with a boy at The Bitter End, a South Carolina hunting lodge owned by board member Carlton Spence. "Carlton is the salt of the earth," says Dr. Perallon. "He provides the boys a hunting trip every year at the Bitter End and I've been lucky enough to act as a chaperone and guide several times. It's a unique experience, sitting in the tree stand with a boy – you can't put a price on it. I remember an early morning hunt – quietly waiting for the deer to come out – and glancing out of the corner of my eye to see the boy nodding his head – dozing on me! I think he finally got a deer, but not that morning!"

Dr. Perallon has become the good friend of a former ranch boy named Jason Claro. Jason married a girl who had been a patient in Perallon's dental practice, and now Jason and Dr. Perallon share many good memories of the Ranch together. "Jason has grown to be quite an impressive man," says Perallon. "And he has told me that he credits the Ranch with much of his success in life."

Drs. Roy Campbell & Craig Raby

In the 70s and 80s, the late Dr. Roy Campbell, a long-time board member and supporter of the Ranch, provided free medical service to the boys regularly. Dr. Campbell was a family physician and recruited other medical colleagues to treat the boys as well, including Dr. Craig Raby, a dermatologist who is now retired. Campbell and Raby went out of their way to treat Ranch boys.

Over the past 70 years, there have been many more medical professionals who have stepped up to treat Ranch boys. Those Medical "Pardners" are all to be commended.

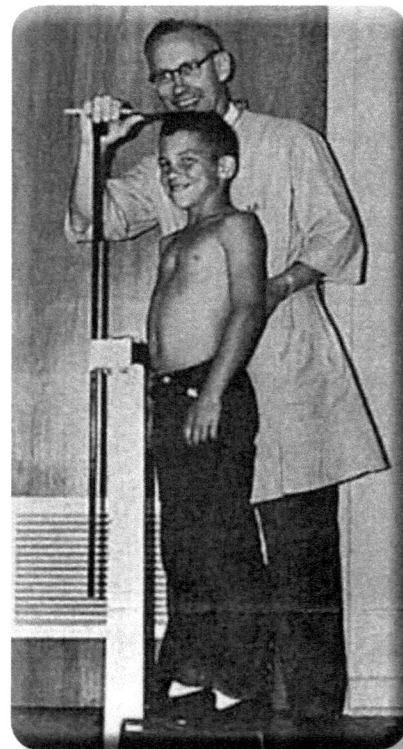

Dr. Roy Campbell at work

Chapter Four: Loaves and Fishes

Throughout the decades, whether it was a 50-pound bag of popcorn or a side of beef, the boys at Rodeheaver Boys Ranch were fed, and thanked God for their meals as they were built, body and soul, into men of character. Even in the leanest of years, God was in control. Time and time again, He sent devoted board members and supporters to the rescue. Often, the miraculous Biblical story of Jesus and the loaves and fishes (Mark 6 and Luke 9) – the act of feeding many with little – seemed very real. God's miracles happened regularly at the Ranch, and still do. One huge miracle happened in the late 1980s when long-time board member Sheriff Walt Pellicer approached his friend Carlton Spence, then CEO of ICS Logistics, one of the nation's largest cold-storage facilities for refrigerating and transporting food. The two were attending a Shriner's event when Pellicer came up to Spence and said, "I've heard you're in the meat business. Do you ever have any leftover food you can donate to a boy's ranch?"

Never having heard of Rodeheaver Boys Ranch, Carlton Spence was touched by Pellicer's description of a hungry bunch of boys out on a big ranch in Palatka – growing boys who were in constant need of good food. Spence's first donation – a truckload of food – was so overwhelming that the staff immediately let him know how much the food was appreciated and how hopeful they were that there was more where that came from. As Carlton Spence began to regularly funnel food to the Ranch, he decided he'd better go and check out these boys who were so quickly devouring his "leftovers."

What he discovered when he went to check it out was that Rodeheaver Boys Ranch used 100% of his donation to support its mission – building boys. A practical, down-to-earth man who generally contributed to things he could see, weigh and measure, Carlton Spence was soon captured heart and soul by the intangible yet undeniable presence of God everywhere he visited at the

Ranch. When asked what the Ranch meant to him, Spence replied instantly. "It's my church."

"If you have ever been with the boys in the chapel or watched them doing their homework or attended their Boy Scout meetings," he said, "You know this is not just about feeding and clothing them. It is about giving them a start in life that, in my opinion, is probably superior to that of about 90% of the boys living in regular homes today. The Ranch boys are not perfect – these boys do make mistakes – but I would take any one of them to be my son."

When Carlton Spence received the 1989 Christmas Card from the Ranch, he was touched. There were a dozen of those ragamuffin ranch boys wearing green choir robes, standing at the altar of the chapel, with the beautiful stained-glass depiction of Jesus the carpenter behind them. Each of them was holding a red candle and appeared to be singing like angels. Instantly, Carlton picked up the phone and called then-Executive Director Ashley Jeter, requesting that the Rodeheaver Boys Ranch Chorus sing at his big Christmas party at the Morocco Shrine Temple that year. It was going to be held in less than two weeks and three-hundred people were invited!

1989 Christmas card

Ashley Jeter was appalled. The Christmas Card photograph was a ruse. He had been on a tight deadline to get the annual Christmas Card done when he saw that his secretary had just picked up her church's choir robes from the cleaners and had them in her car. When the school bus pulled in, Jeter grabbed a bunch of boys, took them down to the chapel, put them in choir robes, stuck a red candle in their hands, posed them at the altar and said, "Go oooooh." He snapped the photograph and sent it to the printer. There was no boys chorus, but he could not tell that to Carlton Spence, the Ranch's new "Golden Goose."

For the next week and a half, Jeter met the boys at the bus and dragged them to the chapel daily to rehearse for their upcoming performance. Luckily, his daughter knew how to sing and was able to help. Their performance at Carlton's Christmas party was a big hit, possibly because they seemed so uncertain and sang so hesitantly. Obviously, the boy's chorus needed more practice and encouragement ... support from 300-plus sympathetic donors poured in!

Support for the Ranch, from the time Homer Rodeheaver sang its praises and sought "Pardners" at every revival meeting across the nation, has usually come from the religious and civic community as well as through the annual mailouts including the Christmas Card and the Back to School Appeal.

Going back to school is always an important time in a child's development, and for the Ranch boys, it was magnified for several reasons: 1) Many of them were far behind in their schooling when they came to Ranch; 2) Most of the boys had not been disciplined in constructive ways that were conducive to good social behavior or study habits; 3) Funds for new back-to-school clothing were low on the list of priorities ... well behind procuring food and shelter for the boys; and 4) With as many as 8 to 10 boys per cottage, studying and homework help was at a premium.

"Education will never become as expensive as ignorance."
Ken's Favorite Sayings

FOUR: LOAVES AND FISHES

In order to provide the educational brain-food ("Loaves and Fishes") so desperately needed to build boys, the Ranch partnered with the Putnam County School Board in 1979 to bring out a daily tutor named Ted Callahan, an English teacher. Now living in Savannah, Georgia, Callahan reminisced recently about his twenty-one years of tutoring at Rodeheaver Boys Ranch. "The Lord blessed my work," he said, noting that no boy ever failed a grade after he began tutoring them. "I did a lot of praying over them, with them and for them." One of Callahan's jobs was to contact the English teacher at school every couple of weeks and get supplemental material to coincide with what the boys were learning in school. "For example, if the teacher was working on grammar – nouns, pronouns, adjectives,

Ted and Ernestine Callahan

etc., my job was to create lesson plans to reinforce that work." Doing homework with the boys was also part of his daily assignment, and he would help them on any of the subjects that challenged them.

"Many times I helped the boys bring up their grade level and sometimes it didn't work, but whether it did or not, the Boys ranch became home, family, a caring center," said Callahan. "When one hurt, all hurt, and when one was joyful, all were joyful. Everyone covered each other's back. Yes, there were hardships but everyone worked together to solve the issue and then moved on. Rodeheaver is a place of great memories – an excellent place to work, an enjoyable place to live, and a wonderful place to share the love of the Lord Jesus."

Ted Callahan's wife, Ernestine, was a business teacher at Palatka High School, and about once a month, Ted would provide special attention to a boy he felt needed it. He would invite the boy to spend the weekend with him and Ernestine. Over the years, many boys grew and benefitted from that special attention given them by that caring Christian couple, the Callahans. Since retiring in 2000, the Callahans have stayed in close contact with several of the former Ranch boys, and, in 2016, an alumni reunion was held. More on this in Chapter Seven.

The Vehicle Improvement Program

In 1992, one of the most enduring fundraisers was launched – the VIP (Vehicle Improvement Program). A car donation and auction program, VIP was then and continues to be a win-win proposition. Donors get a tax break, the boys working with VIP get hands-on training about the mechanics of automobiles, boats, tractors and other vehicles, the dealers get a good price on a car they can sell at a profit, and the Ranch receives much-needed revenue. Over the years, the VIP has brought in much more, including famous radio personality, Paul Harvey. Read Chapter 5 of this history to learn the "rest of the story" about this VIP connection with another VIP!

Another fundraiser and "Fun-raiser," began in 1994 when a friend of Ashley Jeter's came out to the Ranch to visit historic Horse Landing, the site of one of the most well-known battles of the Civil War. The May 24, 1864 Battle at Horse Landing between the Second Florida Calvary commanded by Confederate Captain John Jackson Dickison and a Union gunboat, the *Columbine*, resulted in the sinking of the *Columbine* at the exact location where the Ranch dock extends into the St. Johns River today.

The Battle at Horse Landing Marker reads as follows:

BATTLE AT HORSE LANDING

At this site, on May 23rd, 1864, Captain John Jackson Dickison, with men from the 2nd Florida Cavalry and a battery from the Milton Light Artillery, disabled and captured the Federal gunboat, Columbine. At the time, Union forces controlled the land east of the St. Johns River. The elusive Dickison had made several raids across the river, capturing two outposts. Hoping to trap the Confederates on the east side, Union ground troops moved toward Welaka, and the Columbine was sent upriver. Dickison however, had already crossed the river and set the ambush here at Horse Landing, where the channel and current would bring the boat to within 60 yards of shore.

The Columbine, under the command of Acting Ensign Frank Sanborn, was described as 117 feet in length and "a thing of beauty". The Columbine returned fire, but was soon disabled and surrendered. All but three of her crew and the army troops aboard were killed or captured. The Federal dead are reportedly buried on this rivershore. There were no Confederate casualties. After removing all the supplies and armament possible, the Columbine was burned and sunk, to prevent recapture.

It is the only known incident in history where a cavalry unit sank an enemy gunboat. Dickison was known in the Southern press as the Swamp Fox (and as the Knight of the White Camellia, by the ladies). The Federals referred to him as "Dixie", and land west of the St. Johns was "Dixie's Land".

An interesting footnote: A lifeboat taken from the Columbine was later given by Dickison to John S. Breckenridge, Confederate Secretary of War, to aid in his escape to Cuba at the end of the war.

THIS MARKER WAS PLACED HERE THROUGH DONATIONS BY
MR. AND MRS. JIM GARY, THE 3RD FL CO. A REENACTMENT UNIT,
AND THE FLORIDA CONFEDERATION
FOR THE PRESERVATION OF HISTORIC SITES, INC.

Ashley Jeter's friend was a Civil War Re-enactor of battles such as Olustee and Brooksville, and as he and Ashley chatted, walking along the St. Johns River on the site of the Battle at Horse Landing, an idea germinated. This would be a perfect place to hold Civil War Re-enactments and raise money for the boys ranch at the same time!

The following year, on a weekend in December of 1995, about 200 re-enactors and a few more spectators had a great time blowing up pastures and storming makeshift fortifications. It was decided that a date would be set for future re-enactments (the weekend of Thanksgiving) and the U.S. Army Corps of Engineers came in to help build a substantial fort, bring in some heavy equipment, set up work crews, all as the result of a small grant from the Tourist Development Board. The result was that over five-hundred re-enactors and 1,000 plus spectators came for the second battle and the Ranch made a small profit, as well as giving the Ranch boys and staff an enjoyable event right on the Ranch property.

The Battle of Horse Landing Re-enactment at Rodeheaver Boys Ranch became an exciting annual event, drawing re-enactors from throughout the nation and serving as a major attraction for the Ranch for nearly ten years. Unfortunately, the event evolved into more of a liability than a benefit, for several legitimate reasons involving human nature and a tendency for some to ignore rules and regulations. Today, in the Ranch Museum, there is a rack of beautiful Civil War/1800s regalia worn by participants, and there are several photos of Ranch staff wearing costumes and enjoying the drama of the event. Often, a history buff will drop by Rodeheaver Boys Ranch to visit the site of the Battle of Horse Landing, which will always remain part of the living history of the Ranch.

Today's living history is represented by the Ranch boys who reside there right now and those former Ranch boys who have been built into men and have become good citizens of our nation; former Ranch boys like Lt. Commander Derek Cribbs:

Lt. Commander Derek Cribbs (1990-1996)

Derek Cribbs came from a rough family situation in Palatka, Florida. He went to Rodeheaver Boys Ranch for the first time when he was in 3rd grade.

"Mom was on her third marriage at the time and she was involved with drugs," recalls Derek. "It was a good time for me to leave." Derek stayed at the Ranch for two years until his mother pulled him out. With Derek and his younger sister in tow, their mother left town. After about a year, they landed back in Palatka. "We were living with my grandparents in a small, single-wide trailer," says Derek. "It seemed like everybody was fighting everybody about everything, so I asked to go back to the Ranch." This time, Derek stayed at the Ranch for three years. Again, his mother pulled him out and, again, the home situation was as unstable as ever. Luckily, the Bailey family of Palatka knew and loved Derek, and took him in until he graduated from high school. "The Baileys had been my babysitters when I was about two years old," says Derek. "He was in law enforcement and she was a nurse. They are fine people."

Within days of graduating from Palatka High School in 1998, Derek joined the Navy. During the past twenty-two years, the Navy has been home for the former Ranch boy. Derek has excelled, being commissioned as a Surface Warfare Officer and earning a mechanical engineering degree at Old Dominion University and a Master's degree of Business Administration (MBA) from Naval Post Graduate School in Monterey, California. A devoted husband and father, LCDR Derek Cribbs serves as the Material and Logistics Officer at Destroyer Squadron FOUR ZERO in Mayport, Florida.

"The military was a good fit for me," Derek says. "Like Rodeheaver Boys Ranch, it has structure, with defined duties and responsibilities. I can thank the Ranch for teaching me about a strong work ethic and goal-setting. It was the only stability I had in my life until the Bailey family took me in, and even through high school, I had difficulty separating myself from my biological mother's way of doing things. My younger sister never had the opportunity to go to the Ranch and she's in prison right now. She's been in some bad places and I might have been in those same situations."

Although he has been highly successful at overcoming the challenges of his childhood, Derek is humbly grateful to the people who helped him along the way. "Looking at my family situation, I could be in jail today, but instead, I'm a leader of men," says Derek. "I know how crucial a good work ethic is – regardless of what your position is in the workforce. If it hadn't been for the amazing qualities I learned at the Ranch, I would never have gotten where I am."

As a family man, Derek now looks at his wife and young children and remembers the loving, home-like atmosphere provided by his Boeing Cottage parents, the Delottes, who also gave him his first taste of faith in God. "I've

The Cribbs Family:
L-R: Gator (8), Kimberly, holding Theo, Derek Holding Drew, and Charlie (4)
Theo and Drew are twins ... now 2 years old

had a jaded history with religion over the years, but now my wife and I want a relationship with Jesus for our family. It was instilled in me at the Ranch."

As a boy, Derek's world was filled with turmoil; a confusing, unstable life where it seemed like "everybody was fighting everybody about everything." Rodeheaver Boys Ranch gave him an anchor in the midst of a turbulent sea of trouble. Now, nearly three decades since he first stepped foot on the Ranch, Derek Cribbs is convinced the Ranch was the best thing that ever happened to him. There are future leaders at the Ranch today who, like Derek, need the structure, stability and compassion to grow up healthy and strong. These boys need the basics of food, clothing, education and spiritual growth to become future leaders. The Ranch "Pardners" of today are helping them set and achieve their goals.

"Fame and fortune ought to add up to something more than fame and fortune."
Ken's Favorite Sayings

Billy Santiago (1994-1999)

My father brought me to the Ranch in 1994 when I was 13 going on 14 years old. I'd been living with him and he had some personal issues that kept him from being the best he could be at those times. I didn't understand how evil spirits were working on him then, but I do now. We had some difficult times and Children Service(s) got involved at times which led to being at the Boys Ranch. The hardest thing for me was that he never answered my calls or letters. I was changing and I wanted to prove to him that I was good. I called him every last Sunday of the month per cottage rules, but he never answered. My cottage parents, Charlie and

Sarah and Billy Santiago

Jane Morris, sat me down after a year and explained to me, "Look, son, don't be upset with yourself. You have been trying, but now it comes a time when it's time to let it go. We're proud of you." There were many people at the Ranch who touched my life – Marshall and Linda Vining, Ashley Jeter, Mr. & Mrs Lonbaken, Preston family, Horner family. The names could just continue on, but our most helpful/loving person was our tutor, Mr. Callahan. He is a man who does not age and has a heart of gold.

Before I got to the Ranch, my grades were horrible, but Mr. Callahan took the time to sit down and ask, "What are your struggles? How can I help?" He went above and beyond to communicate with the teachers – he did it for all the boys. That goes a long way. I didn't have attention from my personal family, but the "New Family" at the Ranch cared and showed concern – within a year, my grades were amazing. All of us boys had our proud moments for sure.

I was raised Catholic at first, but then the chapel was eye-opening – all that loud singing. I came to know Jesus is there for me and He loves me – it's the same Holy Spirit. I believe in the Bible. I also know that the staff at Rodeheaver were all people of God. They were strict and persistent, but still showed us the love we needed. They never gave up on us. I was shy, but I made friends. We were paid an allowance of $5 and boy did we have to earn it. Good progress report/good behavior, etc. I raised a steer and a pig for 4-H and learned to work on and understand vehicles through the Vehicle Program provided at the Ranch. I also enjoyed riding horses. I remember Phil Preston and Jack Horner worked in the barn. They were great folks and are missed. My first horse to ride, Midnight, had a mind of her own. When she was done, she took me all the way back to the barn. What a scary first ride! Phil Preston stayed beside me and told me to hold on, laughing the whole time. Good times thinking about it now.

Today, I work as a Service Technician at a GM dealership – I've been doing it for 15+ years. I enjoy fixing things and helping others in need when I can. I learned at the Ranch to be a lender and not a borrower, and I'm grateful to be able to do that. Only God's blessing could allow me to do His work. My wife,

Sarah, and I have two wonderful boys – Rocky, 9, and Felix, 2, and I try hard and am still working to be a good father and take good care of my family. My father finally did come to see me when I was 18 and leaving the Ranch, but by then, I had learned about making good choices and I didn't agree with some of the choices he was making at the time. I hope someday we can get together again, but for now, taking care of my family is the most important thing to me. I'm glad the Ranch taught me how to be a responsible man, and I'm trying to plant that seed in my sons with God's help. Thank you, Rodeheaver, for understanding life. I don't know where I'd be if I hadn't showed up there when I did. God's timing with all the amazing staff and kids was wonderful. He could not have picked a better time for me to be there. I thank God for this opportunity and all the brothers I grew up with. I love you all and we will meet again, if not in this lifetime in the heavenly life praising and having Thanksgiving together. Thank you again.

The endless supply of loaves and fishes, clothing and shelter, education and spiritual growth, all packaged in the love and compassion of Jesus Christ, were provided in the early years to the Ranch boys by many on staff and by the contributing "Pardners" like James E. Thomas, H. E. Westbury, R. T. (Tommy) Clay, Sr., Drs. Roy Campbell, Robert Mitchem, Richard Perallon, and Steve Chapman, William Penn, E. W. (Walt) Pellicer, John Browning, Jr., Bill Huntley, Ed Hedstrom, Neil Freeman, Dan Martinez, Ben Bates, and Carlton Spence. Some of these devoted "Pardners" have gone to their heavenly reward and many new, enthusiastic "Pardners" have come onto the Board of Rodeheaver Boys Ranch since 1995, but none have done more to make it the beautiful jewel it is today than the recently retired Executive Director, Ken Johnson. "When Ken Johnson came to the Ranch in 1996, he was a Godsend for the boys and for the board," said Carlton Spence, who to this day remains actively involved in the day to day activities as well as the overall well-being of the Ranch. "Ken Johnson," said Spence, "saw the big picture of what Rodeheaver Boys Ranch was meant to be from the very beginning and immediately set about making it everything that Homer Rodeheaver dreamed it would be."

Chapter Five:
Welcome Home, Mr. & Mrs. Johnson

God led Ken Johnson to Rodeheaver Boys Ranch. Ken knew it when he drove through the Ringhaver Arch and down Boys Ranch Road. This was his destiny and there was no denying it.

Ken had served as a Youth Educator Pastor in Milton, Florida for nearly twenty years, and VP of Faith Bible College – the administrator of Faith Christian School and his wife, Lois, was a high school English teacher. Milton was where they had raised their three children, Mark, Jonathan and Brooke, and it was home to Lois, who was not at all eager to leave her comfort zone and move to a remote ranch way out in the country. Ken became Executive Director in early 1996, and Lois didn't join him until after her school was finished in June. She was still hoping and praying that Ken would "come to his senses," but he didn't. Lois cried her eyes out as they made that six and half hour drive from Milton to Palatka, finding it so hard to accept that this was really what God wanted for Ken, and therefore, for her. When they reached the Ranch and came to a stop in front of what would be their new home, they were met by a bunch of rough-looking, raggedy boys holding a homemade sign on smudged poster paper that read:

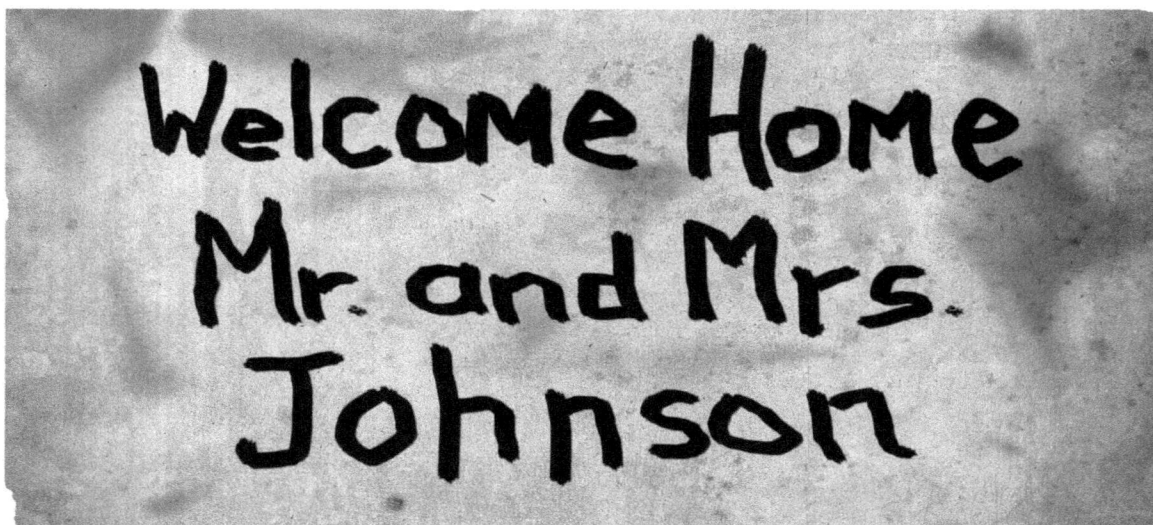

"My heart melted," says Lois Johnson. "I looked into the eyes of these boys. They seemed like little birds in an empty nest. They needed us and yes, we needed them, especially me. God's hand was in this, just as Ken had told me. I knew then that I belonged here as much as he did." Lois, with tears, seeing her new little lost birds standing in front of her future home, said to Ken, "Let's go and take care of these boys!" Lois fell in love with each boy as he came and knew that there was help for each one no matter what and where he came from; she knew her husband could help him. She smiled when each boy came to the Ranch and cried when it was time for each one to leave. After every chapel service, Lois stood near the entrance door to shake their hands; she would tell them she loved them and would be there if they needed a listening ear. She saw hundreds of young men come and go, and they all left with a piece of her heart. "God bless them all; I shall never forget the boys I met in our 23 years. Boy did those years pass quickly. I wish I could go back and start all over again."

Originally from Lumpkin, Georgia (Stewart County), Ken is a lifelong Georgia Bulldog fan. He played a little bit of each sport that a country boy could play with his three younger brothers, but most of the day during summer breaks, he spent his time driving a tractor in those Georgia red clay fields. Ken remembers that two of his Dad's key lessons were: "Son, always plow to the end of the row," and "Set your eyes on the far mark and keep it there. You will plow in a straight line that you can be proud of when it's time to see the harvest."

Dr. Mac and Mary Ann Johnson

Ken's Dad, the late Dr. Mac Johnson, was a Baptist Pastor – what Ken calls "a pastor's pastor," who eventually became President of Faith Seminary and Bible College in Milton, Florida. He served as Ken's major role model and taught him to "Be a man, know your job, and take care of your people" which Ken has always done. A framed photograph of Ken Johnson's parents, Dr. Mac and Mary Ann Johnson, was always prominently displayed in his office.

After moving to Chattanooga, Tennessee when he was 15, Ken Johnson graduated from Chattanooga Central High School, and then attended Middle Tennessee State University, Bob Jones University, and Faith Seminary. He holds a Doctor of Ministry in Psychology from Faith Seminary.

Ken met his wife, Mary Lois Miller, at college in Tennessee and they were married in 1972. Their three children, Mark, Jonathan and Brooke, were nearing adulthood when Ken got God's call to come to the Ranch.

Celebrating Mac and Mary Ann Johnson's 50th Anniversary
Standing behind are Ken and siblings, Rick, Tena, Ann, Jim and Alton

FIVE: WELCOME HOME, MR. AND MRS. JOHNSON

Their three children have become good citizens and productive adults. Son Mark (wife Ralenda) is an Assistant State Attorney working in the homicide division in St. Augustine, Florida. Mark and Ralenda Johnson have three children, Lilly, Ben and Max. Son, Jonathan Johnson (wife Debbie) is employed with the Innovations Group where he is traveling in the Southeast. Daughter, Brooke Hanby (husband Justin) resides in Sidney, Australia. Brooke is an Audiologist

Ken and Lois with their teenagers, Jonathan, Brooke and Mark

(Doctor of Audiology) and her husband, Justin Hanby, is a Criminal Defense Attorney and has his own firm. Justin also heads up the Black Dog Society in Sidney, representing all Australia in raising awareness of the leading cause of death in that beautiful country: Suicide. Justin is a champion swimmer, having forged the English Channel and other great bodies of water globally in order to raise awareness and money for this serious cause. Brooke and Justin have two children: Geneva and Lincoln Hanby.

L-R: Ben, Lily, Mark, Ralenda, Max, Lois and Ken, Lincoln holding Ken's hand, Justin, Brooke, Geneva, Debbie, Eli, Jonathan

Ken is past president of the Florida Association of Christian Child Caring Agencies (FACCCA), past president of the Association of Christian Children's Ministries International (ACCMI) and past president of Central Putnam Ministerial Association. He is a longtime member of the Palatka Airport Advisory Board, a Member of the Azalea City Kiwanis Club (Kiwanis member for 30 years). Ken lists his hobbies as "flying, backpacking, bicycling, shooting sports and being an obedient husband."

An "obedient husband" to Mary Lois Johnson since 1972, Ken has been blessed to have this special lady in his life for all these years, and during his tenure of 23 years at Rodeheaver Boys Ranch, Lois was an integral part of his success as Executive Director. Born in Murfreesboro, Tennessee to Godfearing parents who were married more than 60 years, Lois had three sisters, Patsy, Joan and Ellen and one brother, Steve. She spent much of her girlhood helping her mother in the garden, planting, weeding, pruning, picking and canning, but her goals were to be a wife, mother and school teacher. "God was grooming me for the Ranch," she says, "and for knowing how to build boys." In the first Ranch book, published in 2013, Lois was quoted as follows:

> "*Nurturing a grapevine is much like working with the young men here. To plant a young vine, you must take it out of the previous soil, knock off the dirt and get it in a pail of clean water just long enough for it to pull in the amount of water to quench its thirst. Then, place it in its new home, set this new vine in a hole surrounded by good soil, place a straight and narrow stick by it so that it will have a guide to lead it upward. Next, fertilize and water as needed and constantly remove weeds and pests that would rob it of its nutrients. Then don't forget to check it daily to be sure all is well.*"

Lois graduated from Kittrell High School and studied at Tennessee Temple University, Trinity University and Faith College. She received her Master's degree in Secondary Education/English and earned a Bachelor's degree in Theology. She

taught in four different schools from Tennessee to Florida for thirty-five years and absolutely loved every day of her "Dream Job," adoring the light that shines in the eyes of a child who understands a new concept! As with all of her former teaching positions, Lois Johnson's last full-time teaching job at Peniel Baptist Academy in Palatka, Florida, had a profoundly positive influence on her students. There was a day when the door to Lois's classroom opened and two young men walked in. They were former students and they knew that Mrs. Johnson did not appreciate her classroom being disturbed, but they boldly walked right up to her and then sank to their knees, presenting her with a dozen red roses. "Mrs. Johnson," one of the young men said, "We're both going to St. Johns River College now and our professor told us that we have a better understanding of English than any students he's ever taught. We're here to thank you for teaching us so well."

"You should keep on learning as long as there is something you do not know."
Ken's Favorite Sayings

Although she was at first reluctant to come to Rodeheaver Boys Ranch, Lois knew by the look in her husband's eyes and the tone of his voice that God had truly given him a particular calling to be there. They soon recognized that it was "Holy Ground," a place of God that would change a boy's life and heart. In their 23 years there, Lois always said that each boy was a Book to be written and each Book would be filled with drama; with some comedy peppered in.

Dear to her heart and in her constant prayers were the cottage moms who came to the Ranch and lived in the "trenches," forgetting their own comfort and seeking to show young boys the true meaning of life; wiping a boy's tears in the night when he was afraid because of things he'd witnessed in his past. These courageous, compassionate women cooked, cleaned, visited his school, ran him to the doctor – did all the things a mother would do for her son. They prayed to God to change his life, and when He did, they shouted for joy! Lois took each cottage mom under her wing, nurturing and encouraging them and always being there when they needed to talk and pray. She was the jewel in Ken Johnson's crown and served as safe harbor for him, staff and boys when storms threatened the Ranch.

Ken had many goals for the Ranch when he and Lois came in 1996, one of which was to see "790 acres of some of God's most beautiful land blossom because of the love that people have for helping." Ken knew about the love that people had for the Ranch because he was brought in to run the Ranch by a strong, devoted board of directors. When he became Executive Director, the president of the board was Ben Bates, Jr., and immediate past presidents were Dan Martinez, Neil Freeman, Ed Hedstrom, Bill Huntley, John Browning, Jr., and Walt Pellicer. Freeman, Huntley and Pellicer have since passed away, but the others remain as dedicated to the Ranch today as they have always been.

Ken's Second Office at the Ranch

The first year that Ken was on the Ranch, he was surprised to discover there were few Bibles there, and he ordered Bibles for the staff and the boys who did not have them. The chapel and the study of God's Word became central to Ranch life.

Ken began writing a weekly newsletter specifically for the Board and staff, titling it "The Ranch Rigamarole," noting that, although the colloquial definition of the word "rigamarole" was "a long list of foolishly involved or time-wasting procedures, and that most people feel that communication is a foolish waste of time," the folks at Rodeheaver Boys Ranch felt that "communication is like the blood in the body ... without it, we get sick and die." The Ranch Rigamarole was Ken's humorous attempt to make all the little details of Ranch life available to the board and staff – details that, for whatever reason, had not been made available before.

Having come ahead in the Spring of 1996 when Lois was still finishing up her year of teaching in Milton, Florida, Ken was deeply worried when he got a call from her that she had walked in on a robber in their home in Milton. The criminal had roughly pushed her aside and run away, only to be caught by police shortly thereafter. Apparently, that same robber had shot somebody at the cleaners in town earlier. Both Lois and Ken took this as a sign that she needed to leave Milton and get to the Ranch as soon as possible.

Ken coming in for a landing

John and Linda Jones came to the Ranch in 1996 as cottage parents at Westbury Cottage. Soon after they arrived, Ken took in his first boy as the new Executive Director. That boy was 14-year old Timothy Officer, whose father was in the military in England and had sent his son to Rodeheaver Boys Ranch at the urging of his base chaplain. John and Linda Jones were Timothy Officer's cottage parents, and Timothy was destined to make his mark on the world as well as on the heart of everyone who knew him.

In early 1997, Ken had a couple of large trees removed from the side of Ranch Road to accommodate his private Cessna 150 Commuter plane landing and taking off. A pilot who enjoyed flying and sometimes flew to Milton, Florida and other nearby destinations for meetings and family visits, Ken also used the runway to have boys flown in from various places in Florida. He had a sign placed on the side of Ranch Road to make drivers aware that a plane could be approaching. Lois remembers when she and Ken were approaching the road for a landing and had to swoop back up because cars were paying no attention to their landing.

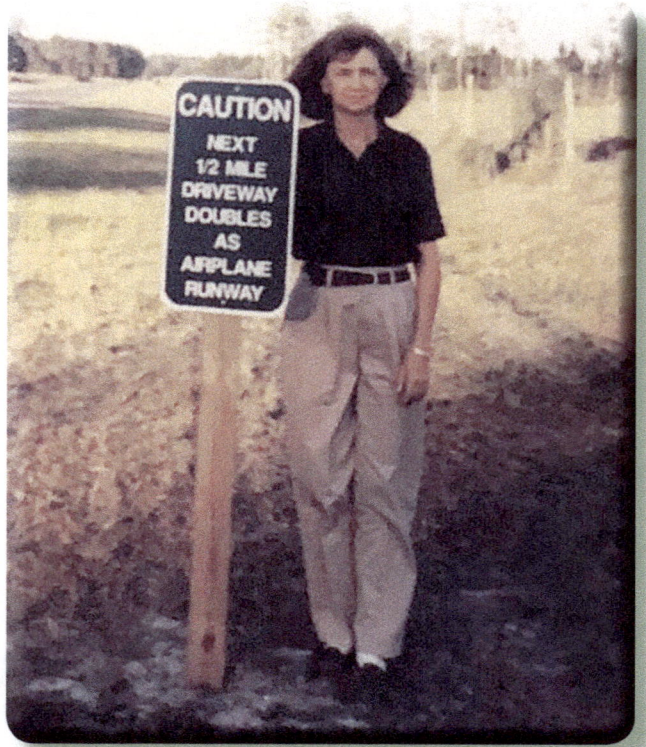

Lois standing by runway sign

There was a hangar for Ken's plane next to their house (where the Ranch Museum is today). A 1950 Tractor and 1950 Chevrolet Truck (designating the year the Ranch was founded) are kept in the hangar, which, when it had Ken's airplane in it, was a fascinating point of interest for the boys, board, staff and visitors to the Ranch. Ken, as all were soon to discover, is a strong man with a wide array of interests and talents, but just one main focus – that of serving God.

One way to serve God was to acquire a fine staff. Almost immediately, Ken began gathering his most trusted colleagues to assist him in building boys. Steve Watkins, a retired U.S. Navy Lieutenant Commander and a fellow pilot, became Director of Ranch Life in January of 1997. He and Ken worked well together, as Ken directed and Steve coordinated all the daily functions on the Ranch.

Steve Watkins recalls how he and his wife, Cathy, first met Ken and Lois Johnson after he was assigned in 1982 to NAS Whiting Field in Milton, Florida as a navy fighting instructor. On the first Sunday that the Watkins family attended Faith Baptist Church in Milton, they were told that the pastor, Brother Mac Johnson, was out of town preaching at another church and his son, Dr. Ken Johnson, was preaching that day. The Watkins so enjoyed the service and fellowship that they joined the church without ever having met the pastor.

They soon became friends with Ken and Lois Johnson, and their children, who were close in years, became friends as well. Ken Johnson was then administrator of Faith Christian School where Lois was a teacher. In the fall, the Watkins enrolled their children in the school. Another family in the church that befriended them was a couple named Jeff and Donna King, who, as Steve said, "miraculously fit into the Rodeheaver Boys Ranch story in the future."

Their three years at Faith Baptist Church were formative ones for Steve and Cathy Watkins. Steve remembers, "Although Cathy and I had both been in Baptist Churches most of our lives, neither of us had an understanding of true Bible salvation. Under the preaching and teaching of Brother Mac Johnson, Cathy and I both came to fully understand Christ's sacrificial payment for our sin and by faith rested in His finished work on the cross. We will be forever thankful for God's leading us to Faith Baptist Church for our growth in Christ and the lifelong friendship we established with the Johnson family."

As with most military families, the Watkins moved on to Steve's next tour of duty, which was aboard the USS Constellation, an aircraft carrier home ported at NAS North Island in Coronado, California. They were there for two years and then the Watkins family moved to Rota, Spain, where Steve flew passengers and cargo all over Europe and North Africa for the next three years. There, Cathy Watkins and other military spouses began a small Christian School. During his first year in Spain, Steve developed a medical condition that could have jeopardized his flight status. He was required to return to Pensacola, Florida for evaluation and a waiver to continue flying, and being only a few miles from Milton, he spent a few days with Ken and Lois Johnson. "The folks at Faith Baptist Church prayed for me during the process and thankfully the waiver was approved," recalls Steve. "I think God had determined that our lives were to stay connected in some way."

From Spain, Steve was ordered back to Jacksonville in 1990. Jacksonville is Cathy's hometown. She was born the second child of Glenn and Margaret Pinner and grew up with an older brother and younger sister. She learned to play piano at the age of eight, added voice lessons at age ten, and began playing for her small neighborhood church and later for other churches at weddings and funerals. These talents would hold her in good stead many years later at Rodeheaver Boys Ranch. When she was just 18 years old, her father died of lung cancer. Five months after their first meeting, Cathy married Steve Watkins. She calls it "one of the fastest and best decisions of my life!"

Cathy feels that God's hand was evident from the beginning. Steve joined the Navy, and as their children, Ben, Sarah and Katie Watkins came along, they began an exciting life of traveling for Uncle Sam. Cathy found joy in meeting new people and considers their global life in the military a wonderful opportunity to train their children in the joy of life. After coming to Christ in 1983, Cathy now knew her ultimate purpose was to live for Him and make Him known, walking each day through prayer and study of the Bible.

"A few kind words take only seconds to say, but their echoes can go on for years." Ken's Favorite Sayings

After six years at NAS Jacksonville, on board the USS Saratoga at Mayport Naval Station and then at NAS Cecil Field, Steve retired from the Navy in July of 1996. He had no concrete plans except that he knew he wanted to serve the Lord in some capacity. Son, Ben, was playing baseball on scholarship at the University of North Florida, daughter, Sarah, was a senior at Trinity Christian Academy in Jacksonville, and their youngest, Katie, was in 8th grade at Trinity.

One afternoon, Steve received a surprise phone call from Ken Johnson who informed him he was now Executive Director for Rodeheaver Boys Ranch in Palatka. "Ken told me that he had felt the call to work there and believed that everything he had accomplished in his life was preparing him for the opportunity to minister to troubled boys in that agricultural setting. Although Steve knew nothing about the Ranch, as a native Floridian (from Brandon, Florida), he had driven by the Rodeheaver Arch dozens of times since childhood.

Realizing how close Ken was to Jacksonville, Steve immediately invited him to come for a visit, but Ken, unable to leave the Ranch, invited Steve to come visit him. "Again," says Steve, "The hand of the Lord was at work in our lives. Ken didn't know I had just retired nor did he know I was looking for a new career. I accepted the invitation with no expectation other than reuniting with my old friend."

What Steve found on that first visit in late 1996 was that his old friend had a daunting task ahead of him. The Ranch barn and paddock were in disrepair, with grounds, cottages and facilities unkempt, much of the property had become a landfill from years of trash accumulation, the dock and river area were a dangerous eyesore covered in scrap building materials. This incredibly beautiful property on the St. Johns river had been so neglected that potential donors were no longer welcome because of the poor impression they would get of the ranch.

> "Society is always taken by surprise at any new example of common sense."
> Ken's Favorite Sayings

But both Steve and Ken saw that the greatest need at that time was spiritual. Homer Rodeheaver's original vision of the Ranch as a Christian haven had to be fulfilled using the principles found in the word of God. "After that first visit, I knew that Ken had the same vision," recalls Steve. "As we talked about me joining the staff, I began to see myself as a contributor to what he envisioned for the ranch."

After prayer and discussion with his family, Steve came to Rodeheaver Boys Ranch on January 2, 1997. With their oldest daughter a senior in high school, Cathy and the family stayed behind in Jacksonville until after graduation. Steve moved into the unfurnished Ranch Life Director's house, with just a bed and a chair for the next five months. That began twenty-one years of life and ministry at the Ranch for the Watkins family. "During those years," says Steve, "Cathy and I were blessed by the marriages of all three of our children and our daughters, Sarah, married to Ashley, and Katie, married to Matt, have given us ten grandchildren. With God's amazing grace we endured the loss of our son to cancer in 2003. We were privileged to work with some wonderful people and to have a positive impact on the lives of hundreds of young boys. It is such a blessing to hear the stories of success from boys who are now young men, many with families of their own."

While Steve worked alongside Ken as Director of Ranch Life, Cathy renewed her love for horses that she had learned as a girl during summers on the Pinner farm. Serving as equine assistant, Cathy trained young boys (many of whom had never been close to farm animals) in grooming and learning to saddle and ride. She also used her talents in music by playing piano along with Lois Johnson in the chapel and teaching the boys piano lessons. "I pray that my legacy as a wife, mother, grandmother and friend left a positive impact for Christ at Rodeheaver," says Cathy, remembering the blessings of helping mentor young cottage moms and working with and teaching the boys. "The Ranch will always hold a special place in my heart and I pray that the Hope of Christ will draw many others to see the vision that Rodeheaver Boys Ranch holds for future boys and staff that make it their home.

Steve and Cathy Watkins retired from active participation in the Ranch ministry in January 2018. "We were blessed to be a part of the Ranch's return to the original vision of its founder, Homer Rodeheaver," says Steve. "Today the Ranch is a beautiful 800-acre facility that the staff and boys are proud to show to visitors and donors."

Steve Watkins and Ken Johnson

One memorable day in 1997, Ken and Steve flew over to Bear Island in the middle of Crescent Lake to check out the campgrounds recommended by board member, John Browning, Jr. "We took off from Bear Island and were headed back to the Ranch, flying right over the Putnam County Fairground, when Steve noticed that we had black smoke coming

out of the exhaust pipes," recalled Ken, who was piloting the plane. "We knew if the engine locked up, we'd have to do a dead-stick landing." Their descent in altitude had already begun in preparation for landing at the Ranch and they had to make a quick decision. With limited engine power, they lined up the plane with Highway 17 (which was crowded with fair traffic) and set the wheels down in front of a police car that had straddled the lanes. With the policeman directing traffic, they taxied the airplane into the parking lot of San Mateo Seafood (John Browning, Jr.'s restaurant) just as the engine came to a complete stop. Ken recalled, "A couple of old World War II pilots came over to where we had landed. One of them said to me, 'Listen here, yesterday you could fly a plane. Today, you're a pilot.'"

Although neither Ken nor Steve fly now, and Ken's airplane was sold years ago, their piloting skills guided many boys over the years, with Ken in the pilot's seat and Steve his trusted and competent co-pilot. Just as Ken and Steve worked smoothly to run the Ranch and raise the bar on raising boys, their wives, Lois Johnson and Cathy Watkins, partnered in gardening, music, caring for the animals (especially the horses) and being there always for the cottage moms and the boys.

Lois loved her gardening at the Ranch, including learning about bee-keeping, working in her vineyard and tending an orchard out behind the barn where Cathy Watkins was working with the horses and the boys. An extraordinary horsewoman, Cathy Watkins taught the boys about riding and caring for the horses and touched their lives by her example of hard work, faith

L-R: Cathy Watkins, Linda Jones, Carolyn Branch and Lois Johnson

and courage. While Cathy worked with horses and Lois was out in the vineyard, they knew when the school bus was coming in, because the pigs could hear it a mile away and would start squealing; they were always so excited when the boys got home from school and would give them their treats.

Having been born in nearby Umatilla (about 60 miles from the Ranch), Mark Warren first laid eyes on Rodeheaver Boys Ranch as a boy sitting in the front seat of a pickup truck while hunters in his family rode around looking for deer. Mark was just 9 years old when he witnessed his step-father commit suicide, but his childhood tragedy was tempered by the kindness of farmers in Umatilla who came to the rescue of his mother. Their example inspired Mark to dream of helping boys someday, and because of them, he developed a strong interest in agriculture, earning a degree from the University of Georgia in Agricultural Education and eventually being hired as Assistant Director of FFA (Future Farmers of America) by the Georgia Department of Education. The FFA Director was a man named Melvin Johnson (Ken Johnson's uncle). "Before I knew Ken, I had hired his sons, Mark and Jon, as teen camp counselors," recalls Mark. Married to his childhood sweetheart, Bonnie, Mark was working for the Florida Farm Bureau when he came to Rodeheaver Boys Ranch in 1997. At that time, Mark and Bonnie Warren had two sons, Jared and Caleb, ages 2 and 3, and were expecting their daughter, Cara. Living at the Ranch, Bonnie, who had her teaching degree, homeschooled their children and Mark, as Farm Director, finally realized his dream of helping boys. He also worked hard to restore the long-neglected Ranch, using little or no equipment. He remembers that there was not even enough money to buy wood to build sheds. Scotties Hardware offered to donate some used wood and Mark picked it up after 9 p.m. at night. Little by little, they worked to make things better. There were four cottages with 8 to 10 boys in each cottage. "We filled a niche back then ... we got the toughest boys and loved and cared for them until they learned to love God and themselves."

> "Since the tongue is in a wet place, it's bound to slip once in a while."
> Ken's Favorite Sayings

Working hand in hand with the boys at the barn, building fence, feeding cattle, caring for the 50 to 60 horses that had been donated to the Ranch, teaching them to weld and carve, plant and sew ... all of it contributed to building boys and rebuilding the Ranch. In those days, discipline was swift and decisive. "We loved them with tough love. When they misbehaved, they got punished fairly and it was over," recalls Mark. "Then it was time to go fishing."

Devoting himself to the running of the Ranch as well as the marketing to potential supporters, Ken traveled to places like Chattanooga, Tennessee and New Orleans, Louisiana, telling the Ranch story. He also became a familiar face locally, joining the Central Putnam Ministerial Association and civic organizations like Kiwanis.

Ken and Lois worked together to improve the Ranch, relying on God, the constant support of the Board of Directors, and their staff of good people like Jeff and Donna King, Steve and Cathy Watkins, Mark and Bonnie Warren, and many others who gave their all to the boys.

In addition to gardening and helping cottage moms cope with their challenges, Lois ran the Ranch General Store. She and former Ranch chef, Patti McClure, filled the shelves of the store with hundreds of jars of jams and jellies from the vineyard and orchard. Often, Cathy Watkins and relief cottage mom Barbara Rowland would get out in the vineyard with Lois and crawl on their knees, weeding, fertilizing and watering. Then, in autumn, they would get together and gather all the fruits of their hard labor. Yes,

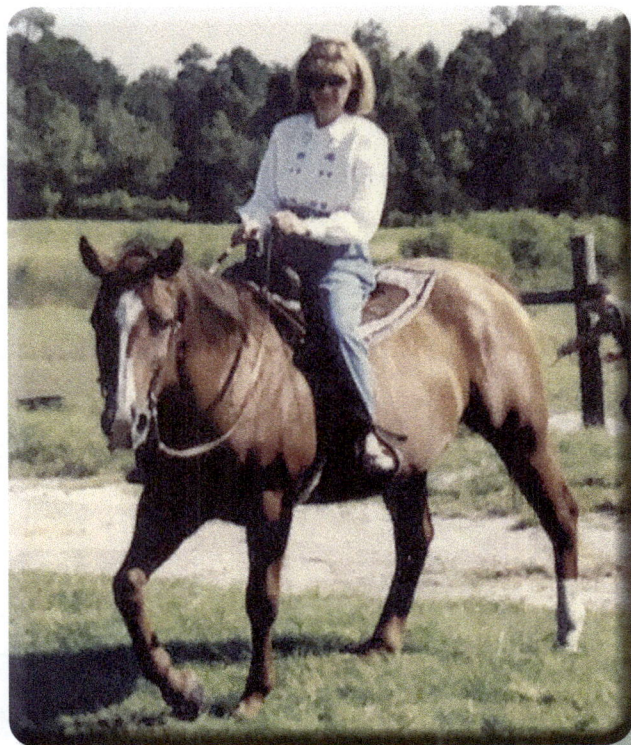

Lois horseback riding

gardening was God-directed at the Ranch, and many of the women there helped to make the vineyard and orchard lush with beautiful fruit.

Often, Lois and Cathy would go horseback riding, taking their husbands with them, or some of the boys who were helping in the barn. Trail riding was an enjoyable past-time then and it still is today.

Chapel on Wednesday and Sunday evenings at the Ranch became special times of worship when the boys and staff would gather and pray and sing hymns from the Ranch hymnals, usually accompanied on opposite sides of the altar by Cathy on the piano and Lois on the organ. Ken Johnson and Steve Watkins would be in the front of the small congregation, both of them leading prayer and teaching the boys their Bible verses as well as memorization of

"If two people ride the same horse, one must ride behind."
Ken's Favorite Sayings

the books of the Bible. Inspiring guest speakers like Ken's son, Mark Johnson, who was attending Stetson Law School, and Jeff King, a pastor with Rock of Ages Ministries, often testified at the services.

Just as Homer Rodeheaver envisioned a Ranch filled with boys worshipping and singing God's praises, the Wednesday and Sunday night Chapel services were the fulfillment of that vision. One of the songs in the Rodeheaver Boys Ranch Hymnal was Homer Rodeheaver's favorite hymn, "If Your Heart Keeps Right," first verse and chorus below:

"If the dark shadows gather, As you go along,
Do not grieve for their coming, Sing a cheery song.
There is joy for the taking, It will soon be light,
Ev'ry cloud wears a rainbow, If your heart keeps right.
Chorus:
If your heart keeps right, If your heart keeps right, There's
a song of gladness in the darkest night;
If your heart keeps right, If your heart keeps right,
Ev'ry cloud will wear a rainbow, If your heart keeps right."

A man whose heart continues to "keep right" is Carlton Spence. Carlton and Ken bonded immediately, and when Ken voiced a need at the Ranch, Carlton rushed to fill it. He still does that today.

During his first year at the Ranch, Ken mentioned to Carlton that there was no large sheltered area where the boys could gather when they were working outside, and it began raining. He thought a pole barn would work well as a shelter from the rain. Carlton agreed, and construction began immediately. What began as a 50- foot-wide and 150- foot long covered pole barn ended up being a 215 by 80-foot pavilion. Later, a guest lodge with four hotel rooms, a board room, a living room, eight showers, and eight toilets was built next to the large covered pavilion. Carlton's daughter, Cindy Spence Sadler McCormick, was instrumental, along with Lois, Cathy Watkins and Donna King, in the décor of each of the four guest rooms at the Lodge, designing them in a tasteful, comforting manner similar to the guest rooms at Carlton's Bitter End Plantation in South Carolina. Riverside Builders were the skilled craftsman who built the Lodge and many of the buildings at the Ranch, including the Executive Director's home where Ken and Lois Johnson lived for several years until his retirement in 2019.

Carlton Spence became President of the Board of Directors in 1997 and has been instrumental and influential in nearly every aspect of Ranch life since Sheriff Walt Pellicer asked him to help feed some hungry boys back in the late 1980s. His monetary contributions have been monumental over the years, as he filled one need after another, and his personal devotion to the cause of the Ranch has translated into many other avenues, including serving the need to bring in other fervent supporters of the Ranch.

1997 was a banner year for the Ranch. Under Ken Johnson's leadership, the number of boys increased that year from 23 boys to 47 by the beginning of 1998.

The annual Civil War Re-enactments were a big draw at the Ranch for several

Ken and Lois at a Civil War shindig

years and the staff got involved in hosting the festivities that occurred in the dining hall. Ken and Lois, Steve and Cathy and all of the staff dressed in costume in the spirit of the event.

The boys began building their tree houses in 1997, a sugar cane mill was established, beekeeping became an important part of Ranch life, and Ben Watkins (Steve and Cathy's son), the left-handed pitcher on the baseball team at the University of North Florida, brought his team out to the Ranch to volunteer. Board member and Orthodontist Steve Chapman organized a triage of dentists to provide for the individual boys' dental needs, Maintenance man Jerry Foster began keeping things in order, Ben Bates received the Ranch's first Wagon Master Award (a unique tribute given to outstanding board members by the staff at the Ranch) after he and Carlton Spence assisted in establishing new Personnel Policies & Procedures Manuals, Employee handbooks and Safety Manuals, and Carlton Spence invited the board and staff to tour ICS Logistics, Beach Trading and his other businesses, treating them to a delicious dinner and productive board meeting.

Carlton Spence received the second Wagon Master Award in 1998. A former Boy Scout who has lived by the Boy Scout Oath all his life, Carlton Spence was instrumental in establishing a new Boy Scout Troop, Number 337, at the Ranch in 1998.

The Boy Scout Oath is still adhered to at the Ranch:

**ON MY HONOR I WILL DO MY BEST
TO DO MY DUTY TO GOD AND MY COUNTRY
AND TO OBEY THE SCOUT LAW;
TO HELP OTHER PEOPLE AT ALL TIMES;
TO KEEP MYSELF PHYSICALLY STRONG,
MENTALLY AWAKE, AND MORALLY STRAIGHT.**

Greg Buchanan was the first Scout Master of Troop 337. Greg and his wife, Lisa, came to the Ranch in 1998 to serve as Relief Cottage Parents, and over the next eighteen years, worked in many capacities including serving as Ranch Cooks for almost seven of those years. At the time of the first Ranch book, in 2013, Greg was Activities Director of the Ranch, Director of the VIP Program, and still Scout Master, as well as Cub Scout Leader. Lisa Buchanan was the VIP Title Clerk, handling all of the voluminous paperwork that goes with receiving, recording and acknowledging donated vehicles at the monthly automobile auctions. Brett Buchanan, who came to the Ranch with his parents in 1998 at four years old, became one of several Eagle Scouts produced through Troop 337. The Buchanans left the Ranch a few years ago and their service has never been forgotten.

Also, in 1998, Ken Johnson furthered the cause of the Ranch by appearing as a guest on the Christian Radio Stations WTGF-FM and WECM-AM, where he had been a radio talk show host for eight years prior to coming to the Ranch. The reception to his guest appearances was so positive that he was invited to come back regularly.

One day, Ken Johnson and Mark Warren were in Palatka and they passed Gator Equipment Company, a supporter of the Ranch. Mark pointed out a Michigan Front-End Loader in the yard and suggested that Ken ask for it. "When?" Ken asked. "Right now." Mark responded. Ken walked in and said to Stewart Smith, "I need that front-end loader right there. It would be a blessing to the boy's ranch." Smith answered, "Would tomorrow be too soon?" Because God and Gator Equipment blessed the ranch with the front-loader donation, the river area was soon cleaned up beautifully.

**Merry Christmas from
One and All – Both BIG & Small**

Mark Warren was featured on the Ranch's 1998 Christmas card, sitting tall on a stately brown horse and smiling down on a young boy with a miniature horse named B.J.

B.J.'s parents, Miniature horses Brian and Jenny, had been donated to the ranch in 1997 and when B.J. was born, Cottage Mom Linda Jones wrapped her jacket around the tiny colt and held him close like a newborn infant. He became their "Cottage Colt," learned to open the front door and would actually go into the living room, sit on the couch and watch football with the boys. Lois remembers that Mark Warren was the "Daniel Boone" of the Ranch, adored by all the boys, and that, "B.J. (Brian Junior) the miniature horse, thought he was one of the boys." B.J. also drank coffee with the cottage parents. He had his own cup.

Sheriff Walt Pellicer at the Ranch Grape Arbor

Law Enforcement Week was held in 1998 at the Ranch Chapel, beginning on Sunday night with Rick Look of the Florida Department of Law Enforcement, Monday night with Bill Thees of the FBI, Tuesday with Richard Davis of the Florida Highway Patrol, all accompanied by fellow officers, and the grand finale on Wednesday night with Sheriff Taylor Douglas presenting retired sheriff Walt Pellicer with a 42 Year Law Enforcement Plaque in front of his entire family, as well as a tribute to Walt for his nearly 50 years of support for the Ranch.

At the beginning of 1999, Ken traveled to Tallahassee for a committee meeting on HR Bill 197 and Senate Bill 2, sponsored by Senator Daniel Webster and Representative Johnny Bird, and successfully testified on behalf of FACCCA homes for the handling of adoptions if the opportunity occurred.

James and Kay Whitley came to the Ranch as cottage parents in April of 1999 and were wonderful, compassionate caregivers for the next eleven years.

Hurricane Floyd visited Palatka and the staff and boys evacuated to the Peniel Christian School auditorium. That was the last time the Ranch was evacuated during a storm, as it was determined to be safer than anyplace else due to the sturdy buildings that had gone up in recent years.

Judge Ed Hedstrom received the Wagon Master Award in 1999.

Tom and Jim Miller of Miller Enterprises visited the dining hall and decided they were going to help build a new portico and roof out by the Flag Terrace.

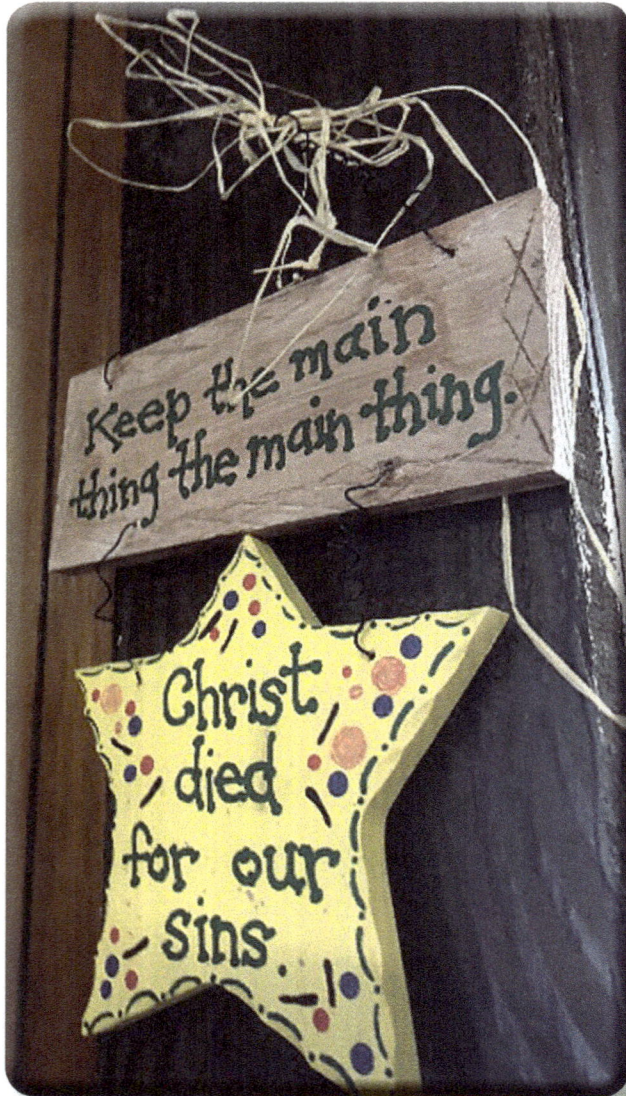

A 1999 special moment Ken remembers best is the speech one of the boys gave at school and practiced with him. The speech was about the Five Actions of Achievement:

1. Dream or visualize.
2. Convert the dream into goals.
3. Convert your goals into tasks.
4. Convert your tasks into steps, and
5. Take your first step and then the next.

Ken was so impressed by the boy's speech that it made it into the Ranch Rigamarole that year!

Boeing Cottage

Gary Feld 7-12-89 Ocala	Justin Forehed 12-28-86 Jacksonville	Jamie Hanson 2-17-84 Sebring	Bryan Lofton 4-11-88 Pensacola	Royce Lofton 1-6-85 Pensacola	Shannon Mercado 7-3-85 Citra	Eric Shoemake 12-22-88 Kingsland, GA	Joshua Takiya 7-22-84 Palatka	Ricky Thies 10-23-86 DeLeon Spr

Rodeheaver Cottage

Brandon Day 3-16-82 Jacksonville	Chad Farley 3-13-83 St. Augustine	Marcus Girdley 6-22-84 St. Augustine	Michael Hughes 1-28-83 Lake Worth	Roger Lofton 1-6-85 Pensacola	James Martinez 6-14-83 Orange Park
Jeremy Mattson 7-29-83 Jacksonville	Bruce Murphy 8-8-83 E. Palatka	Chad Murphy 3-8-85 E. Palatka	Jay Pollino 11-6-83 Key Largo	Devin Starling 9-20-85 Brooksville	Patrick Timberlake 6-23-82 Pomona Park

Westbury Cottage

Andrew Brown 11-10-85 Lebra	Jarrid Couch 12-2-83 Gainesville, GA	Timothy Hardaker 7-20-83 Lakeland	John Jones 1-20-84 Orange City	Nathan Lioomb 12-30-82 Okeechobee	Adam Mihalik 3-4-82 Keystone Heights
	Gabriel McMahon 4-30-82 Orlando	Timothy Officer 8-8-82 England	Matthew White 1-7-84 Zionsville, IN	Joshua Widdoews 8-3-83 Jacksonville	

Phillips Cottage

Steven Barone 11-28-82 Jacksonville	Michael Billingsley 7-30-83 Fitzgerald, GA	Michael Lee 7-14-83 Palatka	Lorne Moore 11-28-83 Cocoa	Brandon Marmon 8-10-82 Port St. Lucie	Ronny White 7-18-83 Sarasota

Thanks for going the extra mile as we struggle down life's highway. You've given us hope for a new direction and now **We're On Our Way!**

Happy Holidays
The Boys of Rodeheaver

1997 Christmas card

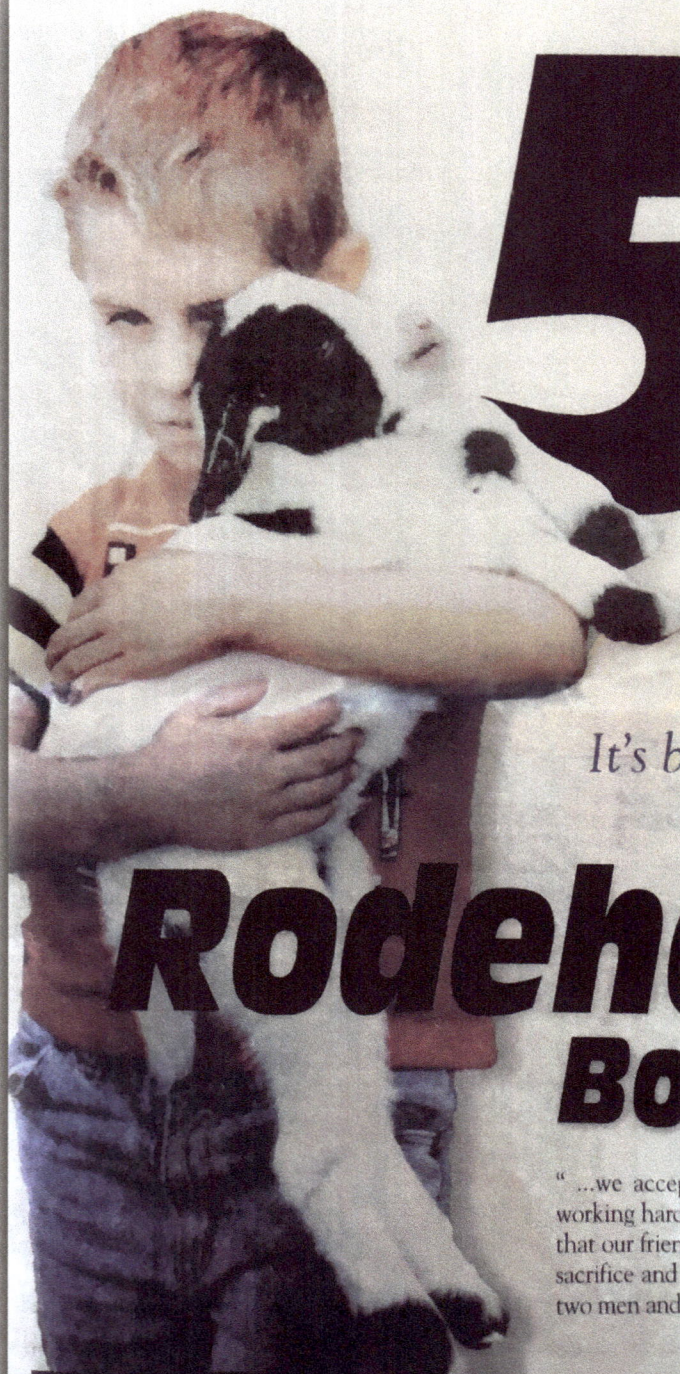

50th

Anniversary Celebration

It's better to build boys than to mend men…

Rodeheaver
Boys' Ranch

" …we accept the challenge to keep waking up each day, working hard to raise the boys, and to hope and pray real hard that our friends will also continue, with a compassionate heart, sacrifice and perseverance in this great vision that began with two men and a small group of friends 50 years ago."

-- Ken Johnson, executive director

8 - Ranch History   10 - Success Stories   2 - Celebrity Visits

CHAPTER SIX:
Y2K ... ALL IS WELL

The year 2000 (Y2K) marked the 50th Anniversary of the Ranch and a huge celebration ensued at the Annual Meeting on Sunday, April 16. The Board and past officials of Rodeheaver Boys Ranch were listed in the magazine insert which ran in the Palatka Daily News on the Friday prior to the meeting. Nearly 1,000 people were in attendance for the annual barbecue, and one special guest, Bruce Howe, came from Winona Lake, Indiana, to celebrate the anniversary. Bruce Howe and his wife, Ann, had been regulars at the Annual Meeting for years and continued to attend until the year before he passed away in October of 2015. "Bruce loved the Ranch boys and always brought them a special present when we came to the Annual Meeting," said Ann Howe. "He would sit on the porch of the Lodge or in the pew at Chapel and hand out a gold dollar coin to each boy who came to say hello ... needless to say, they all came to say Hello!"

An avid ambassador for Rodeheaver Boys Ranch, Carlton Spence used his position as CEO of ICS Logistics, one of the world's largest Industrial Cold Storage companies (founded in 1980) to help finance the 50th Anniversary Edition of the Palatka Daily News. "We have what it takes to keep things moving," was the company slogan for ICS Logistics and it definitely was extended by Carlton to keep things moving at the Ranch. ICS Logistics ran two full-page ads as the centerpiece in the 50th Anniversary magazine, and Carlton Spence was the master of ceremonies for the day in addition to supplying the beef for the barbecue.

The message from Ken Johnson, Executive Director, titled "Ranch marks five decades of caring" was printed in the magazine as follows:

Greetings to all our friends and collaborators in the great work of helping children and young men. I hope this note of challenge and thanks finds you and yours well and happy.

Fifty years of service is a milestone in any organization, especially one that depends almost completely on the gifts and support of others. This legacy of 50 years would have been impossible – and I do mean impossible – were it not for the thousands of like-minded, giving friends, such as you.

Exactly how do you define 50 years at Rodeheaver Boys Ranch? Do you talk about money? Food? Clothing? Shelter? Livestock? Machinery (or the lack of it)? Activities? School work? Chapel services? Personal witness? Teamwork?

Believe me on this, I could talk for hours on any of these things, and they are important, but they come up short in trying to define 50 years. At least I think they do.

In defining anything, you have to look at the very essence of the thing you're attempting to understand. Abraham Lincoln said it best when he said (and I paraphrase), "To really understand anything you have to bound it on all sides, the north, south, east and west ... and be able to break it down and explain it to a child."

I believe this defining process, honestly done, could not ignore the attributes of the human spirit reacting to the urges of its Creator, to sense, consider and do something about the plight of suffering children and their families.

These attributes would have to include vision. The greatest book in the world states, "Where there is no vision the people perish." Looking back on the beginning 50 years ago, Homer Rodeheaver and his friend, Harry Westbury, saw a need and went about trying to meet that need ... the need for providing a home and life for boys from wherever.

Vision would not be complete without compassion. This is "sorrow for the sufferings or trouble of others, and an urge to do something about it" ... urge being the operative word here. Caregivers here at the ranch, down through the years have had this necessary trait. Again, the greatest book in the world contextually

states that, "Compassion makes a (big) difference."

But all of you know that a feeling or an urge doesn't get the job done, especially for 50 years. Vision and compassion are wonderful traits, but without the next, they would be just "good intentions." The next defining attribute is sacrifice, which is "foregoing something of value for the sake of a more pressing claim" ... that claim being the life and happiness of a boy who would otherwise be left to the mercy of the streets or dysfunctional extended family. For 50 years, the staff has sacrificed to be here, and friends have sacrificed to help them to do the job ... neither is more important than the other.

Now the bottom line ... even after vision, compassion and sacrifice ... there is an attribute we dare not forget – perseverance – the trait of continuing in some course of action, in spite of difficulty or opposition. With this, we accept the challenge to keep waking up reach day, working hard to raise the boys, and to hope and pray real hard that our friends will continue, with a compassionate heart, sacrifice and perseverance, in this great vision that began with two men and a small group of friends 50 years ago.

We give thanks every day for the opportunity to be working here on the Ranch.

The year 2000 is a milestone, one at which to look back and count the blessings, but also it is a mark to begin a new race of challenges in this day and time.

We accept the challenge.

Do you?

Ken traveled to Winona Lake, Indiana in 2000 to help the Reneker Museum of Winona Lake History honor Homer Rodeheaver. His tribute to Rodeheaver was so well received that he was asked to return the next weekend and do the Billy Sunday Mt. Hood Dedication for the State Historic Site.

After long-time tutor Ted Callahan retired in 2000, Ken worked with the

School board in Palatka to find a new tutor. Larry Litzell came to the Ranch as the new tutor and was there for several years.

That summer marked Ken Johnson's first backpacking trip on the Appalachian Trail with Judge Ed Hedstrom and his son, Scott Hedstrom, Roy Rowland, and ten Ranch boys. Ken chuckles when he remembers, "We were a pretty ragtag group that year – no money for backpacks, so we got them from the Army Surplus Store, and they had holes in them. The boys were learning to dig holes and we were constantly reminding them to leave nothing but tracks and memories. We'd sit around the campfire and talk about ghosts and spirit bears, gnomes and goblins and they'd throw candy wrappers here and there." Ken remembers, "The boys stayed up late and woke up weary. One morning, we woke the boys and were getting ready to hit the trail when Ed looked around and said, 'What do you think ... that a bunch of Gnomes are going to come after you and pick up your trash?'" The boys learned many lessons on that backpacking trip, not the least of which was to be mindful of their responsibility to the environment. In remembering that first backpacking trip, Ken Johnson notes that he and Ed Hedstrom still go on annual backpacking trips to this day and still enjoy it immensely.

> "There are those who watch it happen, those who wonder what happened, and those who make it happen."
> Ken's Favorite Sayings

Funds were found in 2000 to do a complete rework of all the metal on the Brad Robinson Building. "A beautiful job was done by Charles Smith who brought in Adel Steel from Georgia," recalls Ken.

The year 2000 marked the beginning of an annual tradition that Ranch boys still eagerly anticipate – the hunting trip to Carlton Spence's Bitter End Plantation in South Carolina. That year, 13 boys earned the right (through good grades and behavior) to hunt at Carlton's place, and several of the Board members and staff accompanied them as guides. That same scenario has played out nearly every year since then.

It was in 2000 that Bobby Cothren's Stellar Group transformed what had been called "Skipper's Corner" after the late Skipper Pearce into a Scouting activity center, which has since become the popular weight room for boys and staff.

The late Sam Taylor, Treasurer for the Ranch, received the 2000 Wagon Master Award – always a special tribute to deserving Ranch "Pardners," and Sam Taylor had earned that distinction through giving years of dedicated accounting to the Ranch.

Tom Knapp, Sharp Shooter

A world record holder in shotgun and skeet shooting, Tom Knapp, visited the Ranch and put on a shooting exhibition that amazed everyone who witnessed it. Knapp held seven clay pigeons with his left hand and arm – threw them up in the air and shot them before they hit the ground. Knapp, who is now deceased, made an impression on those present that is still remembered.

On November 2, 2000, the Ranch held their first Boy Scout Court of Honor with Judges Hedstrom, Parsons and Nichols at the Palatka Courthouse, and later that month, the troop held their first-ever Boy Scouts of America Flag Retirement Ceremony, a solemn and moving evening event featuring the Boy Scouts proceeding down a lighted path in total silence.

The Ranch Christmas Card featured remarks from three Coaches who supported the VIP Program, Bobby Bowden, Butch Davis and Steve Spurrier.

2000 Christmas card

On January 12, 2001, Steve and Cathy Watkins' son, Ben, was married to Julie Johnson in the Chapel at the Ranch.

Ben Watkins and his beautiful sisters, Sarah and Katie

Ben Watkins, left-handed pitcher for UNF

Watkins wedding day – January 13, 2001

Sadly, Ben passed away from cancer on May 25, 2003, just two years after marrying his sweetheart and beginning their new life together. His death was a devastating blow to all who knew and loved him, and yet, his parents Steve and Cathy, were then and remain comforted by Ben's profound faith in the Lord Jesus Christ. Steve says, "We all miss Ben but we know from his testimony for Christ that we'll see him again."

SIX: Y2K … ALL IS WELL

2001 was a milestone year for the Ranch in more ways than one. Ken Johnson recruited another old friend and strong man of God, Jeff King, to come and help the Johnsons, Watkins, Warrens, cottage parents and volunteers build boys. Jeff King and his wife, Donna, had known the Johnsons and the Watkins for decades – even before the days when all of them attended Faith Baptist Church in Milton, Florida back in the 1980s.

Donna and Jeff King

Jeff became the Ranch Development Director and his wife, Donna, a nurse by profession, became the Ranch Historian and Museum Curator, compiling much of the material that was featured in the first Ranch Book published in 2013 and a great deal more that is now on display at the Rodeheaver Boys Ranch Museum. A football player at the University of Tennessee and Middle Tennessee State University (MTSU), Jeff discovered Christ while in graduate school at MTSU. A big man who was also involved with the Horse Science Riding Program at MTSU, Jeff jokingly called himself "a reformed long hair hippie football player." He got to know Ken Johnson in 1970s while attending Faith Bible College in Milton, Florida. "I learned so much about the Lord and about life from Dr. Mac Johnson, Ken's Dad," said Jeff, remembering that he went to the theological seminary where Dr. Johnson was President to take a two-year course and ended up staying for nine years as an instructor and Dean of the Seminary. Prior to coming to the Ranch, Jeff held the position of Prison Prevention Field Director for Rock of Ages Ministries, developing a character curriculum for presentation in public schools and implementing it nationally. When Ken Johnson called Jeff and asked him to come to Rodeheaver Boys Ranch, former Executive Director Ashley Jeter was nearing retirement. Jeff and Donna arrived in May and stepped directly into the fray, quickly becoming integral builders of boys on the Ranch.

Soon, the Kings were actively involved in the civil war reenactments that occurred annually on the site of the Battle at Horse Landing. Donna greatly enjoyed researching the Civil War history and dressing up in period costumes, and Jeff was her gallant Southern gentleman. All of the Ranch family participated in hosting the reenactments at that historic site, and in 2001, the marker for the Battle of Horse Landing was erected. It remains there to this day.

Shortly after coming to the Ranch, Jeff King rose to the challenge when board member Kenny Downs reported that famed radio personality Paul Harvey had made a negative comment on his show about charitable organizations that raise funds through automobile donation. Because the VIP Automobile Program was one of the major fundraisers for the Ranch and had been since 1992, Jeff wrote a letter to Mr. Harvey and invited him to come to the Ranch and see for himself how the program worked and the great value it brought not only to the Ranch but to the boys and the community. In part, Jeff wrote:

> We personally collect donated cars, and the boys actually work on the vehicles as part of our vocational program. The cars are auctioned off here at the ranch once a month, and we currently raise about 25% of our monthly budget from these auctions. The big difference in our program is that we do not have a middleman to collect and auction our cars. We do it all ourselves, and the entire process helps us fulfill the mission of the ranch, which is more than housing and feeding the boys; it's also teaching them a trade.

Paul Harvey's one negative remark about automobile donation, like many of God's blessings, turned out to be a positive for the Ranch. After making a positive remark on his program in response to Jeff's letter, Paul Harvey received a solid invitation to visit the Ranch and make a guest appearance on the First Coast as a fundraiser. Several of the Ranch's "Pardners" chipped in to get him to Palatka and it was well worth the effort and expense.

"Most of the time when we ask God to help us, help is already on the way."
Ken's Favorite Sayings

On June 22, 2002, a sold out "Evening with Paul Harvey" was presented at the Morocco Shrine Auditorium in Jacksonville, with an introduction by Palatka Mayor Karl Flagg; Jacksonville Mayor John Delaney served as Master of Ceremonies. Among the major sponsors were ICS Logistics, Inc., The Stellar Group, Ring Power Corporation, The McCormick Agency, Morocco Shrine Temple, and Nimnicht Chevrolet. Not only did the formal "Evening with Paul Harvey" bring in a great deal of money, but lasting national attention after Harvey spent some time at the Ranch.

Eating homemade ice cream with the boys in the dining hall; dining at the home of Ken and Lois Johnson with Jeff and Donna King, Steve and Cathy Watkins, and Ed and Joy Hedstrom; being chauffeured around in a limousine

Paul Harvey changed his mind about the VIP Program!
Here, he is pictured with Herb Wilson with the caption:
"Would I buy a used car from Herb? You bet! Paul Harvey"

provided by Nimnicht Chevrolet; being put up in the Lodge; and, of course, being introduced personally to the workings of the VIP Program; all of these factors impressed the famous man more than anyone thought possible. Today, on the Ranch website (www.rbr.org) one of the late Paul Harvey's radio shows in June of 2002 can be heard in its entirety. Focused on his great weekend visit to the Ranch, Harvey extols the virtues of founder Homer Rodeheaver and then details several touching "snapshots" of his impressions of the Ranch, even to the rain that fell almost constantly while he was there.

On September 20, 2002, Ken Johnson received a letter from Paul Harvey delivered by Federal Express. A substantial check was enclosed, but even more valuable than that was Paul Harvey's remembrance that it was not a long-distance call to God from the Ranch, but a local call. He stated that he felt God's presence there, especially in the beautiful chapel where a stained-glass window showed Jesus in His role as a carpenter, working to build the skills and characters of young boys who would grow into fine men.

As always, the Ranch boys were rewarded for getting good grades at school and, in 2002, their devoted tutor, Larry Litzell, took the honor roll boys to Islands of Adventure in Valdosta, Georgia – just one of many rewards that still come to Ranch boys as a result of their hard work and dedication.

When former Sheriff Walt Pellicer passed away in 2002, there was standing room only at the First Baptist Church of Palatka's auditorium where his memorial service was held. All of the Ranch boys were taken to pay tribute to a man who had served as a supporter and board member of Rodeheaver Boys Ranch for as far back as anyone could remember. Tommy Clay and Judge Ed Hedstrom, two other long-time Ranch "Pardners," spoke at the service in memory of their old friend. Today, Walt's son, Walton Pellicer, is a devoted board member of the Ranch. The legacy continues.

Ken Johnson was installed in 2002 for his second year as President of the Florida Association of Christian Childcare Agencies (FACCCA) in Tallahassee, and remembers spending some quality time with then-Representative Joe Pickens (now President of St. Johns College, where many of the Ranch boys begin their college careers).

In early 2003, Dr. Mac Johnson, Ken's father, passed away suddenly at age 69 due to complications with his heart. It was a sad day for the Johnson family, and for the many who had been nurtured and brought to Christ by Dr. Mac Johnson over the years, including Steve and Cathy Watkins and Jeff and Donna King. Dr. Mac Johnson had been President of the Georgia Farm Bureau and Chairman of the Deacons of the Baptist Church before going into full-time ministry. By the time he passed away, Dr. Johnson had preached all over the world, his hope being that his son, Ken, would follow in his footsteps and join his worldwide ministry. However, on a visit to the Ranch, Dr. Johnson had confided to Ken, "Now I see this is where you should be."

"Ask the question! You already have 'no' in your pocket." Ken's Favorite Sayings

On February 14th, 2003, Valentine's Day, Steve and Cathy Watkins and Ken Johnson took several Ranch boys on a four-day camping trip to Carlton Spence's Bitter End Plantation in South Carolina. Because Lois Johnson was teaching and couldn't join them, Ken's mother, Mary Ann, went with them. "It hadn't been long since Daddy died," recalls Ken, "This was her first trip to do anything. One of the boys was talking in the van on the way about what he wanted to do when he retired. It struck Mother funny and she laughed for miles. It was the first time I'd heard her laugh since Daddy died. It was one of the best trips either of us had ever had."

Dr. Steve Chapman became President of the Board in 2003, and that was also the year that he received the Wagon Master Award for his longtime service to the Ranch and for caring for so many of the Ranch's needs over the years. "Whenever anything needed done, Steve Chapman can always be depended on to pitch in, from fixing fence to fixing teeth, and he's earned his title as the Orthodontist's Orthodontist," said Ken Johnson, paying tribute to Chapman's consistent devotion, which continues unabated to this day.

That year, some of the boys had the privilege of deep-sea fishing off the coast in St. Augustine and 2003 was also the first year that scouts went camping at Philmont in New Mexico, the premier camping spot for Scouts. Ranch boys Jonathan Harper and Casey DeHaas worked on Eagle Scout projects, building playgrounds for two different churches in Palatka.

It was in 2003 that a special visitor named Donald "Duck" Harper came to Rodeheaver Boys Ranch for the first time as the guest of his sister, Ruby, and her husband, Carlton Spence. "Duck" has been a fan of bluegrass music for many years and he immediately recognized the beautiful spread of the Ranch as an ideal place for a bluegrass festival. "You need to make this happen for the Ranch," Duck told his brother-in-law Carlton. "This could be a huge funding source and a way to get the Ranch well-known throughout the country." Duck suggested that Carlton call Adams and Anderson, the top bluegrass festival organizers in the country, and invite them to the Ranch. Carlton caught his brother-in-law's vision and began to pursue Adams and Anderson vigorously,

Donald "Duck" Harper and Carlton Spence

but quite unsuccessfully. Norman Adams informed Carlton that he had no interest whatsoever in taking on another bluegrass festival, and, in fact, he and his partner were looking forward to reducing their load and retiring. Undaunted, Carlton continued to call Adams month after month to invite him and his partner, Tony Anderson, to the Ranch. He reasoned that if he ever, once, got them there, they'd see the Ranch as the perfect venue, and realize what a benefit the bluegrass festivals would be for the boys.

Finally, Adams and Anderson agreed to drop by the Ranch on a Florida vacation with their wives, Judy Adams and Susan Anderson. Of course, once they saw the lay of the land, the lodge and pavilion, ate in the dining room and attended chapel with the boys, they were hooked, just as Duck and Carlton had predicted. Bluegrass, with its Christian values, patriotic, family fun atmosphere with great country/gospel music, was tailormade for Homer Rodeheaver's vision of a boys ranch. Once again, God was working through good Ranch "Pardners" like Carlton and Duck!

Once Adams and Anderson had agreed to hold a bluegrass festival at the Ranch, there was a great deal of preparation that had to be done prior to the first festival. A festival RV Park had to be built, the size of the pavilion had to be doubled, new paving had to go in – a multitude of things had to come together to make it feasible for a large festival to be held on the ranch.

And then, there was the repair to the Dining Hall as the result of an unexpected and unwelcomed arrival. There have been several dramatic arrivals to the Ranch over the past seventy years ... Homer Rodeheaver's visits, President Johnson's historic visit, airplanes swooping in, Paul Harvey's arrival in a chauffeur-driven limousine, RV campers, helicopters, horse-drawn wagons, trailers hauling fishing boats, and most of these arrivals have been welcomed with open arms; however, the abrupt arrival of a pickup truck at 5:50 a.m. on Saturday, January 24, 2004, was not one of them. Just as morning dawned, a pickup truck carrying two passengers and being driven by an inebriated young man from Interlachen, Florida, crashed into the middle

of the Dining Hall at such a high rate of speed that, after almost hitting the flagpole in front, it raced through the front wall, crashing into tables and chairs and finally coming to a halt at the kitchen counter. Miraculously, neither of the young passengers were injured, although a breathalyzer test revealed that the driver had a blood alcohol level of .12 – four points over the legal limit. Had there been a bit more daylight and had he been driving at a reasonable rate of speed and in good condition, the driver might have seen the small sign in plain sight at the right hand side of Ranch Road that reads:

Zero Tolerance. No tobacco.
No Alcohol. No drugs.
(Inside or Outside)

The timing of the "drive-through" at the Dining Hall was especially frightening as, often, fishing tournaments or special occasions on Saturdays will begin with an early breakfast right there just as the sun is rising. For several years, photographs of the crash scene remained on the bulletin board in the dining hall – a vivid reminder to the boys about the dangers of drinking and driving. It took weeks for the dining hall to be repaired and time was of the essence because the first ever Palatka Bluegrass Festival was scheduled at Rodeheaver Boys Ranch for February 12, 13, and 14th of 2004!

"Carlton Spence and Bobby Cothren lined up Coxwell Construction of Jacksonville to do the landscaping and roadwork – pro bono," recalls Ken Johnson. "Rick Oreair Electric did all the electrical work at cost, Pritchett Trucking did the hauling at cost, Stevola furnished the limerock and Ring Power furnished the machinery. It was a miracle that we had everything ready for the first festival, including 300 RV sites that were completely full!"

In all, about $1.5 million worth of improvements (and repairs) were accomplished for less than a third of that figure in less than six months! There was no question that Homer Rodeheaver was smiling from heaven throughout the entire process. In the meantime, Ken Johnson and Steve Chapman traveled to Dunellen, Florida because they wanted to see a Florida Bluegrass Festival in action at the Withlacoochee Bluegrass Festival. "That festival was on the banks of the Withlacoochee River just as our festival was going to be on the banks of the St. Johns River," recalls Ken. "We duplicated several of the things they had at that festival, including the green room and porch behind the stage so the stars could really enjoy themselves. The visit Steve and I made back then was one of the reasons we were so successful at our festival!" Ken notes that Steve Chapman has a kind way about him that transcends his duties as a past president and member of the Rodeheaver Foundation. "Steve took the time to come into the dining hall after our first festival and congratulated the staff on what a good job they did," recalls Ken. "That kind of acknowledgment means a great deal."

**Bluegrass Festival Organizers Tony & Susan Anderson and
Judy & Norman Adams in 2012 at the
6th Annual Palatka Fall Bluegrass Festival at Rodeheaver Boys Ranch**

With the infrastructure in place, the annual bluegrass festival grew bigger and bigger each year until, in 2008, the Palatka Bluegrass Festival at Rodeheaver Boys Ranch became a bi-annual event with one held in February and one in the Fall – either October or November. Through the years, people who attended the bluegrass festivals became regular supporters and passed the word about the Ranch to others across the country. Jeff and Donna King became Bluegrass ambassadors for the Ranch and traveled to several festivals a year to share the Rodeheaver story. Some of the top names in Bluegrass music have become regulars to the Ranch, including Rhonda Vincent and the Rage, The Hagar's Mountain Boys, The Baker Family, the Dave Adkins Band, and The Little Roy and Lizzie Show. Emcee Sherry Boyd is on hand for every bluegrass festival at the Ranch and is one of the biggest cheerleaders for the boys. Of course, the Ranch boys are there to help park cars, serve barbecue, give tours, help stock the Ranch Store and help the staff in any way that is needed during the big three-day bi-annual event, including helping cook and serve dinner to visitors in the Dining Hall.

Left to right: Judge Ed Hedstrom, Steve Watkins, Marc Spalding, Dr. Bob Mitchem, Bobby Cothren, Carlton Spence, Dr. Richard Perallon, Sherry Boyd, Ken Johnson & Jeff King at the 2012 Fall Bluegrass Festival.

The Dining Hall, from the time of the "Grits & Gravy" photograph in Trucking Magazine in 1953 on, has been as central to the building of boys physically as the worship of God has been to them spiritually. One of the big events in the dining hall is the 5:30 a.m. breakfast for the boys and their fishing guides at the annual Rodeheaver Boys Ranch Bass Tournament every spring. Thankfully, the tournament breakfast on Saturday morning began months after the pickup truck crashed into the Dining Hall. Otherwise, with the tables filled with hungry boys wolfing down breakfast at 5:50 a.m. in preparation for a day of fishing, it could have been the worst tragedy in Ranch history.

The Tournament began when Jerry Shawver, a math professor at Florida State Community College in Jacksonville and a member of the First Coast Christian Bass Club, had fished a Bass Masters Classic Tournament and been asked to speak to Ranch boys about fishing in 2004. Greg Buchanan and Steve Watkins approached Shawver after his talk, and Greg said, "You know, Jerry, it would be nice if one day some of you guys could come down here and take these kids out fishing." Jerry instantly agreed.

Jerry Shawver and Ranch Boys

The following year, Jerry Shawver, Al Brim, Ben Strawn and Roy Wires got together with Greg Buchanan and Steve Watkins and organized the first ever Rodeheaver Boys Ranch Bass Tournament. That first year they only had about twenty boats but Jerry remembers, "We helped the boys make a lifelong memory and we learned that the boys can teach us as much as we teach them."

As with most of the great ideas that occur at the Ranch, God has blessed the boys' bass tournament and it grows each year, with more and more anglers wanting to participate one on one with a boy in a fishing tournament. In the past, fishermen from the First Coast Christian Bass Club, St. Augustine Bassmasters, Jacksonville Bass Club, Jacksonville Bass Finders, North Florida Christian Bass Club and Po Boys Bass Clubs have participated, bringing new donated fishing rods, caps, tackle boxes and plaques for the boys as prizes each year. "There are no rewards for the boaters," says Shawver, "It's all for the boys."

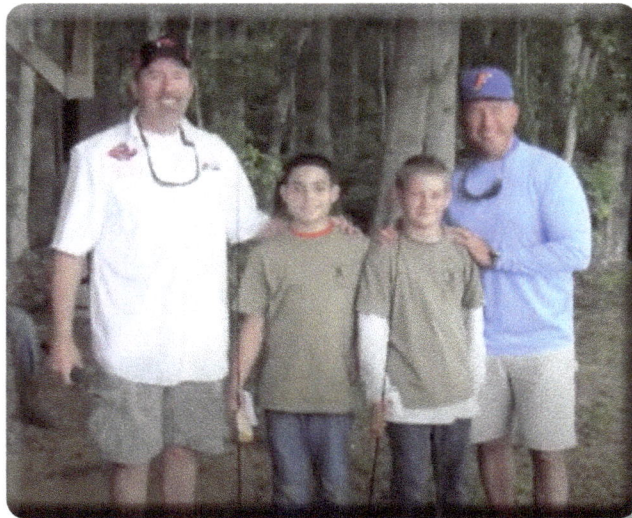

Jerry Shawver, Ranch Boys and Mike Oglesbee

At the Annual Meeting in 2004, the Ranch was honored with a visit from FSU Coach Bobby Bowden and his wife. Bowden gave a rousing keynote speech of praise for the Boys Ranch and Don Holmes, who emceed that year, led the applause. The room in the Lodge where the Coach and his wife stayed is now officially called "The Bobby Bowden Room."

When board member Ed Beckler passed away in late April of 2004, the drive to the river was dedicated to his memory by Henry and Helen Hirschman. Henry funded Ed Beckler Park, he said, because Ed had never wanted any recognition but now that he was gone, he could do nothing about it. The bear columns on either side of the drive into Ed Beckler Park are there because it is an actual bear crossing. Ken Johnson remembers Ed as "a modest man, a humanitarian, Rotarian and philanthropist – a man who did much for the community."

Tutor Larry Litzell resigned in 2004 to take a full-time pastorate in a church in Interlachen, Florida. He was missed by both the boys and the staff.

Hurricane Charley made landfall just west of Ft. Myers, Florida on August 13th with maximum sustained winds near 150 mph. The hurricane moved north, hitting Punta Gorda, Port Charlotte, Orlando and up to Palm Coast, causing significant damage along the way; fortunately, Rodeheaver Boys Ranch sustained little damage. Mark Warren got a bunch of boys together to load up a meat cooker and 1,100 pounds of meat (courtesy of Carlton Spence's ICS Logistics) to take to Arcadia, Florida. Mark had been informed by the county extension agent that Arcadia needed meat, and, thanks to God, Rodeheaver had it to share!

"Pray like it all depends on God and work like it all depends on you." Ken's Favorite Sayings

That September, Ranch "Pardner" Jack Langdon's Aunt Jenn Newby and mother, Pearl Langdon, financed the efforts of the Ranch boys to create the world's longest ice cream sundae for the Guinness Book of World Records. They created and devoured a 50-foot long ice cream sundae, but it melted before a World Record could be reached.

The Bluegrass Festival of 2005 was a great success, with RV sites increased to 365 and a new staging area, as well as the pavilion being extended 45 more feet. The festival was growing and so was word of the good work being done at Rodeheaver. When Ken and Lois Johnson traveled that year to Combes, Texas to see missionary Bob Cole at the First Baptist Church of Combes, Ken spoke to the congregation about the Ranch and they began supporting the boys annually. Today, under the leadership of Pastor Steve Weist, the First Baptist Church of Combes, Texas continues to support the Ranch monthly.

Bobby Cothren became President of the Board in 2005, and Rick and Patti McClure came to the Ranch as cottage parents on the 1st of June. A few months later, Teddie and Elizabeth Betonio came to be cottage parents at Boeing Cottage, bringing with them a beautiful family. The Betonios were from the Philippines. The youngest boys traditionally live in Boeing Cottage and the loving compassion of the Betonio family was exactly what a young boy needed. Elizabeth Betonio, with her Masters Degree in Education and

Teddie with his Masters Degree in Nursing, provided nurturing and thoughtful parental care for their Ranch Boys and their own five children, Amos, Esther, Genesis, Jerusalem and Ruth Betonio.

Teddie Betonio had been in charge of the choir at his former church and he held the belief, as did Homer Rodeheaver, that peace could be achieved if everyone just sang together. When his cottage full of rowdy young children got wild, Teddie would sit down at the piano and gather them around him to sing. "After they've sung for a while," he said, "the anger just comes out of them and peace takes over. Pretty soon, they are ready to settle down."

Each year, Teddie and Elizabeth began in September to prepare their young children for a Christmas Cantata to be performed at Wednesday night chapel service the last week before Christmas. If a boy insisted that he couldn't sing, Teddie convinced him otherwise. "They can all sing," he insists. "It's just a matter of practice ... like everything else in life."

Betonios' Boeing Cottage Chorus - Christmas Cantata – 2013

SIX: Y2K ... ALL IS WELL

The Betonio's left the Ranch in 2014 but have remained in close contact with many of the friends they made during their nine years as Boeing Cottage Parents. Elizabeth Betonio shared several Ranch boy memories for this 70th Anniversary Edition of the Ranch History, among them the following:

Robbie's Story: Sometimes Elizabeth's heavy Filipino accent led to amusing stories, and this is one of them: "At Boeing Cottage, we had two washing machines – labeled WM(A) and WM(B). The white clothing went into WM(A) and the colored into WM(B). I instructed the boys carefully, training three to four boys at a time on the procedures of washing their clothes. I usually put in the laundry detergent and was there when one of the boys transferred the washed clothes into the dryer. One day I noticed there were colored clothes mixed in with white clothes. I called the boys together and the colored clothes belonged to Robbie. The following conversation ensued:

Elizabeth: Robbie, was it clear to you when I told you to separate your colored clothes from your white clothes?

Robbie: (with confidence) Yes, ma'am!

Elizabeth: If it was clear to you, why did you mix your colored clothes with the white ones?

Robbie: But Mrs. Betonio, you said that I should separate my white clothes from my "collared" clothes, so I put all my "collared" clothes into this washing machine!

After we finished laughing, I apologized for my accent and he apologized for not understanding. It was a sweet learning experience.

William's Story: At Boeing Cottage, we had a "quiet time" after lunch. The boys could read their Bibles quietly, write a letter home or just take a nap. I was doing dishes on a certain Sunday when I heard noises at quiet time. It was William playing with his clothes hangers – there were several broken ones on the floor. I reminded him about "quiet time." In a few minutes, I caught William in another boy's room playing with his belt. I asked him to come practice his memory verse from the Bible in front of me while I finished the dishes. He was having trouble memorizing his verse, Hebrews 11:6, one that the boys recited at every chapel service: "And without faith it is impossible to please God, for he that cometh to God must believe that He is, and that He is a rewarder of them that diligently seek Him." He recited the verse over and over while I was doing the dishes and all at once I felt God speaking to me through William. I commended his effort and sent him to his room for "quiet time," and I stopped what I was doing and went to my room and knelt down to pray. This verse was for me as well as for William. God spoke to me through this boy.

London's Story: London Jett was my daughter Esther's age and they became best friends at RBR. One year, they shared an interest in a 4-H project, raising pigs for Putnam County Fair. Then in 2014, my family left the Ranch and Esther left her dear friend, London, behind. Fast forward to 2020 when Esther, now a nurse, took care of a young patient named London at Shands Hospital. It was exciting for them to be reunited after six years and I told London, through "Messenger" that I still loved him and he was in my prayers. He kindly replied and said he was grateful for my love and care for him at the Ranch. He left Shands and seemed to be getting better, but in February 2020, our sweet London passed away. That sandy-haired, blue-eyed boy found a place in our hearts and now has a place in heaven.

❧

Papa's Story: God allowed my father to visit the USA from the Philippines and stay with us for almost six months at RBR. The greatest thing God did on that visit was save my Papa in the tiny office at Boeing Cottage. For 26 years, my Papa was unmindful and uncaring about God's Word and every time I told him, he hated it, but on the morning of February 14, 2014, as I was reading and studying the Bible, he asked me about it. God gave me the greatest opportunity to testify about God and His Salvation through Jesus Christ, our Lord. It was amazing that my Papa just listened attentively, and the salvation message was freely expressed. On that day, he prayed the sinner's prayer and accepted His gift of salvation and dedicated his life to Him. God still answers prayers and He always will.

❧

Betonio Family Wedding – Marriage of Genesis and Nate Johnson

That year, Herb Wilson resigned from managing the Ranch VIP to assume ownership of the feed store in Palatka and Mark Warren resigned as farm manager to take a job as Flagler County Agricultural Extension Agent in Bunnell, Florida. Change, as always, was met with resolve at the Ranch, and God took care of the rest.

When Bobby Cothren was given the Wagon Master Award in 2006, Ken Johnson said, "Bobby Cothren is probably the most unselfish person I've ever met. With his practical and professional abilities, marketing strategies and his ability to choose people who are very good at what they do, few people can put a team together like Bobby can." Bobby and his wife, Cheryl, have been stalwarts of the Ranch for nearly two decades, being present at and generously supporting nearly every event, including the 2002 visit by Paul Harvey.

Bobby Cothren, Paul Harvey and Cheryl Cothren

As with all of the other improvements going on at the Ranch, the RV Park grew from 356 sites to 516 in 2006, and again, all of the sites were filled for the Bluegrass Festival despite the cold and rain that year. After the heavy rains, Bobby Cothren brought in his Stellar Construction and partnered with Ring Power to do an intense drainage project for the RV Park that took nearly a year to complete. When a need arose, invariably the Ranch "Pardners" filled it and more.

Ken, like his father before him, faced health issues with his heart and in 2006, he underwent five heart bypasses at Flagler Hospital. His 24/7 job as Executive Director of the Ranch had to be put on hold for a few days until he recovered and, again like his father before him, he jumped back into his personal ministry undaunted and with renewed energy – just in time to celebrate his Tenth Anniversary at the Ranch!

"A real friend has the ministry of presence."
Ken's Favorite Sayings

Longtime Ranch "Pardners," Bill and Bonny Huntley had donated enough money a couple of years prior to 2006 to build, furnish and maintain a new cottage for the boys, and the beautiful new Huntley Cottage was dedicated in 2006 at the Annual Meeting in April.

Rick and Patti McClure took over the kitchen responsibilities for the dining room – an extremely important job that they fulfilled beyond all expectations. Helping the McClures in the kitchen and working all over the Ranch were dedicated volunteers, Jerry and Joyce Flannery and Al and Nancy Mathies, Ray and Ginny Dobbins, Dick and Ruth Donaghy and Wilbur Driggers. Our volunteers came from across the country, drove to Rodeheaver Boys Ranch and spent months living in their RV's and working for the Lord during their retirement years. Many of them are still here in 2020 and many have passed on from this earthly plain. They are all so well remembered and so deeply appreciated for the love and devotion they gave to the boys.

**Many thanks to a few of our great volunteers pictured in 2012:
Ray & Ginny Dobbins, Jerry and Joyce Flannery,
Russ and Sharon Terjung, Dick & Ruth Donaghy
(not pictured: Wilbur Driggers, Al & Nancy Mathies)**

In 2006, as with most years, the Ranch Boys did well with their 4-H Pigs at the County Fair – winning 14 ribbons and coming away with money from pig profits for their bank accounts. The boys spend months fattening their pigs in anticipation of showing them at the Fair and, most often, the pork is donated back to the Ranch by the same generous donors who buy the pigs. Once in a while, though, a boy becomes attached to a pig and somewhat reluctant to face the final act when they all know the pig is going to be sold and slaughtered to feed hungry boys. This was the case back in the early 2000s when the following classic and completely self-explanatory letter was shared with the Ranch staff and stored for safekeeping by bookkeeper Peggy Yundt:

Dear Mr. Eubanks

Thank you for buying my pig. His name was Bob. He will listen to you if you are nice to him. He loves pig-popper. I hope you haven't eaten him yet. I would like you to give him this message.

TO: Bob
Oink, Oink, Oink,
Oink, Oink, Oink,
you are someones dinner.
Oink, Oink, Oink,
Oink, Oink, Oink,
I don't like it either.

Well I was wondering if Bob and you will write me back please. I hope Bob tastes good.

by
Jeremy Mattson

Among the AB Honor Roll boys that Ranch Tutor James Hughes and Cottage Parent Teddie Betonio took to Universal Studios in Orlando in 2007 was Raymond Minks, who had come to the Ranch in 2002 at age 11. Raymond was a studious boy who loved to read, especially about history. When he got to the Ranch, he came with a certificate from First Grade stating that he had not missed a spelling word all that year. Raymond did so well at school that he ended up assisting James Hughes in tutoring the other boys. He and James became friends and still remain close to this day, as Raymond considers Hughes to be his mentor. Raymond began his Eagle Scout project of building a second pavilion at the Ranch Campground and then, in 2007, he left the Ranch to join his family. He returned in 2008 to complete his Eagle project before earning his Eagle Scout designation. "I can't think of a project that I would have liked better than the one I did," he says. "It is helping boys now and for many years to come."

Raymond Minks & Greg Buchanan – Eagle Scout Ceremony – May 2007

After leaving the Ranch to reunite with his family when he was in 10th grade, Raymond earned academic scholarships to college and graduated from Truitt-McConnell College, a Baptist Institute in Georgia, with degrees in business administration and history. He married his college sweetheart, Katelyn and they have three children with Biblical names: Enoch, 5, Reuben, 4 and Hadassah, 2 and two rescue dogs named after Star Constellations:

a Doberman named Orion (the hunter) and a Newfoundland named Ursa (the bear). The Minks family lives near Atlanta, where Raymond works as Operations Manager for a trucking line.

Raymond says that the Ranch taught him a lot of basic life skills like time management and dealing with people, and that he became a Christian at the Ranch. Raymond also became a musician when he was at the Ranch, starting with base clarinet in middle school. He now plays tenor saxophone. Over the five years at Rodeheaver, Raymond says that he did just about everything, from working in the barn and the VIP to hunting, fishing and camping. "Those were formative years for me," he says. "I learned so much about life."

The Minks family attends Eastside Baptist Church near Atlanta, where Katelynn's parents run a food pantry. A devoted and patient father to his three children and a man who is grateful his wife can be a "stay-at-home Mom," Raymond was also grateful to be an "essential worker" during the 2020 Pandemic, as his trucking company delivers groceries. As "essential" as Raymond was in 2020, he considers Rodeheaver Boys Ranch to have been an essential part of his boyhood.

Former Ranch boy, Jonathan Harper, married his beautiful Mandy on July 21st in 2007 at the Palatka Baptist Temple where her family attended, and where Jonathan had met her while helping on an Eagle Scout project, building a playground. Jonathan Harper was 14 when he came to the Ranch and remained there through high school graduation from Palatka High. He was one of the Ranch's first Eagle Scouts and Karen Hughes, then Principal of Palatka High as well as a long-time board member of the Ranch, made a special book for him and presented it to him at his Eagle Scout Ceremony. His Eagle

Jonathan & Mandy Harper & Family

Scout Project was the outside remodel – painting and repairs of the house of Yvonne Brandt who served as secretary and public relations assistant for the Ranch for twenty-two years. He distinguished himself both at high school and in college, where he became a computer engineer, having worked his way through ITT as an employee of his great Uncle Carlton Spence's company. Today, Jon and Mandy Harper, the parents of three beautiful children, are big supporters of Rodeheaver Boys Ranch and attend as many events as possible. "My time at the Ranch was one of the blessings of my life," says Jon, who enjoys being a hunting guide, mentor and role model at his Uncle's plantation when the Ranch boys come in the fall, and continues to have a heart for all of the Ranch family. "Jon Harper is a wonderful role model for the boys of the Ranch," says Ken Johnson. "He has worked hard and earned a good life for himself and his family. When I look out on a room filled with boys at an event and I see Jon's smiling face, it touches my heart."

"You are doing a lot of things right, so take a deep breath ... breathe ... be thankful ... and don't let up."
Ken's Favorite Sayings

Cathy Watkins remembers that her mother, Margaret Pinner, took Jonathan Harper into her small two-bedroom bungalow on one of the old brick streets in Palatka, and set him up in one of her bedrooms. "Jonathan settled into being one of her boys (as she helped other Ranch boys, too). He lived with her for two years and she loved his dry sense of humor. She was proud of Jonathan's gift for all things technological and bragged about his instructor at ITT using him as his teaching assistant. When Jonathan graduated, his mother and grandmother traveled from West Virginia and Cathy's mother (whom he called Granny) attended the ceremony. Margaret, who has gone on to her heavenly reward now, is remembered fondly by all who knew her at the Ranch.

Through her mother's loving ministry, Cathy Watkins got to know Jonathan Harper more intimately than she knew most of the Ranch boys because her husband, Steve, purposely spared her many of the details of their lives before coming to the Ranch. Over the 21 years they were at the Ranch, Cathy got to know the boys mainly through working with them at the barn, as they

prepped horses together, curried, scraped hooves, saddled and bridled the horses and rode out on trails together. She particularly remembers the Sapp brothers, Michael and his younger brother James. Michael suffered from a speech impediment, but he somehow found it easy to talk to Cathy while horseback riding. "No stuttering, no hesitation or breathing problems," Cathy remembers. "It was a real insight into the use of equine therapy for not only physical but emotional cases." Mike's brother, James, worked with Cathy at the barn as well and still keeps up with Steve Watkins on Facebook. James is now married with two sons.

In the summer of 2001, Michael Sapp got some much-needed help from Tutor Larry Litzell, Ken and Lois, and Jeff and Donna King. Litzell found a three-week speech therapy program at the University of Virginia Medical School that would accept Mike, the only caveat being that someone had to be with him all three weeks. "Larry went up there the first week, Lois and I the second week, and Jeff and Donna the third week," remembers Ken Johnson. "The boy could actually talk with confidence when he came home to the Ranch!"

> "Access to power must be confined to men who are not in love with it."
> Ken's Favorite Sayings

Cathy remembers, also, that there was a period of two or three months when the Ranch had a shortage of cottage parents and Steve, as Director of Ranch Life, took three boys into their home. The three were Jimmy Melanson, Justin Wessel and Melvin Ealy. She remembers special qualities that each boy possessed. Jimmy had the friendliest personality and if there had been a contest at the Ranch, he would have won "Mr. Congeniality." Justin was a cute little redheaded boy with freckles who could be just charming enough to get him out of doing chores, but he was trustworthy when tasked with doing something he enjoyed – like running errands to the office. Melvin, the youngest of the three boys, was grateful for whatever was given him and would seek out the giver to personally thank them.

So many memories flood Cathy's heart and mind as she looks back at her years – good, bad, happy and sad. "I choose to remember the best of those years," she says, "because I know God had and has a plan for each boy and staff member who spent time together, sharing what wisdom and knowledge each could pass on." It is Cathy's prayer that the Bible verses that were part of their memorization and helped them earn trips home, penetrated their minds and hearts, especially John 3:16-17 "For God so loved the world that He gave his Only begotten son, that whosoever believes in Him will not perish but have everlasting life. For God sent not His son into the world to condemn the world, but that the world through Him might be saved."

It was in 2007 that the groundbreaking for the new Langdon-Newby Activities Center happened, with Jack Langdon holding the golden shovel and architect Bob Taylor posing with Board Members Dan Martinez and Bobby Cothren, and all of the Ranch boys, who were extremely excited at the prospect of having a special activities building for Boy Scout meetings and recreational activities. The building was completed in 2010 and continues to be the site of pizza parties, table tennis tournaments, movie nights and more. Dedicated to Jack Langdon's mother and aunt, much of the funding for the building was provided by the Rodeheaver Foundation along with Thomas A. Miller and Joseph E. Miller.

Groundbreaking – Langdon-Newby Activities Center

In 2008, Dwight and Malynda Scifries presented the Ranch with a new 21' center console boat for recreational use by the boys and staff. The "Sweet Malynda" could fish the river and offshore and provided a great deal of entertainment to all. Dwight and Malynda Scifries of Montezuma, Indiana became friends of the Ranch back in 1997 and, after nearly twenty years of visiting, supporting and making improvements in the 4-H, Boy Scout and Youth Sports Shooting programs, they became cottage parents in 2016. Dwight, an expert in firearm safety, sought contributions to establish the Youth Sports Shooting Program at the Ranch, purchasing several air rifles, .22 caliber target rifles and assorted hunting rifles for the older boys as well as a large firearm safe for storage. Malynda, an accomplished school counselor, helped with the educational aspect of the Ranch.

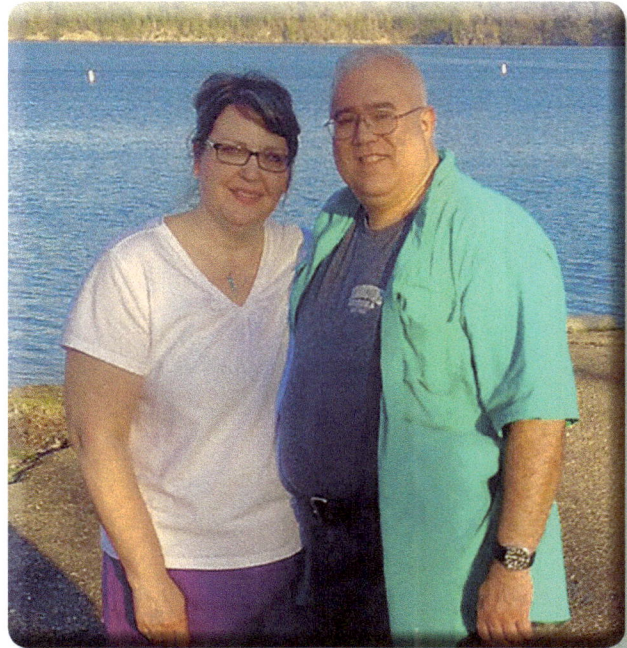

Malynda and Dwight Scifries

The boys have always had a great affection for the animals on the Ranch, and the Scifries' Labs, Reuben and Judah, held a special place in their hearts.

Ranch boys with Labs Reuben and Judah

**Special Friends and Ranch Ladies
on Malynda's birthday
L-R: Donna King, Malynda Scifries,
Lois Johnson and Cathy Watkins**

Steve Watkins was certified in 2000 as an NRA Boy Scouts of America Shooting instructor trainer, and in 2002, with a generous gift from Dwight's close friend, the late Dr. Michael Berger, the ranch was able to construct an outdoor shooting range with a large covered pavilion for firearm safety training and shooting. The Scifries have since retired, but as with so many others, remain close to the Ranch and keep the boys in their hearts and prayers.

Don and Joan Inman visited the Ranch for the first time in 2006, having worked with children at the Patrick Henry Girls Home in West Virginia. They had read about the need for cottage parents at Rodeheaver Boys Ranch in the Christian magazine, *Sword of the Lord*. Don and Joan came on as cottage parents for Westbury Cottage in 2008, and their daughter, Debbie, married Ken and Lois Johnson's son, Jon, in the Chapel on February 23rd, 2009.

Here's "the rest of the story" on Jon and Debbie! Jon Johnson was the "go-to guy" for any repairs that needed to be done around the Ranch, and he was especially adept at working in the Vehicle Improvement Program (VIP). From the very beginning of his time at Rodeheaver Boys Ranch, Don Inman did mechanical work at the VIP, and there he got to know Jon Johnson. The two soon found another passion in common – Fishing! Don and Jon went fishing regularly, except when Jon occasionally went to West Florida to visit

his girlfriend. On a weekend fishing trip, Don encouraged Jon not to take another trip to West Florida until he had met his daughter, Debbie Inman, who was coming to join them at the Ranch. It was love at first sight for Jon and Debbie. He never took another trip to see his girlfriend in West Florida again.

Dr. Robert Mitchem received the Wagon Master Award on October 2, 2008. His love for the Ranch is boundless and he has spent hundreds of hours of volunteer time out in the woods of the Ranch, building tree stands, deer and turkey feeders, and guiding hunters. A tremendous benefactor, Dr. Mitchem works closely with the staff to do whatever needs to be done.

The first fall Bluegrass Festival occurred in October, 2008 and was a great success. That same year, Ken Johnson worked as staff advisor, helping Brett Buchanan on Brett's Eagle Scout project of building the wooden bridge to Lois Johnson's beautiful, carefully created and tended Butterfly Island.

In 2008, Bobby Cothren's Stellar team won the annual "Ben Watkins Golf Tournament" and Bobby was elected President of the Rodeheaver Boys Ranch Board for the 5th year in a row. It was also the year that John Browning, Jr. donated an impressive and extremely valuable arrowhead collection to the Ranch, to be placed in the future Ranch Museum.

Another milestone occurred in 2008 when Ken Johnson finally sold his airplane due to heart challenges, trading it for a 97% restored and completely drivable 1929 Model A with a rumble seat. This vehicle happened to be the same model that Carlton Spence's Dad, Hezekiah, had driven when courting Carlton's mother Margaret "Sugar" Spence. Carlton purchased the Model A and took his Mother riding in it several times before she passed away on October 22, 2013.

"You cannot make use of the runway behind you or the sky above you." Ken's Favorite Sayings

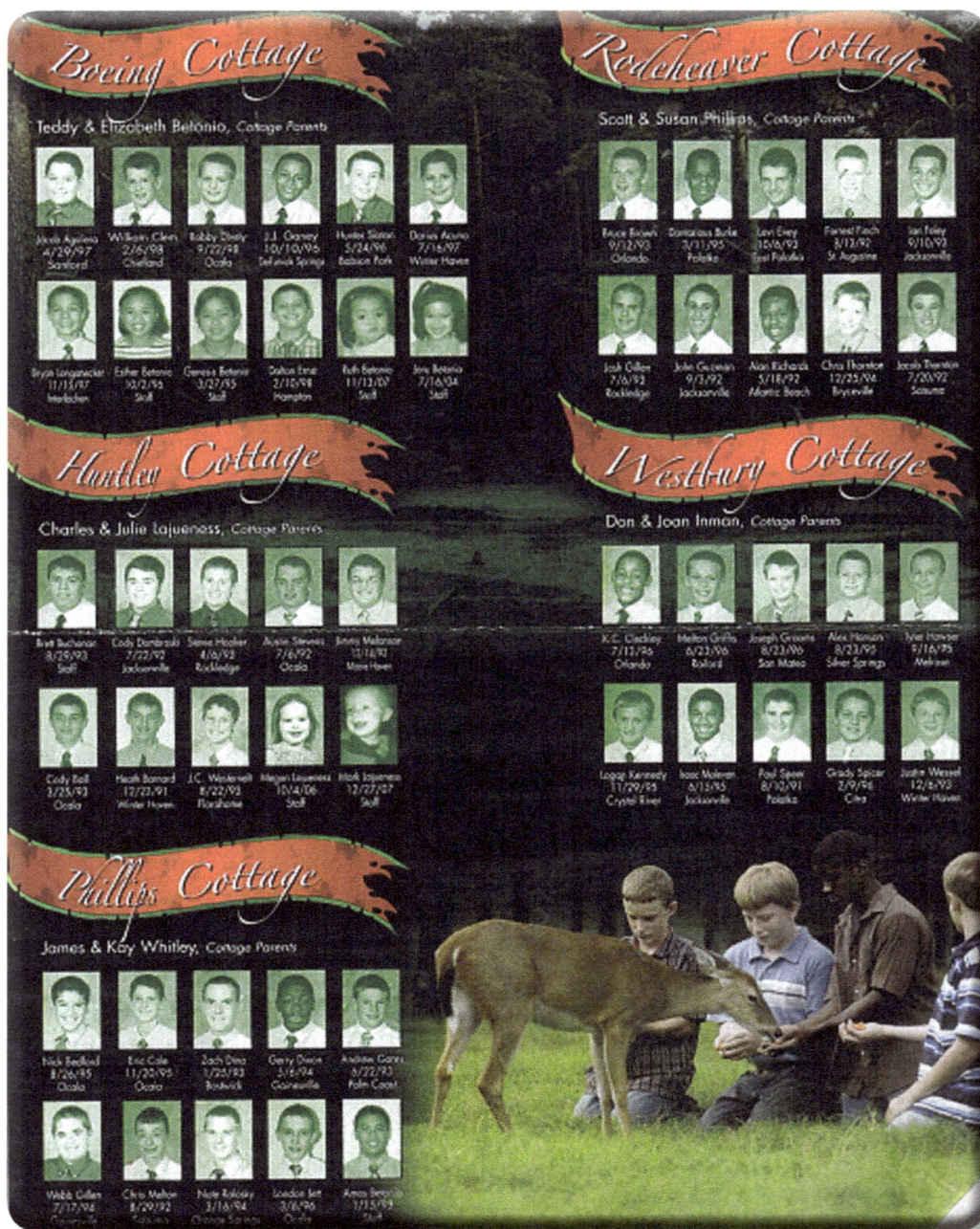

2008 Christmas card

Coach Urban Meyer of the University of Florida came on board in 2008 as a radio and television spokesman for the Ranch's Vehicle Improvement Program and brought a great deal of attention to the Ranch. It was a thrill for four Ranch boys to meet Coach Meyer and Heisman Trophy Winner Tim Tebow!

Coach Meyer and Ranch Boys

**Ranch Boys with
Heisman Trophy Winner Tim Tebow**

After twenty-one years of loving and compassionate service to the Ranch, Yvonne Cooper Brandt was medically retired in 2009, and given a special retirement dinner and tribute by Board President Bobby Cothren and Foundation President Dan Martinez, along with grateful staff and former Ranch boys Jason Claro and Boogie Feggins.

"Yvonne raised a wonderful family," says Ken Johnson. "She was an absolute thoroughbred when it came to expressing herself. We had the common bond of enjoying the English language and we enjoyed working together." One specific memory of Yvonne, who passed away within a year of retiring, was that when Ken Johnson came to the Ranch, he approached her with his usual directness and said, "We can be friends and if we agree on that, I'll expect you to be my friend." Yvonne was a loyal friend both to Ken and to the Ranch. When she caught someone delving into the files of former Ranch boys in the records room, she got him right out of there and made it clear, in no uncertain terms, that those records were confidential. "She was fierce about protecting the best interests of the Ranch and caring about the boys," Ken recalls, "and when she passed away, her entire large family sang beautifully at her graveside."

Historically, over the past seven decades, devoted Ranch "Pardners" have eagerly shared the Ranch and its story with good friends who have become new "Pardners" to the Ranch. Just one example of this beautiful evolution is when Sheriff Walt Pellicer brought his friend, Carlton Spence, to the Ranch back in the late 1980s and Carlton Spence brought his friend, Bobby Cothren to the Ranch in 2000, and Bobby Cothren brought his good friend, Wayne Robison, to the Ranch in 2009. "Wayne and Eleanor Robison of St. Augustine are two of our most precious friends and donors," said Ken Johnson, noting that Wayne Robison runs his company, Rulon International, and his entire life in deep devotion to God.

Rulon International is a St. Augustine-based wood ceiling and acoustical wood walls manufacturer that has developed a unique way to give back to the community locally and worldwide by creating toy guitars for sick, underprivileged and disabled children. In 2016, Wayne Robison, President and CEO of Rulon International, came up with the idea of turning scrap wood into guitars with the goal of creating 10,000 of the small, wooden toys to sick children around the world. Beginning with a donation of guitars to an orphanage in Haiti, the project evolved into Rulon sending unfinished guitars for the children to paint and decorate to give to others – and so it goes. When God directs one to help another, it leads to that one helping the next one and so on. With the catchphrase, "Allowing the Melody to Move us Forward," on his company website, Wayne Robison invited Ranch boys to participate in building guitars in their woodworking shop to be donated to others. "The blessing goes on; it doesn't just stop with the child," said Eleanor Robison, Wayne's wife and helpmate in life. Today, every guitar is manufactured in-house and the paint used on the guitars is recycled as well, devoid of chemicals. "I don't think we'll ever stop," said Tim Tyler, ttyler@rulonco.com, Rulon's Guitars for Children Program Leader.

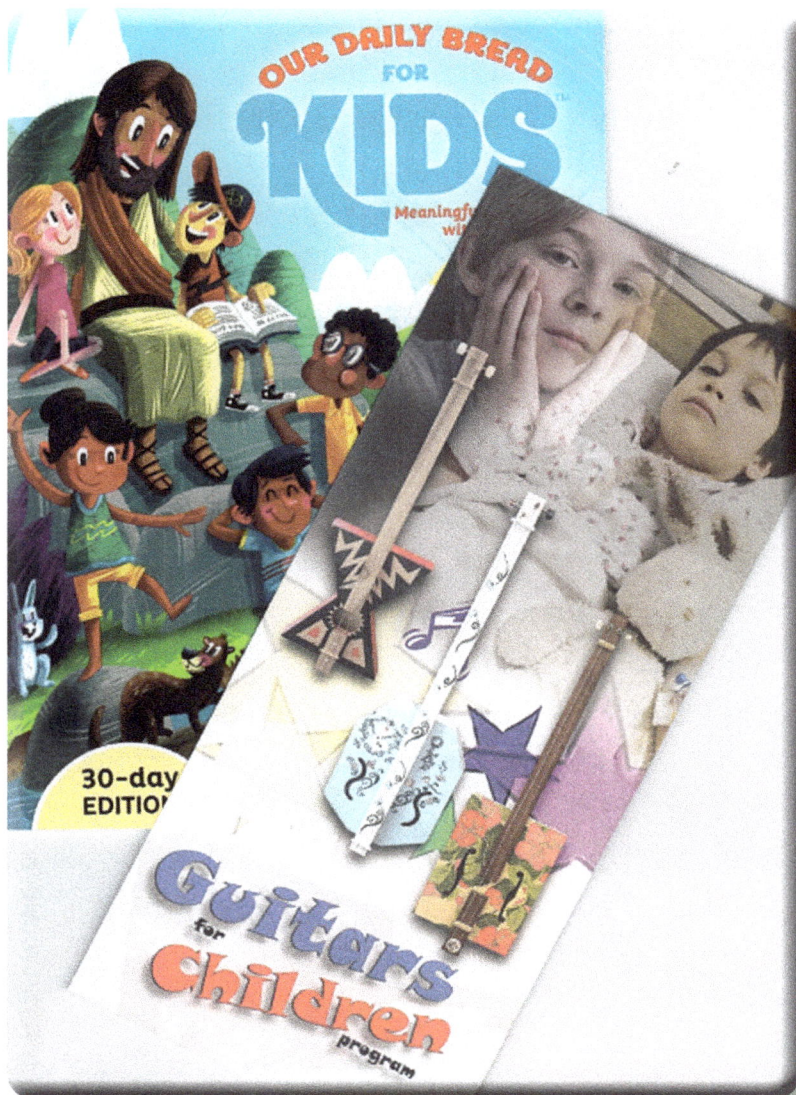

"God has blessed us and given us the opportunity to give worldwide," says Wayne Robison, who was one of 14 children raised in a Pennsylvania Dutch Mennonite Baptist family. "Dad and Mom taught us to care for the fatherless children, widows and the rest of the world, too, and that's what we do. Also, each guitar is accompanied by a little inspirational book and a music CD – both developed for us by the Daily Bread people in Chicago specifically designed towards children." Robison is touched by the letters he receives from children around the world, and he is also touched closer to home by the boys he meets at Rodeheaver Boys Ranch. Talking of the competency of Ken Johnson and Brad Hall as Executive Directors, and the boys that Rulon has helped with living expenses after they age out at the Ranch, Robison notes "God has blessed us even in these times of trouble, and it's our responsibility to give back." He marvels at how God has a plan for our lives, remembering the day that Bobby Cothren said to him, "You know, Wayne, I'd like to take you out to a boys home that I work with." Thankful that God directed Bobby to take him to the Ranch, Robison now employs some former Ranch boys and, through his company and his actions, shows them that God is in control every day, in every way.

SIX: Y2K ... ALL IS WELL

In 2009, Ernie Cremer was presented with the Wagon Master Award, a highly deserved tribute to a man who is one of the original "Pardners." From the time he was a toddler he rode the tractor with his dad, Ed Cremer, Harry Westbury and Homer Rodeheaver as they cleared the land, marking the area where the Ranch was going to be built by tearing up a sheet and tying strips on trees. As far back as he can remember, the Ranch has been an integral part of his life, and like his father before him, Ernie Cremer lives his life in service to the Lord. Ernie's timber company, Cremer Wood, Inc. has the Christian motto: "You're taller than trees on your knees." Having given immeasurable help to the Ranch for most of his life, Ernie took over the cattle program in 2009, further endearing him to the Ranch and the boys. In accepting the 2009 Wagon Master Award, Ernie remembered his Dad's devotion to the Ranch and how he always took special gifts to the boys at Christmas – harmonicas, yoyos, compasses – and did much more for the Ranch than people ever realized. Ernie has seen several generations of boys put on the right path by living at Rodeheaver Boys Ranch and says that he brings as many people as he can to see the Ranch and the boys. "You just have to see it once to understand," he says, adding that he has brought his Sunday School classes out to the Ranch often. Ernie and his wife, Sandra, have been married for 49 years and have a devoted, loving family that are part of the rich fabric of Palatka, Florida.

And, speaking of loving family and rich fabric in Palatka, Lois Johnson compiled, typed and published a series of seven different cookbooks as fundraisers for the Ranch, featuring recipes from local, and even national and international contributers. The books are available for purchase at the Ranch store. The 2009 Volume III was dedicated to Rodeheaver Boys Ranch & Bluegrass Friends, and the recipes are, as always, delicious!

Rodeheaver Boys Ranch & Bluegrass Friends Recipes Vol. III

"It's Better To Build Boys Than To Mend Men"

A few recipes:

PANCIT GUISADO OR FRIED NOODLES

Elizabeth Betonio
Ranch Cottage Mom

½ c. Boiled chicken
½ c. Boiled pork or ground pork,
  (or you can use all chicken)
4 pieces Garlic
1 or 2 T. Soy sauce
1 med. Onion
1 c. Shredded cabbage
2 or 3 c. Carrots (shredded)

1 can Chicken broth
1 c. Noodles
½ c. oil
Salt (to taste)
Pepper (to taste)
Scallions or onions or lime (to
  taste)

Sauté garlic & onion; add the chicken & pork in your frying pan. Boil the chicken broth seasoned with soy sauce, salt and pepper to taste. Add the carrots, the meat and cabbage. Let it cook for a while (Do not overcook vegetables) Add the noodles (add boiling water if necessary to cook your noodles in the right texture. Garnish with chopped spring onions, squeeze lemon or lime juice on top before serving.

MY FAVORITE SALMON PATTIES

Lois Johnson
Ranch Store and Hostess

1 can (14-oz.) Alaska Pink Salmon
2 c. Soft bread crumbs
⅓ c. Finely minced onion
¼ c. Milk
2 Eggs

2 T. Parsley, minced
1 T. Lemon juice
¼ tsp. Salt
¼ tsp. Dill weed
dash Pepper

Drain salmon, reserving 2 T. liquid; flake. Combine the bread crumbs, minced onion, milk, eggs, parsley, lemon juice, salt, dill weed, and pepper including the 2 T. of liquid. Shape into 8 (1-inch) thick patties. Pan-fry on both sides in 2 T. oil or butter until golden brown. Great with those hot "cat-head" biscuits and Grandma's tomato-gravy.

COCONUT POUND CAKE

Judy Adams
Georgia Bluegrass Girl

2 c. Flour, self-rising
2 c. White sugar
5 Eggs
½ c. Milk

1 c. Oil
1 tsp. Vanilla
1 tsp. Coconut Flavoring
1 c. Coconut

Beat oil, sugar, and eggs together then add flour, milk, vanilla, flavoring, and coconut. Grease and flour a tube or bundt pan well. Carefully, pour in batter. Bake one hour at 350°. Let cool 20 minutes, then turn out.

TOPPING

1 c. Sugar
½ c. Water

½ c. Margarine
1 tsp. Coconut flavoring

When cake is cooling and still in the pan, take a toothpick and punch holes in it carefully. For the icing, bring syrup to a boil. Pour over cake that is still in its pan as soon as possible. Let icing cool 20 minutes only, then carefully take out of pan. Cover tightly

THE FIRST BOOK OF MOSES,

CALLED

GENESIS.

CHAP. 1.

e creation of heaven and earth, 3 of the
ht, 6 of the firmament, 9 of the earth sepa-
ced from the waters, 11 and made fruitful,
of the sun, moon, and stars, 20 of fish and
wl, 24 of beasts and cattle, 26 of man in the
age of God. 29 Also the appointment of
od.

the beginning God created the heaven
and the earth.

And the earth was without form, and
d; and darkness was upon the face of the
p: and the Spirit of God moved upon
face of the waters.

And God said, Let there be light: an
re was light.

And God saw the light, that it was good
God divided the light from the darkness

God called the light Day, and the even
God called Night: and the evenin

17 And God set them in the f
the heaven to give light upon th
18 And to rule over the light fr
night, and to divide the light
ness: and God saw that it wa
19 And the evening and the
the fourth day.

20 And God said, Let the w
abundantly the ing cre
life, and fo
in the ope
21 And G

CHAPTER SEVEN:
A NEW DECADE & A FIRM FOUNDATION

The year 2010 marked the 60th Anniversary for Rodeheaver Boys Ranch, and a grand opening ceremony was held for the long-awaited dedication of the Langdon-Newby Activity Building, with special consideration given to Jack Langdon whose mother and aunt had been so devoted to the Ranch.

Dedication of the Langdon-Newby Activities Center on Feb. 24, 2010
L-R: Jeff King, Steve Watkins, Jack Langdon, Greg Buchanan – Ranch Boys!

It was in 2010 that Russ and Sharon Terjung began volunteering at the Ranch and brought about some wonderful advances in both technology and Ranch boy studies. Russ was a retired IT Specialist who worked wonders with computers, and Sharon is a retired teacher who worked wonders as a tutor with the boys. The Terjungs had summered in Winona Lake, Indiana for most of their lives and recognized the Rodeheaver name from having seen Homer Rodeheaver and heard him in their youth.

Russ Terjung working wonders with computers

Lois Johnson's sister, Joan, and her husband, Glenn Lester, delivered from Tennessee a 1950 Chevrolet Three-Quarter Ton Farm Truck to the Ranch for the 60th Anniversary celebration. Also courtesy of Joan and Glenn are the televisions in the lodge and the floating ramp at the river for fishing and swimming activities. The Lesters, who live in Tennessee, have been long-time supporters of the Ranch and often attend the Bluegrass Festivals and other events during the year.

The 60th Anniversary year was when Marc Spalding was elected President of the Board at the Annual Meeting and Bobby Cothren was honored for having served five years prior. Marc Spalding grew up in Palatka and went to school with the Martin twins, Terry and Jerry and their older brother, Larry. "Back in 1964, my father, William 'Bill" Spalding, was a developer and a contractor who was part of the groundbreaking committee on the barge canal when President Johnson came to the Boys Ranch," recalls Marc. "It seemed to me,

as a youngster, that the boys at the Ranch got to do a lot of things – they got to go to games and shows and on trips – sometimes it made you question whether the Martin twins were telling the truth, but they were." Marc notes that there were so many people who cared about the Ranch and tried to do all they could for the boys ... and that there were hard times, too, that nobody talked about. He remembers it all, and became even more involved in 1985 when he married Linda Kaye Johnson, the daughter of Edgar Johnson, who, with his wife, Ethel, had opened their home and their hearts to Ranch boys, often bringing them home on weekends, almost adopting one Ranch boy.

So, it was just a natural progression that Marc Spalding, who had always known and cared about the Ranch, would become President of the Board. Now an active member of the Rodeheaver Foundation, Marc remembers his Presidency well. "Being president, you become much more cognizant of the day to day struggles of the Ranch and you gain a lot of respect for the great job that is being done by the staff," he says.

Marc Spalding

Personally, Marc treasures those intimate times with Ranch boys and getting to know them one-on-one. "You rub shoulders with a kid for a few hours in a tree stand and you form a bond," says Marc. "Being part of the Ranch family means a great deal to me – always has and always will."

In 2010, after eleven years at the Ranch as devoted cottage parents, James and Kay Whitley retired on May 24, and went to Winston-Salem, North Carolina. "The Whitley's loved the boys and they were really missed after they retired," says Ken Johnson. "We still keep in touch." Among the Ranch boys the Whitley's still keep in touch with are Nick Bedford, who is now in the Marine Corps. They also mourned the early demise of London Jett, a special Ranch boy who passed away in February of 2019 and left a void in many hearts.

Kay and James Whitley were Nick Bedford's cottage parents in 2008 and 2009 when he was in 8th and 9th grade. Prior to coming to the Ranch, Nick lived with his grandmother, Mary Ann Bedford, and his great-grandparents. Mary Ann worked at Ocala Christian Academy, which Nick attended, and he was active in sports and church, but becoming rebellious. His mother was going through a divorce and Mary Ann felt that he needed more than she and his great-grandparents could give him. Nick saw the brochure for Rodeheaver

Kay and James Whitley

Boys Ranch and wanted to go there. It was an answer to prayer for Mary Ann.

"The first thing I remember is pulling off the main road and driving three miles to the Ranch. It is such a peaceful place and you leave the outside world behind. I just felt this was the place for Nick. We met Mr. Watkins and then we went to the Whitley's cottage. They were such sweet Godly people. Over the next two years, we were able to visit with the Whitleys frequently and check on Nick," recalls Mary Ann. "We became friends because we had the same hopes and dreams for Nick."

Nick Bedford's 13th birthday

Nick celebrated his 13th birthday at the Ranch. He learned discipline and how to keep his room clean and do his own laundry. He got to go on camping and two hunting trips, shot two deer – activities he wouldn't have had the opportunity to do if he had not been at the Ranch.

After two years at the Ranch, he went back to Ocala to live with his mother, and he graduated from Ocala Christian Academy with honors. While he was at the Ranch, Nick became friends with tutor, James Hughes, and came to be involved in civil war re-enactments. That's when Nick's interest in the military began. He joined the Marines in November of his senior year and left for basic training in July. He's been deployed twice, to Honduras and to Japan, and he now works on helicopters at Camp Pendleton in California. Nick is married to Kelsey and they have a 3-year old daughter, Aubrey. He plans to go to college and eventually become a pilot. His grandmother gives a great deal of credit to the Ranch and the Whitleys for helping Nick become the responsible man he is today.

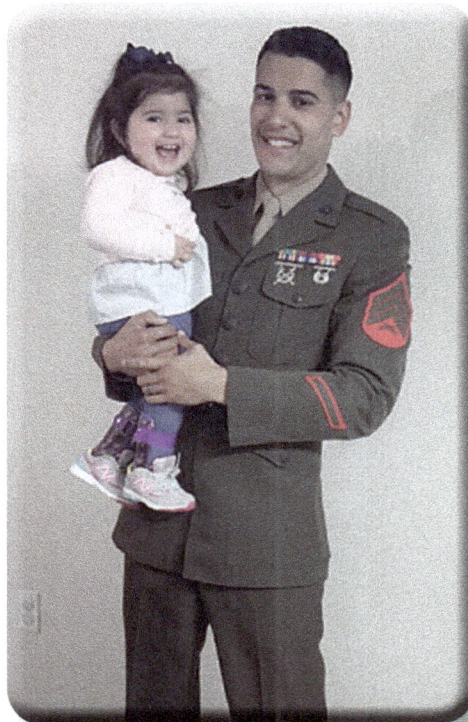

Nick Bedford with daughter Aubrey

It was in 2010 that 27 Ranch Boys were baptized at Faith Baptist Church in Palatka, with Dr. Mike Hudson, Rev. Eddie Parcher, Rev. Dave Thomason and Dr. Bennie Reynolds officiating.

Ken and Lois traveled to Switzerland in September of 2010 to visit their daughter Brooke, who was doing some training in Audiology. They were accompanied by Lois' sister, Joan, and Joan's husband, Glenn.

Bobby Cothren introduced Sidney Hobbs of St. Augustine to the Ranch and Sidney's daughter, Madison, whose birthday was near Christmas, decided she

Madison Hobbs 2013

wanted gift cards for the boys rather than birthday gifts at her party. A beautiful, generous angel, Madison was a philanthropist from the time she turned six years old and always made her birthday a time of sharing rather than receiving gifts. Her father's service to the Ranch as a board member has been a prime example of why the Hobbs family raised a daughter like Madison. She brought cards to the Ranch for the boys' Christmas shopping for several years.

"Madison is still the most amazing person I know," said her Dad, noting that in 2013, she was 13 years old and is now a 20-year old sophomore at the University of Georgia and still thinking of others first. "From the time she was about ten years old when Bobby Cothren brought us out to the Ranch until she was sixteen, we had birthday parties for her and she requested gift cards for the boys. Since we stopped doing her parties, she's kept up the tradition and still gives the boys gift cards at Christmas each year."

As to the retirement of Ken Johnson and the hiring of Brad Hall as Executive Director of the Ranch, Sidney Hobbs said it was with a heavy heart that he heard of Ken's retirement because of his great admiration for Ken, but his outlook brightened when Brad Hall came to the Ranch. "The Lord looked after us and found a great replacement for Ken in Brad Hall. Change is hard, but it's good." Hobbs has great hopes for the Ranch's future, knowing that God is in control as He always has been.

And speaking of Christmas, Attorney Don Holmes (long-time board member and President of the RBR Board in 2020) helped bring about a Christmas miracle for a young Ranch boy named Shawn Turberville in 2010. Shawn's family wanted their grandson home for Christmas at the last minute and sent a plane ticket, but there was no one at the Ranch to take him to the airport. Don called the Ranch on Christmas Eve day and asked Ken if there was anything the boys needed for Christmas and Ken told him about Shawn's dilemma. Don picked up the boy on Christmas Eve, took him to dinner and put him on the airplane. "It was a huge gift he gave to Shawn," says Ken Johnson, "and one that is not forgotten." Shawn's beloved grandmother, Bonnie, who cared for him most of his life, had been diagnosed with cancer, and passed away very shortly after his Christmas visit.

2010 Christmas card

"A drink of cool spring water, biting into a juicy apple, a glance at the woman of your dreams across a room ... some of life's greatest pleasures."
Ken's Favorite Sayings

In 2011, photographer and artist Edie Kynard of Palatka helped Jeff King put together a new Ranch publication called the Wrangler Magazine, which was an instant success.

In one of the first Ranch Wrangler Magazines, a tribute was paid to Yvonne, Richard Earl Cooper, and Noah Cool (known as Grandpa Cool), all of whom passed away within a few weeks of one another. Grandpa Cool had a special relationship with Don Inman, having helped raise him as a boy, and he was beloved by the boys at the Ranch. Grandpa Cool, who lived for years with the Inman family, passed away at the Ranch surrounded by loving family. Like Noah Cool, the Inman family has always fostered children over the years, and continue to do so to this day. "God blessed us with the knack of working with children," said Joan Inman, cradling her little adopted red-headed Daniel, nearly 3 years old, in her loving arms. "We were at Westbury Cottage for eleven years and cared for 74 boys during that time."

The Ranch Bids Good-bye To Three Of Its Closest Seniors In The Month Of December.

Yvonne Brandt, 74, served as secretary and public relations assistant in the office for over 22 years. She retired in May of 2009 due to her health. She passed away at the end of 2010. Yvonne was a great asset to the ranch and her smiling presence is missed. She was surrounded at the funeral by her loving sons and daughters.

Richard Earl Cooper, 76, served as the ranch driver who picked up bread each day along with running other errands. He was faithful for over 11 years and will be missed as the ranch family makes plans to go on. His memorial service was in the Ranch Chapel.

Noah Cool, 85, known in Westbury Cottage for years as "Grandpa Cool" also went on to be with the Lord. Mr. Cool was in with the first wave at Normandy Beach in World War II. The ranch family misses him as (in our minds) another war hero was laid to rest. Mr. Cool was interred in Ohio, and later a memorial service was held in the Ranch Chapel.

These three seniors loved the ranch and loved the Lord. Their passing reminds us of the "empty shoes" they left behind to be filled by someone who has the kind of heart they had. The ranch continues to benefit from their memory as memorials continue to be received in their honor.

When the Wrangler talked of "Empty Shoes," Yvonne Brandt's shoes were replaced by the running shoes of Sara Josephson, a marathon runner and all-around athletic lady who was there to keep things "running" efficiently when the time came for Yvonne to retire. Sara had come into the office in 2006 as the development secretary, then worked in Yvonne's office in the morning and VIP in the afternoons, until being recommended to take over upon Yvonne's retirement. "Sara's greatest assets are dependability and loyalty," said Ken Johnson. "Her love for the Ranch is unconditional – 100%!"

When Lois Johnson was a full-time teacher, Sara was her Number One substitute if a day off from school was necessary. Lois was so saddened when Sara told her she had found another job and would not be subbing anymore, until one day she walked into the Ranch office and there sat Sara! "I knew she was perfect for the job!"

Sara Josephson
Ranch Executive Assistant - 2019

It was in 2011 that Dr. Mitchem donated his valuable Marion County Cedar Landing Fish Camp property off the south end of Kenwood Lake to the boys ranch – just one of many donations of property from devoted "Pardners" over the years. That year, Dr. Mitchem also gathered a group of volunteers including Leon Bayless, Ed Brock, Mike DuPont, Nick Fectau, Dr. Mark Lewis, Herman Somers, Alan Raybon and Martine Williams to rebuild the top deck of the dock on the river due to safety concerns.

Steve Watkins' mother, Martha Jean McDaniel, passed away in 2011 and her memorial service was held in the Ranch Chapel, with President of the board, Marc Spalding and his wife, Linda Kaye Spalding, in attendance. A couple of months later, Donna King's mother, Billie Clement, a generous Ranch supporter, passed away in Murfreesboro, Tennessee.

"First impressions usually rule the relationship."
Ken's Favorite Sayings

In April of 2011, Ken Johnson was elected President of the Central Putnam Ministerial Association and many prayers went out to Cottage Dad Scott Phillips who underwent radical colon surgery in a Jacksonville Hospital and miraculously recovered.

At the May 2011 Rodeheaver Boys Ranch board meeting, Judge Ed Hedstrom was honored by the board, staff and Ranch boys at his retirement from the bench and for his many years of service to the Ranch and the community. He was presented with a "Rossi Circuit Judge" 410 Shotgun that also shoots a 45 Long Colt – a Judge for a Judge. "Ed Hedstrom has been and continues to be the understood gatekeeper of the Ranch," says Ken Johnson, speaking in the present tense in the year 2020.

In 2011, Carlton and Ruby Spence celebrated their 60th wedding anniversary. The boys couldn't fathom that anyone could be married for

**Cody Ball - 2003 - 2011
Ranch Boys Fishing – Cody on left**

"60 whole years!" That was also the year that Carlton donated several golf carts to the Ranch as well.

Ranch boy Cody Ball received his Eagle Scout designation in 2011, and today, he is a well-respected Florida Highway Patrolman in Ocala, Florida. The "rest of the story" is both heart-wrenching and inspiring. Cody and his younger brother, Kyle, had been taken away from their mother and placed in one foster home after another from an early age, sometimes even enduring painful separations. In 2003, when the brothers were finally put in the custody of their aunt and uncle in Ocala, they were two angry, unruly little boys. Cody was 10

and Kyle 9 when they arrived at Rodeheaver Boys Ranch. "We got into fights nearly every day," recalls Cody. "I even fought with Kyle, but if anybody else tried to hurt him, it was game on ... I made sure they got hurt instead." Cody remembers spending a lot of time in the office with Steve Watkins, Greg Buchanan and sometimes, when he got in big trouble, with Ken Johnson, but it was not always so bad. He loved fishing and many of the good things he had at the Ranch.

Cody maintained his defiant attitude, though, even up to the time he became an Eagle Scout in 2011. "I left the Ranch that year and finished my senior year in Ocala, graduating from Francis Marion Military Academy in 2012," recalls Cody. "My dream had always been to be in the Marine Corps and I told Mr. Watkins that's what I wanted to do. Mr. Watkins was my role model, but he warned me that my nasty attitude was going to be my downfall someday, and he was right." Cody enlisted in the Marine Corps and shipped off to basic training in 2012 and his bad attitude got him discharged from the Marine Corps right away. "It was a wake-up call," remembers Cody. "My aunt and uncle let me go – I was an embarrassment to myself and to the family.

"I remember coming back and sitting on the steps at Huntley Cottage crying and Mr. Watkins asking me what happened. Everything he'd warned me about had happened."

By 2013, Cody had picked himself up and dusted himself off. He was attending the College of Central Florida when he got hired by the Marion County Sheriff's Office, after requesting letters of reference from the

The neighborhood kids love Trooper Cody Ball!

Ranch. "In 2014, I asked for references from Mr. Watkins, Mr. Johnson and Mr. Buchanan for the Florida Highway Patrol. I still had a lot of explaining to do and had to get a waiver, but with their help, I got in and went to the Florida Highway Patrol Academy in Tallahassee. My first assignment was back here in Ocala and that's where I've stayed." Today, Cody and his wife, Billee, have a 7 year old daughter, Aylee, a 2 year-old son, Grayson, and a 5 month old son, Levi. Cody's younger brother, Kyle Ball, stayed on at the Ranch, graduated in 2012 and is now in the Virgin

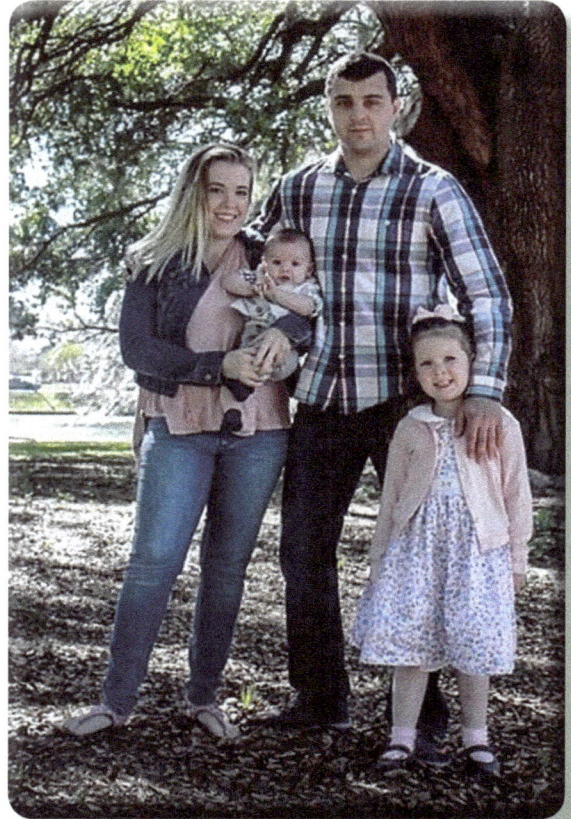

**Cody Ball and Family
(not including most
recent addition, Levi)**

Islands, working construction and doing well. The brothers are still very close. "Kyle calls every other day or so and tells me what's going on in his life," says Cody.

Cody Ball is a man of God who accepted Christ back in 2008 during a Sunday service in the Chapel with Mr. Johnson. "I took the Ranch for granted, but looking back, I didn't realize how good I had it – the camping trips and the spiritual aspect – I could have done so much more if I had known then what I know now." Again, the

**Kyle and Cody Ball at Cody's
Florida National Guard Graduation**

staff at the Ranch helped Cody get back in the military when he enlisted in the Florida National Guard in 2015.

Getting kicked out of the Marine Corps was one of the things that bothered him the most, and now, with God's help, he is a proud member of the military once again. "I realize now that God was closing that door so that I could learn and open it later. I don't know what my path would have been if my heart had stayed like it was," says Cody. Since he has always thought of the Ranch as home, Cody occasionally pays a visit to the VIP and chats with Don Inman, the only familiar face at the Ranch now that Steve Watkins, Ken Johnson and Greg Buchanan are no longer there. "The boys ranch is always on my mind," he says. "I plan to recommend it to boys who need some direction in life. I wish I'd understood earlier how much they helped me along the way."

Joyce Oliver was on the Ranch board for several years and rolled off the board in 2011, but her late husband's bequest to the Community Foundation of Northeast Florida has continued to grow and to benefit many charitable programs in Putnam County including Rodeheaver Boys Ranch. The charity dollars are important, but even more important to the Ranch are the love and concern that she and Frank showed to one particular Ranch boy, Ricky Gurthie, who, at age 4, was the youngest boy ever to be taken in at the Ranch. During the dozen years he spent at the Ranch and for several years thereafter, Frank Oliver took Ricky under his wing and put him to work. Used to hard work at the Ranch, Ricky said that "Mr. Oliver always treated me kind of like he was my daddy. He gave me good advice."

Joyce Oliver

Joyce Oliver says that she is still close to Ricky Gurthie. "Ricky is a sweet young man who will help me any time I ask him. He lives in Hollister now and works for Georgia Pacific. He has a son, Zachary, who is an electrician out at the Mill – a very smart young man. I have high regard for Ricky and his son." In 2011, President Marc Spalding appointed Danny Berenberg, Managing Partner of Gift Council, to the Board of Directors.

On August 21st, long-time Ranch Supporter Bill Huntley passed away and in his memory, the Rodeheaver Foundation submitted a large donation to support Huntley Cottage for many years to come.

**Peggy Campbell,
Long-time Ranch Supporter**

In 2012, Carlton Spence was recognized as the Grand Marshall of the Bluegrass Festival in February. He received a Henry 45 Long Colt Mare's Leg – like Steve McQueen's Josh Randall character carried. On hand to make the presentation were Peggy Campbell, Judge Ed Hedstrom, Marc Spalding, Richard Perallon and Sherri Boyd. This was the first Bluegrass Festival with the new concrete floor, contributed by Carlton Spence.

That year, Dr. Mitchem hosted several turkey hunters and raised a great deal of money for the Ranch from this particular group, as these men came to hunt Osceola Turkeys, required for a grand slam.

After honoring Marc Spalding for his two years as President of the Board, Dr. Richard Perallon was elected the new president in 2012. Perallon also received the Wagon Master Award that year, with a gift of an old Scofield Study Bible, a 14-foot bullwhip and flowers for his wife, Lisa. Dr. Perallon's father was there to honor his son.

Ranch boy Jimmy Melanson graduated from high school and returned to his home in Moore Haven, Florida, with a job.

The Ranch received a new documentary film on Homer Rodeheaver sponsored by the Reneker Museum of Winona Lake History and Development Director Steve Grill for Grace College and Seminary in Winona Lake. Judge Ed Hedstrom was on hand for the first showing of the new film.

The Board voted later that fall to remodel the Executive Director's house for a Ranch Museum and build Ken and Lois Johnson a new home.

Ladies of the Ranch – Joan, Lois, Sara and Lisa
Bitter End Plantation – 2012

A Ranch History Book was commissioned to be written by Susan D. Brandenburg and the Board was encouraged to grant interviews with her. Carlton Spence and Dan Martinez contributed to the cost of book research and printing. Carlton's annual deer hunting trip to the Bitter End added a guest list of ladies that included Susan D. Brandenburg, Lois Johnson, Joan Lester, Lisa Perallon, Beverly Mitchem, Sara Josephson, Andrea Jackson and her mother, Frankie Jackson. All guests had a wonderful time but the fact that only three deer were killed caused some hunters to theorize that having women on the annual Ranch boy's hunting trip was bad luck.

Lois Johnson reported that she loved the day, and confessed that she and her sister Joan had met with the deer and warned them to hide.

Amanda Morgan, Ranch Equestrian

Ken Johnson remembers that in 2012, the Ride for the Ranch under the able leadership of Amanda Morgan had over forty horses and riders and was a great success.

Dr. Joel McQuagge, Equestrian

Dr. Joel McQuagge of the University of Florida, Animal Sciences Department, an expert in Equine Behavior and Management, rode with them and demonstrated horse-training procedures. He was in rare form as a trainer and an entertainer and both the boys and the staff were impressed at how easily he could get an untrained horse to do something in just five minutes. Ken added that several of the staff joked about referring some of the boys to Dr. McQuagge for some powerful "boy-whispering."

Bruce Howe and Ken Johnson in the Renecker Museum, Winona Lake, IN

In researching for the Ranch book, Ken and Lois Johnson, along with Susan D. Brandenburg, traveled to Winona Lake, Indiana, the home of Homer Rodeheaver, and spent time with Bruce and Ann Howe touring the places frequented by "Mr. Homer," as Bruce Howe called him, including the Renecker Museum where much of his memorabilia is displayed, and the famous home of the late evangelist, philanthropist and founder of the Ranch.

In 2013, Carlton and Ruby Spence visited the Ranch and took a tour of the new home built for the Executive Director as well as presenting the Ranch with a new coffee table book about Carlton's Bitter End Plantation written by Andie Jackson and Susan D. Brandenburg.

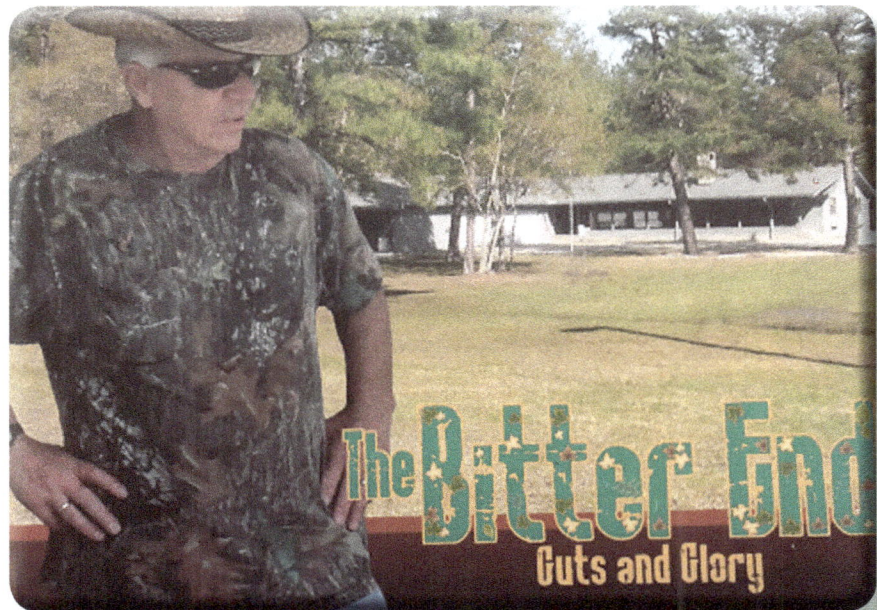

Carl Wenger donated a 1950-8N Ford tractor to the Ranch Museum, and on February 10th, the new Ranch Book went on sale in the Ranch Office as a fundraiser and many books were purchased at the Bluegrass Festival.

That year, the first annual Rodeheaver Classic Car, Truck and Motorcycle Show was held in March and was a huge success. According to Ken Johnson, a lion's share of the work on this show was done by Richard Wilson, Bobby Cothren, Sidney Hobbs and Jeff King. By 2019, the annual show had become a popular and highly anticipated event.

Saint Matthew | **Chapter VI**

The
Lord's Prayer

Our Father which art in heaven,
Hallowed be thy name.
Thy kingdom come.
Thy will be done in earth,
as it is in heaven.
Give us this day our daily bread.
And forgive us our debts,
as we forgive our debtors.
And lead us not into temptation,
but deliver us from evil.
For thine is the kingdom,
and the power,
and the glory,
for ever.

Amen

The
Ten Commandments

I. Thou shalt have no other gods before me

II. Thou shalt not make unto thee any graven image

III. Thou shalt not take the name of the LORD thy God in vain

IV. Remember the sabbath day to keep it holy

V. Honor thy father and thy mother

VI. Thou shalt not kill

VII. Thou shalt not commit adultery

VIII. Thou shalt not steal

IX. Thou shalt not bear false witness against thy neighbor

X. Thou shalt not covet

Exodus 20: 1-7

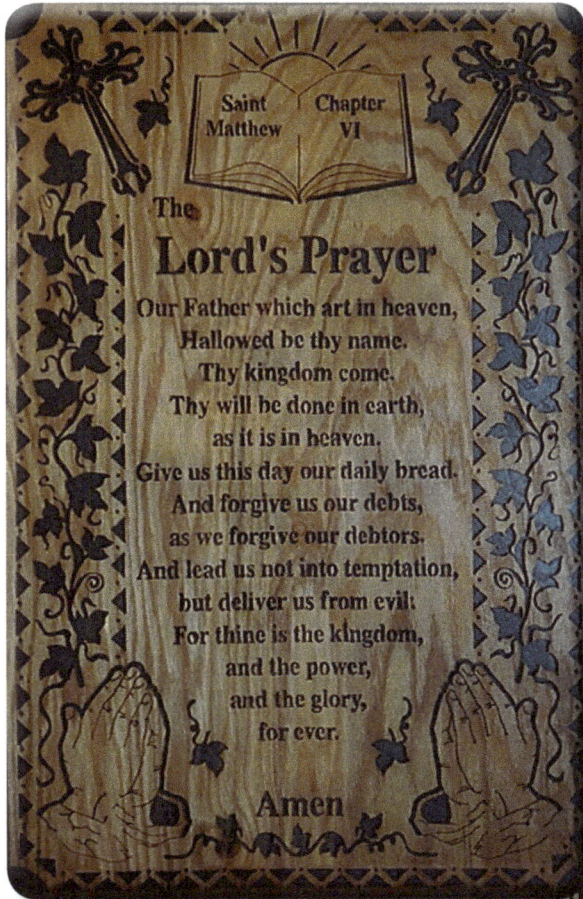

In 2013, the boys and staff girls had 18 pigs entered at the Putnam County Fair and 12 of those placed, with a Reserve Grand Champion in the middle weight class. Under the tutelage and leadership of Cottage Dad Scott Phillips, eight Boys Ranch projects were entered in the woodworking division and all eight came in first in their categories. One was Best in Show and one was Best in Class. No one "works wood" better than Scott Phillips. There are, in fact, two examples of Scott's work in the Chapel to this day, created with the help of the boys, with prayer and many painstaking hours of work. The artistry of the wood carvings perfectly accompanies the beauty of the stained glass windows.

Ann and Bruce Howe - 2013

The Ranch Museum Building was opened and dedicated at the Annual Meeting in 2013 and Richard Perallon was elected President of the Board of Directors for another year. Bruce and Ann Howe from Winona Lake, Indiana were special guests of the Ranch. Bruce loved sitting in the rocking chair and telling boys stories of days gone by at the Ranch. He also loved giving the boys golden dollars, so was always surrounded by boys.

In 2013, Bruce Howe was sitting on the porch in the rocking chair and had a special visit from former Ranch boy Tommy Morgan, a proud Dad and hard worker who was running for the Putnam County School Board, District 2. Tommy's Platform in the race for School Board position was based on what he had learned at the Ranch; to be honest, fair and trustworthy. He told his constituents that he lived by the Code of the Rancher, and that code was on the flyers he passed around as a candidate.

Bruce Howe with Tommy Morgan and three of Tommy's beautiful children. Tommy remembers Bruce from his past visits to the Ranch.

"The Code of the Rancher"

1. **Live Each Day With Courage.**
2. **Take Pride In Your Work.**
3. **Always Finish What You Start.**
4. **Do What Has To Be Done.**
5. **Be Tough, But Fair.**
6. **When You Make A Promise, Keep It.**
7. **Ride For The Brand.**
8. **Talk Less And Say More.**
9. **Remember That Some Things Are Not For Sale.**
10. **Know Where To Draw The Line.**

Long-time relief cottage parents Roy and Barbara Rowland retired in April of 2013 and headed out west for a long vacation. Just about as soon as they returned, they were back at the Ranch volunteering, and they remain dedicated to the Ranch to this day.

Barbara and Roy Rowland

In addition to being in charge of stocking and manning the Ranch Store during Bluegrass Festivals and annual Ranch Meetings and Barbecues, Lois Johnson singlehandedly compiled the Ranch Cookbooks for many years, garnering recipes from cottage parents, boys, friends, family, donors, church members. Anyone and everyone who had a good recipe was encouraged to send it on. The Ranch Cookbooks have been great sellers in the Ranch Store for years. In 2013, Lois put out the newest Ranch Cookbook, entitled "Casseroles, Cookouts, and Slow Cookers." Now the Ranch Museum carries copies of all of Lois's beautifully crafted cookbooks, and they are a big fundraiser at Christmas, as the recipes never grow old.

Ranch Boys Elijah Helmic and Eric Cole earned their Eagle Scout Awards in 2013. Elijah's project was Phase One of the three story wildlife observation tower at the Ranch (Al Mathies and Randy Tillman helped him, and Dr. Mitchem helped with financing). Eric's Eagle Scout Project was to erect a bear-proof feeder tower pole.

> "You are not much of a cowboy if you remember how many times you've ridden a horse." Ken's Favorite Sayings

Long time board member Sam Taylor, who had been the Treasurer for fifteen years, passed away in July. His wife, Orabelle and daughter Nina were also great supporters of the Ranch.

The annual camping trip to Philmont that summer went well for the backpackers, with the help and supervision of Jonathan Harper, Greg Buchanan and Amos Betonio.

Saturday evening, August 9, 2013, Margaret "Sugar" Spence, Carlton Spence's 99-year-old mother, visited the Ranch. She was alert and interacted with the staff. Ken Johnson recalls she was "a real lady, dressed to the nines." This was, Carlton Spence told the Ranch staff, the "next to last item on her bucket list" as she prepared for her 100th birthday. The last item was to visit Carlton's plantation, The Bitter End, once more, but she passed away in October, 2013 (*counting the 9 months she took to be born, she was 100). Ken Johnson took the Ranch boys to pay their respects at her memorial service, and he officiated at her graveside service, noting that she left a legacy of laughter, love and overwhelming positive influence. Carlton completed her final bucket list item before she was buried, taking "Sugar" Spence on a last ride to the Bitter End.

In September of 2013, following up on stories published in the Ranch Book, Susan D. Brandenburg began doing a "Faces of Rodeheaver" series of individual Ranch Boy stories. Former Ranch boy, Timothy Officer, came to the Ranch and met with her in the conference room. The story she wrote as a result of that meeting is one that will be remembered by all who knew Timothy Officer, to whom a chapter in this book is dedicated.

The Rodeheaver Boys Ranch Chapel was blessed to be the site of two weddings in 2013, that of Caleb Warren (Mark and Bonnie Warren's son), and his fiancé, Cody. Ken Johnson officiated at their wedding in September, and Ed Hedstrom's daughter, Dallas Hedstrom, married her fiancé Jimmy Neshawat in the Chapel on November 15th, with Dr. Robert Mills officiating.

> "Being around some people makes me wish I was lonely."
> Ken's Favorite Sayings

Jerry Mattox, Palatka's oldest and longest serving barber, retired ion December 31, 2013. He had cut the hair of hundreds of Ranch boys over his 56-year career, as well as cutting the hair of many of the staff and board members. At 4:50 p.m. on the last day of the year, Dan Martinez climbed into Jerry's barber chair to receive the last official haircut of his career. Minutes later, Danny and several other visitors saw Jerry lock up and bid all a fond goodbye. He received some nice retirement gifts – a fishing reel and several gift cards – and now lives in the same retirement area where Ken and Lois Johnson live.

At 12:01 a.m. on January 1, 2014, the Ranch staff and boys had their traditional special program in the Chapel, praying in the New Year. This tradition began when Ken Johnson became Executive Director in 1996.

In January 2014, Ken Johnson took a group of Ranch boys and staff to the Palatka Kay Larkin Airport Fly-In, to help with parking. The event grew each year and it became nearly impossible to park cars without help from law enforcement.

Tommy Clay came to the January 2014 Board Meeting and was thrilled to see his grandson, Chance Clay, appointed as a new board member. Chance has been called "the Spittin' image of his grandfather."

"Every man or woman needs to learn how to drive a farm tractor for perspective."
Ken's Favorite Sayings

Wayne Robison was the recipient of the 2013 Wagon Master Award, but due to his busy schedule and being out of the country at the time scheduled for the presentation, the Wagon Master Award went to Robison at his Rulon Office. It was delivered, with some ceremony, by Bobby Cothren, Jeff King and Ken Johnson, who were touched by his response to receiving the Scofield Study Bible. He had, in his office, two or three other Scofield Bibles that he had worn out. He was due for a new one.

Donna King went to Murfreesboro, Tennessee to spend time with her father, Don Clement, who was ill. He passed away at age 87 in 2014. Jeff King conducted the memorial service for him. Donna's brother, Joey Clement, well-known to the Ranch boys, hunted at the Bitter End for the past ten years, despite being in a wheelchair.

Bookkeeper Peggy Yundt retired in the spring of 2014 due to her mother's illness. She was an integral part of the Ranch staff and was missed by all.

The Putnam County District School Board sold the Ranch a used school bus for $1.00 in 2014. Board Member and Former Principal Karen Hughes and Superintendent Phyllis Criswell took a special interest in making this happen. It was greatly appreciated.

Ken Johnson and Jeff King gave a special talk to the Palatka Rotary Club that spring, recognizing Dan Martinez, Ed Hedstrom and Bob Webb, their close friend and compadre in the Rotary Club. Bob Webb, a past member of the Rodeheaver Boys Ranch Board of Directors, designed the mail out appeal process for the Ranch in the early 90s, and was much admired by all of his

fellow Rotarians. Ken and Jeff wove their program around a painting "Into the Breach" by Military Artist Stuart Brown, that had been presented to the Ranch by former Ranch boy, Timothy Officer, who was an elite Air Force Ranger. The painting, in this instance, referred to the fact that Bob Webb (Robert W. Webb) was a man who went above and beyond the call of duty as a citizen of Palatka, having been active in Scouting, president of the Palatka Quarterback Club, president of the Putnam County Chamber of Commerce, president of the Palatka Rotary Club, a deacon at the First Baptist Church and Sunday School Superintendent, etc. etc. Sadly, a year later, on May 27, 2015, Bob passed away. He was greatly treasured and is sorely missed. Today, there is a Robert W. Webb Award of Excellence Trophy that is presented to an outstanding senior in Putnam County annually. Bob and his fellow Rotarians, Dan Martinez and Ed Hedstrom, as well as many others on the Rodeheaver Board of Directors, definitely qualify as courageous men who forge ahead "Into the Breach" for Rodeheaver Boys Ranch.

Into the Breach

Bob Webb's son, Douglas Webb, continues serving Rodeheaver Boys Ranch when called to help with special events, and also regularly in an unusual capacity, as the Ranch's "Coyote Man." Doug sometimes spends the night in

"Coyote Man" Doug Webb in February 2020

his truck guarding the Ranch from varmints of the four-legged variety. Since 2007, he's gone out to the Ranch three or four nights a week to keep coyotes, hogs and raccoons, and in season, bobcats from creating havoc. "There are a lot of bears out there in the woods, too, and they are a nuisance, but they're a protected species," said Doug. "When I see a bear, I throw up my hands and yell and try to push it deeper in the woods, away from the cottages and the deer feeders."

"On working with children: Tell 'em, tell 'em what you told them, tell 'em again."
Ken's Favorite Sayings

The thing about Doug Webb is this ... when he is sitting quietly in his truck at night, he spends most of his time communing with God and His creation.

"I know the future of the Ranch is secure," he says. "We're in God's hands."

Tyler Hoffler and Heather Lockhart got married on July 12, 2014 in the Pavilion at the Ranch rather than the Chapel in order to accommodate their

more than three hundred guests. After a brief honeymoon, and as the result of a strong request from Lois Johnson, the young couple reported to the Ranch on August 1 as Cottage Parents.

Board Member and former Palatka High School Principal Karen Hughes and her Sunday School Class from First Baptist Church of Palatka had a back to school cookout and chili supper for the Ranch Boys in August of 2014. Buddy Evans and Ben Bates helped.

It was in the fall of 2014 that Miss Gussie Chavers joined the Rodeheaver family circle, pledging to help the Ranch then and in the future, and Sandy Raburn-Fortner of First Coast Technical College joined the Ranch Board. Sandy's ideas were fresh and very much appreciated. As so often happens when God is in control, Sandy brought Krista Purcell on to be hired by the Rodeheaver Foundaation as Development Director.

Krista Purcell and Ranch Boys

Krista has done a stellar job for the Foundation and the Ranch ever since then and is a key member of the staff going forward in 2020 and beyond.

In 2014, we had a special speaker in our Chapel. Justin Hanby from Australia talked to the boys about his world class swim across the English Channel. The boys were impressed. Justin was also Ken Johnson's guest at the Palatka

Rotary Club. Ken said, "Justin's manhood is not being questioned. Anybody who swims the English Channel is a stud. As to whether or not he'll be in my family – the jury's out on that." Justin joked, "I've convinced his daughter that I'm a good man. Now I have to convince her Daddy that I'm a good man."

Sheriff Jeff Hardy sent Officer Kim Traber to assist the staff with CPR and AED Training once again in 2014. Officer Traber is serious about her mission and a tremendous help to the Ranch staff.

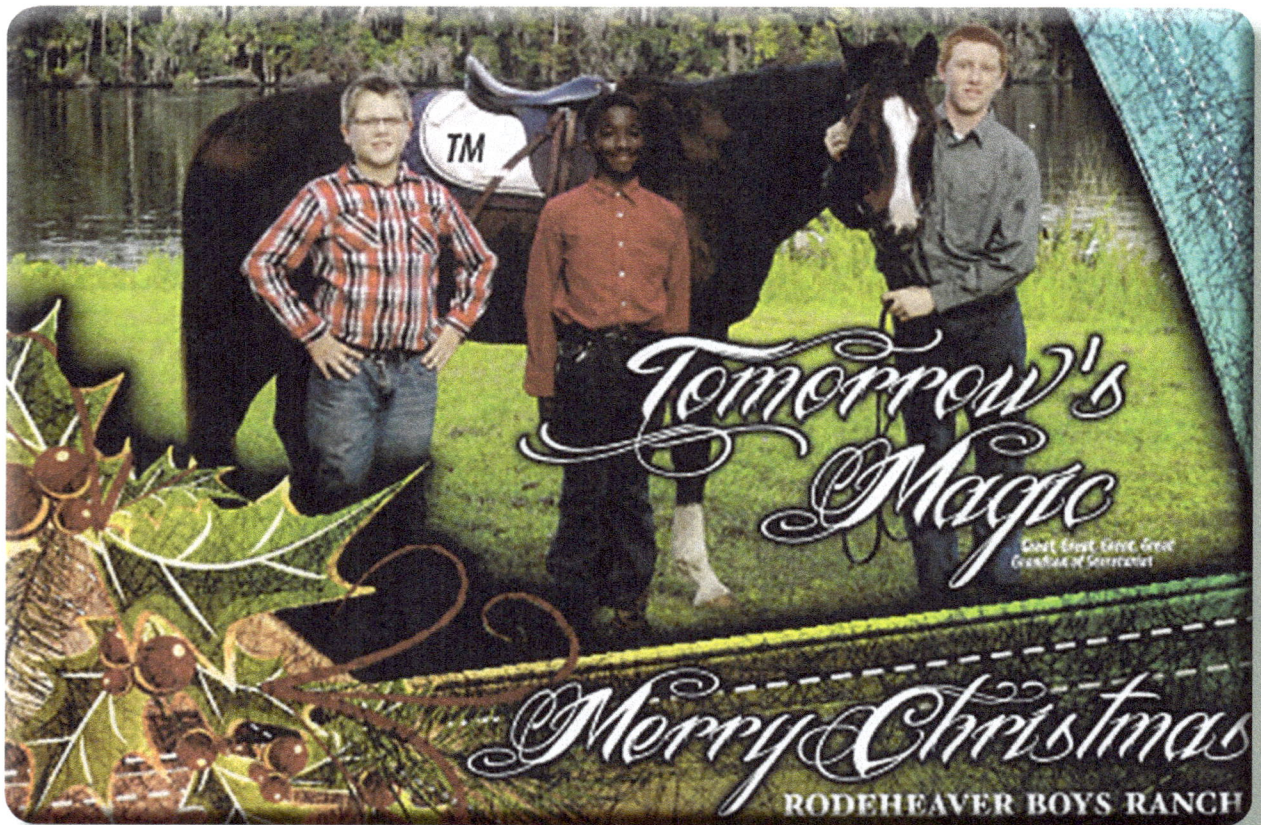

2014 Christmas card

The 2014 Christmas Card featured Tomorrow's Magic, the 4th great grandson of Secretariat. The boys were so proud to pose with this fine specimen and the name Tomorrow's Magic had a dual meaning, as the boys themselves represent the magic of the future.

Board Member Karen Hughes received the 2014 Wagon Master Award. "Karen probably does more behind the scenes for the Ranch than anybody can possibly imagine," said Ken Johnson. "Anytime she talks to anyone and they have an inclination toward charity, they always end up contributing to the Ranch. She is a great promoter and truly loves the boys."

The first of January 2015 was a sad day for the staff at Rodeheaver Boys Ranch as Steve Watkins' father, Alvin Watkins, passed away in Plant City, Florida. It was also a time of worry and stress for the King family, as Donna continued to battle cancer and was hospitalized due to breathing difficulties.

Karen Hughes

Cancer seemed to plague the Ranch in early 2015, when Roy Strickland, the VIP Auctioneer, was diagnosed with advanced colon cancer.

The February Bluegrass Festival went well except that the mercury dipped pretty low and Walmart sold out of every blanket they had. Hot beverage sales and Brunswick Stew sales went through the roof in the concession stand. As always, Darren Sanders of Mid-Florida Golf Carts in Deland loaned golf carts for the festival.

In March, the Ranch hosted a Southern Gospel Festival under Richard Wilson with help from Bobby Cothren and Sidney Hobbs, featuring the Dixie Melody Boys, Jeff and Sherry Easter, The Trinity River Band and the Easter Brothers. Dan Martinez was honored in 2015 at the Annual American values Dinner on Thursday March 12, for the Boy Scouts of America. Dan was the one who funded the Putnam County Scout Executive. Ben Bates was a presenter of the well-deserved award.

Stanley Hodge of Design Signs did the work and also the lettering on new signs in front of the dining hall, the activity building, and the Sign of State Road 19 coming into the Ranch – now touting 800 Acres!

Marie Watts joined the Ranch as the new bookkeeper. She was vetted by the finance committee and does a great job to this day.

> "Praise of someone else has a wonderful way of improving their hearing."
> Ken's Favorite Sayings

The 65th Annual Meeting went well and Don Holmes became President of the Board of Directors.

In May of 2015, Ken Johnson served as the main speaker at the Memorial Service for Law Enforcement Slain in the Line of Duty in the State of Florida at the Ravine Gardens Auditorium. That year, six officers including troopers, policemen and one a canine officer, were lost. The haunting sound of bagpipes ended the ceremony outside.

On May 9th, several guests from Australia visited the Ranch to attend the marriage of Justin Hanby to Ken and Lois's daughter Brooke in the Chapel. A reception followed at the Ranch Pavilion.

Ranch Boy Landon Madden starred in Beauty and the Beast at Palatka High Schools Cinema Arts Department and Nolie (Reynaldo) Gonzalez graduated from Palatka High School.

Ranch boy John Bedgood was honored at the Kiwanis Luncheon for Straight A Students. John graduated early with honors in 2018 and is now employed at Rulon International in St. Augustine.

Ben Bates sent a 54-seat tour bus to pick up the Ranch staff and boys to attend the Billy Graham Festival of Hope in Jacksonville. Not only were they treated with food for the soul by the Rev. Billy Graham, but they were treated with a CP Deli Box Lunch en route.

John Bedgood

Steve Watkins and Jerry Shawver conducted a successful and enjoyable 2015 Rodeheaver Boys Ranch Fishing Tournament with weigh-in by Mike Oglesbee and pictures by Becky Williams and Edie Kinard.

Vehicle Auction volunteer Walter Hawkins, 84, passed away in June. He and his wife, Betty, were always at the staff Christmas Party.

In April of 2015 at the Annual Meeting, Bruce Howe was presented a Lifetime Achievement Award by Ken Johnson, Judge Ed Hedstrom, Tommy Clay, Marc Spalding and Dr. Richard Perallon.

Jeff Struecker, U.S. Army Ranger Hall of Fame

Six Ranch boys traveled with Greg Buchanan and Ken Johnson to the Turning Point Church Men's Ministry Beast Feast in St. Augustine in June of 2015. It is a wild-life dinner with pricey tickets and the guest speaker was Jeff Struecker from Columbus, Georgia, the Sergeant that kept going back to pick up casualties in the Black Hawk Down incident. A highly decorated veteran and, more importantly, a man of God, he spent his last ten years in the military as a Chaplain.

Former Ranch Boy Timothy Officer was killed on August 3, 2015, in a training accident. Time stood still.

Few tragedies have ever touched the hearts of the long-time staff at the Boys Ranch more than the death of this fine young man. For this reason, the remaining five years – from 2015 to 2020 – will be continued in Chapter 9, following a Memorial Chapter to a young hero who gave his life to God at Rodeheaver Boys Ranch.

Chapter Eight:
TRIBUTE TO TIMOTHY OFFICER

Ken Johnson, Timothy Officer and Steve Watkins

Timothy Officer was the first new boy accepted at the Ranch under the new Executive Directorship of Ken Johnson that began back in 1996. Tim was, literally, an Air Force "brat," who was rebellious and had problems submitting to parental authority. His dad, Master Sgt. Timothy Officer Sr., was stationed at Mildenhall Air Force Base in England and, after researching several alternatives, heard about Rodeheaver Boys Ranch in Palatka. Both Ken and Steve Watkins reviewed the application before accepting the boy. He would be a long way from home and family.

When Tim arrived from the UK, it took him no time at all to endear himself to the Ranch staff and fit in with the boys. "Tim just had a way about him that was irresistible," recalls Ken Johnson. "For instance, he was the only boy I ever loaned my car to, and that speaks volumes ... I don't believe in playing favorites."

Having worked with hundreds of boys over the years, Steve Watkins notes that Tim was one of the boys that stand out in his memory. "Tim had the type of personality that immediately won people over," says Steve. "He had a smile that never stopped and from the start, he made a positive impact on other boys and staff. Tim made friends easily and was popular at Jenkins Middle School and later at Palatka High School. He was a hard worker and endeared himself to Mark Warren, our farm manager. He began to develop the self-discipline and respect for authority that were hallmark biblical principles taught and enforced at the Ranch." After two years at the Ranch, Tim had done everything asked of him and wanted another chance to prove himself back with his family. The Ranch and his dad agreed and Tim returned to Mildenhall AFB for a brief time before old family problems re-emerged and he returned to the Ranch. "By now, Tim was a teenaged high school student who felt he was a failure and, though he tried to get back into the Ranch program, he had lost much of the enthusiasm he'd had at the beginning," remembers Steve. "After another year, Tim's dad was reassigned back to the United States and he went home to his family again. For several years, we lost touch with him, although we later heard he had enlisted in the Air Force. Little did we know that Tim was a Special Forces Warrior who had distinguished himself in combat and made ten deployments to Iraq and Afghanistan!"

And then, after fourteen years, Tim was back! "One day in 2013, he just showed up on our porch at the boys ranch," says Steve. "We hugged and cried and hugged and cried and then began catching up on the missing years. Tim told Cathy and me what the Ranch had meant to him, and especially the spiritual things he had learned. We learned that his brother had been killed in Afghanistan and that Tim had accompanied his brother's body home; he said

ther verses he memorized in chapel constantly went through his mind and helped him to stay calm. At this point, I developed an immediate bond with Tim's father because we had also lost a son and understood the pain."

During the next year, Tim became a regular visitor to the Ranch from his home in Savannah, Georgia, where he was assigned to a U.S. Ranger Battalion. It was during one of those visits that Tim went to the Chapel one evening and after hours of searching and praying, came back to Steve and Cathy's house in tears and told them that he had trusted Christ as his Savior. The next morning, he met with author Susan D. Brandenburg in the Ranch conference room and, as a result of that meeting, she wrote the following Ranch Boy Story:

Timothy Officer, Former Ranch Boy

As he sat alone late at night in the Chapel at Rodeheaver Boys Ranch on Sunday, September 15, 2013, Timothy Officer opened the Bible and began to read the familiar verses of John 3:16 (For God so loved the world, that he gave his only begotten Son, that whosoever believeth in him should not perish, but have everlasting life.) and Jeremiah 33:3 (Call unto me, and I will answer thee, and show thee great and mighty things, which thou knowest not.). For the first time, the words filled him and he understood. For the first time, Tim felt the living presence of Jesus Christ and knew his life would never be the same again.

"It took me 17 long years to come back and find what was here all along," marveled Tim the next morning when he visited his mentors, Ken Johnson and Steve Watkins. "The Lord was always pulling me back here, but I was afraid."

Afraid? Timothy Officer… afraid? No way! A fearless, courageous, hard-charging member of the Air Force's elite First Ranger Battalion strike force with many dangerous missions behind him, including five in Iraq and five in Afghanistan, the young former Ranch boy is a hero. In the eyes of Johnson and Watkins, Tim is a shining example of success – a young patriot who bravely puts his life on the line for his country and credits the Ranch for giving him guidance and direction as a boy.

So, what was it about coming back to the Ranch that struck fear in Tim's heart? "I was afraid that these two great men of God would see right through me to the emptiness inside," he admits. "I wasn't the man they thought I was. Inside, I was still that kid who came to the Ranch 17 years ago."

A troubled 14-year old youth with a bad attitude, Tim came to the Ranch from Mildenhall, England in 1996 at the recommendation of a pastor at Lakenheath Air Force Base, where his dad was stationed. As a "military brat," Tim was used to new faces and new places. He adjusted easily. He knew how to flash that smile and get people to like and trust him, and he knew he was smarter than anybody at this "hick" ranch way out in the middle of nowhere. Athletic, well-spoken and personable, Tim was soon quite popular with Ranch staff and boys alike. "I was always a sociable person," he says, "I knew how to make a good impression, but inside, I had complete disregard for authority. I was selfish and didn't care about anything but me."

Three years at Rodeheaver Boys Ranch gave him the structure he so desperately needed and taught him about hard work and self-discipline, but there was a wild streak in Tim. He wasn't afraid of anything or anybody. He craved adventure and took risks that would have terrified other kids his age. When he went into the United States Air Force Special Operations component right out of high school, he found that "basic training was a breeze after Rodeheaver Boys Ranch."

Since 2000, Tech Sgt. Timothy Officer has distinguished himself as an elite warrior, one of only 50 such men in the U.S. Air Force. "It's been an exciting challenge over the years to meet the high expectations of Mr. Johnson and Mr. Watkins back here at the Ranch," said Tim, "They thought I was a knight in shining armor, but I wasn't. I fought for my country, volunteered with the

homeless, worked at Habitat for Humanity, did all the right things, but deep down, I was doing it for me. I was totally exhausted with sin. I would come back from a night raid filled with death and noise and terror, and walk into my apartment at 2 a.m. all alone. I was dead inside. There was really nothing to live for except the next adventure."

Meanwhile, back at the Ranch, the Chapel where Tim spent so many hours as a boy was still there. At age 31, the young champion re-entered that sacred space and came out a new man. "On September 15, 2013, I became a warrior for God," said Tim. "If it hadn't been for the faith Mr. Johnson and Mr. Watkins put in me, I'd be face-down in a gutter somewhere. Instead, my life is now filled with purpose. I'm fighting on a brand new battlefield for something bigger than me."

"We've always loved Tim and so has God," says Ken Johnson. "He's what this Ranch is all about – building men who are physically, emotionally and spiritually fit. What a joy it is to know we've helped build a young servant leader like Tim."

Steve remembers that Tim often called over the next year, asking for advice as he was making decisions about his military career. "He was considering getting out of the Air Force and going into full time ministry, as the Lord was dealing with him. We talked about this often and he respected my opinion because I was a career military man myself. In the end, Tim decided to reenlist and took orders to Air Force Special Forces Command at Hurlburt Field in the Florida Panhandle," Says Steve. "Cathy and I were thankful for Tim inviting us back into his life. And then on August 3rd, 2015, we got a call that changed everything. Tim had been killed that morning in a training accident. Tim had become like a son to Cathy and me and his death has left a hole much like the death of our own son, Ben. Timothy Officer Sr. had two sons buried side by side at Arlington National Cemetery.

Two sons. Two gold stars. Retired Master Sergeant Timothy Officer Sr. thinks about his sons, Timmy and Justin, every single day with both pride and sorrow. On a recent day in 2020, Tim Officer Sr. spent the morning replacing his gold-star flag in front of his Colorado Springs home because the other had become tattered due to weather.

Tim Officer Sr.'s Flag Display

Timothy Officer was a Special Tactics tactical air control party Airman who was killed in a military freefall accident on Eglin Range, Eglin AFB, Florida, Aug. 3, 2015. His brother, U.S. Army Sgt. Justin Officer, buried in Colorado Springs, Colo., was killed by an IED in a dismounted foot patrol, Kandahar Province, Afghanistan, Sept. 29, 2010. Timmy traveled with Justin's casket home to Colorado Springs.

The Family paid a written tribute (obituary) through Emerald Coast Funeral Home in Ft. Walton Beach, Florida, that began: "Our son, Timothy Alan Officer

Jr. went to be with the Lord and his brother on Monday, August 3, 2015. Timmy, as he was known to all, was our first-born son, born in Huntington, West Virginia, August 8, 1982. Timmy entered the world at about 5 lbs. and a bit premature. He would grow into the 6'1", 220 lb. handsome young brother, friend, and warrior most have come to know."

Timmy was fondly remembered as pursuing typical boyhood adventures such as sledding in Michigan with his father and his brother, Justin. Timmy enjoyed youth sports, excelling at baseball, and loved catching fish and all outdoor adventure. Through his father's Air Force career, he was well-traveled. He was a naturally curious, stubborn, and fearless boy who would often disappear, with his little brother in tow, to explore places unknown. These early traits were evident as he served his country in the Air Force for fourteen years as a member of Tactical Air Control Party, a Joint Terminal Attack Controller, or JTAC. As with most combat warriors, Timmy downplayed his role and did not seek attention to himself. General George Patton said, "It is foolish and wrong to mourn the men who died, rather we should thank God that such men lived." His parents do mourn, and they also thank God. "We say goodbye and honor them in death as we did in life," said Tim Officer Sr. "Timmy and Justin live in our hearts and memories forever."

Timothy Officer Jr.'s funeral was held Wednesday, August 12, 2015 at 2 p.m. at The Springs Funeral Services, and he was interred at Arlington National Cemetery, Arlington, VA on October 5, 2015. An article in the Colorado Springs Gazette ran on the day of his funeral.

Colorado Springs man mourns the loss of second son, an Air Force veteran
BY TOM ROEDER tom.roeder@gazette.com
Aug 12, 2015

Tech. Sgt. Timothy Officer Jr. will be remebered at a Wednesday funeral in Colorado Springs. (Air Force)

Retired Master Sgt. Tim Officer Sr. will say goodbye to his airman son at a Colorado Springs funeral Wednesday, four years and 11 months after he buried his other boy, a soldier.

Tech. Sgt. Timothy Officer Jr., 32, died last week in a Florida training accident during a freefall parachute jump. His younger brother Justin died Sept. 29, 2010 after a bombing in Kandahar, Afghanistan.

"I'm so very proud of them, yet so very sad," said the elder Officer.

Raised in a nomadic Air Force family, Officer Jr. followed in his father's footsteps after high school. He enlisted to become a medical technician, but during basic training, he opted for one of the Air Force's most dangerous jobs, a tactical air control party specialist.

His father, who moved to Colorado Springs after retiring from the Air Force, looked on with no small degree of trepidation as the younger man trained to put bombs on enemy targets while serving alongside ground-pounding troops.

"He chose the path, it didn't choose him," Officer Sr. said.

Officer Jr. embraced his new career and quickly became known

as one of the top airmen in his field. In 2003, he earned the Bronze Star Medal for valor while serving with Army troops during the invasion of Iraq.

His father said that's one of more than 10 deployments for Officer Jr., who fought in Iraq and Afghanistan and most recently helped train Jordanian forces to battle Islamic State terrorists.

The love of service runs deep in the officer family. Justin Officer joined the Army after high school and served as a cavalry scout in Iraq and Afghanistan. After Justin was killed in the 2010 attack, Tim Jr. kept serving, earning a spot as a tactical controller supporting the Army's 75th Ranger Regiment.

"That doesn't just fall in your lap," Officer Sr. said.

Proud Dad and Leadership Grad – Sr. and Jr.

The following article was published by the Air Force Special Operations Command on October 15, 2015:

An American hero:
Special Tactics Airman buried at Arlington
By 1st Lt Katrina Cheesman, 24th Special Operations Wing
Photo by Senior Airman Dylan Nuckolls

Three Special Tactics Air Commandos salute the casket of Tech. Sgt. Timothy Officer during his funeral at Arlington National Cemetery, Va, Oct. 5, 2015.

ARLINGTON NATIONAL CEMETERY, Va. *-- Tech. Sgt. Timothy Officer, Jr., was laid to rest at Arlington National Cemetery, surrounded by friends, family and teammates, Oct. 5, 2015.*

Officer was a Special Tactics tactical air control party Airman who was killed in a military freefall accident on Eglin Range, Aug. 3, 2015. His brother, U.S. Army Sgt. Justin Officer, buried in

Colorado Springs, Colo., was killed by an IED in a dismounted foot patrol, Kandahar Province, Afghanistan, Sept. 29, 2010.

His family remembers both as "American heroes who were larger than life itself."

Officer, a two-time Bronze Star medal recipient, was known to many as a man of great sacrifice and intent. As an Airman who controlled air space and precision strikes, he was selected to serve alongside one of the Army's elite special operations units, the 75th Ranger Regiment.

"Timmy was an impressive warrior," said Master Sgt. Richard Douglas, one of Officer's best friends. "He was smart, fast and fearless. Everyone respected Timmy for who he was, and for what he brought to the team."

Officer received a Bronze Star Medal with Valor as a young airman first class in 2003, during the invasion of Iraq, distinguishing himself by heroism when a large artillery shell exploded fifteen feet from Officer and his U.S. Army teammates. Despite the chaos of the explosion, Officer jumped to action and eliminated two enemy killed in action while simultaneously coordinating close air support.

When his crew ran out of ammunition, Officer willingly put his life at risk to run across the battlefield and gather more ammunition. In the end, he contributed to 55 enemy killed and numerous enemy tanks destroyed with precisely coordinated air strikes, and "undoubtedly saved his fellow crewmembers with countless members" of the U.S. Army battalion, "directly aided in the defeat of the enemy," according to his citation submitted by the Army.

Off the battlefield, Timmy was a giant of character, according to Douglas.

"He really tried to be a righteous man. He strove to devote himself to God, and was really focused on doing the right thing," Douglas said, recalling that Officer had considered selling all his *belongings to serve others across the country as a missionary. Instead, Officer decided to stay in the military to continue to serve and support his special operations teammates.*

Douglas also recalled how Officer devoted his time to mentoring others, particularly young teens, who reminded Officer of himself growing up.

"He would mentor the guys at the Boy's Ranch, because he grew up there," Douglas said. "He would go back to give back."

Teammates remembered how Officer would drop whatever he was doing to help a friend, and he often altered the mood of everyone he encountered.

"He would brighten any room he walked into with his humor, charm and an award-winning smile," said Tech. Sgt. Kevin Caroon, a TACP who worked with Officer. "If you ever had a problem, he was the guy you could always lean on, and not only would he not mind, he would insist."

For many, he was more than just a friend; he was family. To his friend's children, he was known as Uncle Timmy. He loved kids, recalls Douglas, and would be the one adult playing with children during parties and events. When any of his friend's children were having issues and needed someone to talk to, it was Officer who would offer to go for a drive with them and just listen.

One friend recounted a time when his four-year-old daughter asked Officer on the phone when she would see him next. Officer answered he would see her as soon as he could. The very next morning, Officer was at his friend's house at 6 a.m. with orange juice, coffee and doughnuts to make sure he was there when she woke up.

It was moments like this one that showcase the cheerful, selfless man behind the battle-hardened veteran, who "brought light to the most bleak moment and always had an answer for those who needed direction," shared Caroon.

While more than 100 people mourned together at the two fallen brothers' resting place, members of the Special Tactics and TACP

communities who couldn't attend the interment simultaneously held their own memorial of Officer, showcasing their dedication to memorializing Officer's life and legacy.

"Timmy was a man of honor and character," said Douglas. "He was an American hero who will be missed, but never, ever forgotten."

Justin Officer

Timothy Officer

Tim and friends

Even when not deployed overseas, just six months before he leapt to his death in a free fall training accident, Technical Sergeant Timothy Officer distinguished himself by quick action and selfless courage. While assigned to the 720th Operations Support Squadron, 720th Special Tactics Group, 24th Special Operations Wing, Air Force Special Operations Command, Hurlburt Field, Florida, Sgt. Officer assisted with a vehicle accident on Florida State Highway 98 in Okaloosa County, Florida. While en route to a local training range rehearsal, Sergeant Officer made his way into an overturned truck which was carrying two large diesel fuel cells, assessed the occupant and started first aid through mangled entryways just large enough to gain entry. Once inside, he observed the occupant in a badly twisted position; he estimated the occupant may have suffered a broken back, pelvis and two broken legs, and he employed a back board for extraction. Sgt. Officer assisted the compacted minivan driver who kept losing consciousness due to grievous injuries, shallow breathing, weak pulse and deep shock. Sgt. Officer kept him stable throughout extraction and remained with the victim until professional assistance arrived. By his prompt action and humanitarian regard for his fellowman, Sergeant Officer reflected credit upon himself and the United States Air Force. For this action, Sgt. Timothy A. Officer was awarded the Air Force Achievement Medal (First Oak Leaf Cluster) for Outstanding Achievement on the 30th of March, 2015.

Timothy and Justin Officer are survived by their parents, Tim Sr. and Stacy; and Sister Kylea. "No one," said Tim Officer Sr., "would willingly sacrifice those they love and admire so deeply, but my unlimited sadness is countered by pride in boys so willing to risk their lives to defend others. Somebody needs to step forward and do these things. I thank God we have men who are willing to do them."

As the Ranch staff assimilated the untimely death of a beloved son to the Ranch, a beautiful tribute wall and table in the Ranch Museum was assembled in honor of Timothy Officer, Jr., and plans were soon underway for the design and construction of a more elaborate and lasting tribute in

the form of a Timothy Officer Jr. Memorial Obstacle Course on the Ranch property. It was to be an obstacle course that Timmy himself would have enjoyed and found challenging as a youth. The Obstacle Course was dedicated on January 13, 2018.

TIM'S MAJOR AWARDS AND DECORATIONS

Bronze Star with Valor Device (one oak leaf cluster)
Joint Service Commendation Medal
Air Force Commendation Medal
Army Commendation Medal (three oak leaf clusters)
Air Force Achievement Medal
Army Achievement Medal
Meritorious Unit Award (one oak leaf cluster)
Combat Readiness Medal
Air Force Good Conduct Medal (three oak leaf clusters)
National Defense Service Medal
Afghanistan Campaign Medal (one oak leaf cluster)
Iraq Campaign Medal (one oak leaf cluster)
Global War On Terrorism Expeditionary Medal
Global War On Terrorism Service Medal
Korean Defense Service Medal
Air Force Overseas Ribbon Short
Air Force Overseas Ribbon Long
Air Force Expeditionary Service Ribbon with Gold Border (three oak leaf clusters)
Air Force Longevity Service (two oak leaf clusters)
USAF Noncommissioned Officer Professional Military Education Graduate Ribbon (one oak leaf cluster)
Small Arms Expert Marksmanship Ribbon (one oak leaf cluster)
Air Force Training Ribbon

USAF TECH SGT TIMOTHY OFFICER, JR.

Memorial Obstacle Course Dedication

January 13, 2018

11:30 A.M.

Welcome

Ken Johnson, Executive Director Rodeheaver Boys Ranch

Prayer

Historical Perspective

Steve Watkins, Ranch Life Director, U.S. Navy Retired

Ranch Museum

Portrait Prints – Jeff King, RBR Development Director

Memorial Funding

Krista Purcell, Rodeheaver Foundation Development Director

Obstacle Course Builders

John Holley and Steve Watkins

Timothy's Military Family and Friends Testimonies

Timothy's Father

Timothy Officer, Sr. USAF Retired

Dedication Prayer

Brad Hall, Pastor First Baptist Church in Palatka

Course Activity/Group Pictures

RODEHEAVER BOYS RANCH

SINCE 1950

CHAPTER NINE: MOVING ON — 2015 – 2019

God moves in mysterious ways, His wonders to perform ... just days after the untimely death of Timothy Officer, a beautiful baby boy was born to Ethan and Brianna Bullock, Huntley Cottage parents, on August 22, 2015. The Lord giveth and the Lord taketh away ... on October 15, 2015, another close member of the Rodeheaver Family, Bruce Howe, died peacefully at age 95 in his home in Winona Lake, Indiana.

Scott and Susan Phillips, Rodeheaver Cottage Parents, retired in 2015 due to Scott's health problems, and relocated to Central Florida. Happily, they remain close to the Ranch family to this day. For many years, Scott led the boys in woodworking classes, one of their favorite activities. Scott presented Ken with his masterful creation, "Guardians of the Nest," at Ken's retirement celebration. The work is now on display in the Ranch Museum.

Brianna Bullock, Joan Inman, Lois Johnson, Susan Phillips, Patti McClure, Barbara Rowland, Cathy Watkins, Elizabeth Betonio and Sara Josephson

Susan Phillips had a special place in her heart for the boys and all of God's creations at the Ranch, and she wrote about it in the original Ranch book in 2013. Here is an excerpt of her story about Lazarus, the Egret:

"One day I was out with a couple of our boys. We were coming back to the Ranch and it was raining, not hard, just a soft rain. We were singing a song and just being silly when I came upon many egrets eating bugs in the field just inside the Ranch entrance. I slowed down and these silly birds flew all over the place, even in front of me. One bird hit my car and flew to the side of the road. I was devastated. I got out of the car and picked it up and drove it the rest of the way to our cottage. This bird was still alive. I brought it to the front porch of our cottage and sat in a chair with it. Its leg was

hurt, so I rubbed its legs, pulled its wings out and massaged them. Seeing them in a field doesn't do justice to their beauty. Their wings are massive. He had his talons engulfed around my hands and he clung to them. Their beaks are huge. This bird was beautiful; and I had the privilege of holding him for about an hour – just massaging him. I was amazed. I set the bird on the chair. The boys asked if he was going to die. I said I didn't know. My husband Scott came in the house and I asked him if he saw the bird in the chair. He said, "You mean the bird standing in your flower garden?" Sure enough, he was standing in the garden. I was so excited! I told the boys that now we needed to name him, because it looked like he'd be fine. One of the boys, Shawn Tuberville, said, "How about Lazarus, because it's like he came back to life." That was perfect. Lazarus walked with a limp and could stretch out his wings. At night we would check on him and shoo him back next to the cottage. In the morning, he was perched on one of the bicycles in the back of the cottage, sleeping with one leg folded under. Having had birds, I knew if they slept with one leg folded under them, that meant they were healthy. Lazarus was going to be fine."

In 2015, Don Holmes won the Wagon Master Award, a well-deserved tribute, indeed, and the boys and staff finished up with 50 handmade guitars for disabled children in hospitals – the project initiated by Board Member Wayne Robison of RULON International in St. Augustine.

Ranch boy Landon Madden played Buddy in the Christmas Elf Play at Palatka High School. Landon was becoming quite a star!

There were annual Christmas parties, as always, sponsored by the Jacksonville Jaycees and Seminole Electric Company Employees and, one of the boys' favorites, the Christmas party at the Palatka Horsemen's Club off

Hampton and Jeanette Stanley at The Palatka Horsemen's Club

of State Road 19 – a party that has happened nearly every year since the Palatka Horsemen's Club began in 1959. Hampton and Jeanette Stanley were charter members and ran the Club for many years. The Club still hosts people who love to ride horseback and the boys from Rodeheaver Boys Ranch are still invited to Christmas Dinner there.

On January 16, 2016, the Rodeheaver Alumni Ranch boys planned a nice reunion in Palatka headed by Jason Claro and Boogie Feggins. Former tutor Ted Callahan helped. They had lodging at the Crystal Cove Resort and ate two meals at the Ranch, with about 80 people touring and enjoying refreshments and photos. Sixteen alumni came and especially enjoyed visits to their former cottages, the dining hall, chapel, activities center and museum. They kept talking about how "fancy" everything had gotten and when one of the current ranch boys complained about the ranch being hard, an alumnus would automatically retort, "You don't know what hard is!"

From The Executive Director

One of the most frequently asked questions when we are traveling or hosting visitors here on the ranch is "How do you find the good people who come to the ranch to work with the boys?"

There are a myriad of possible answers to that question depending on whose asking and why. Of course, when we have a need in personnel, we immediately make it a matter of prayer and invoke the blessings of God in helping us connect up with the right people.

When we say "the right people" we are thinking several things. First of all, we desire Christian applicants who have a Christian world view philosophy. Secondly, they must have a solid stable marriage. You can imagine how important that is. Thirdly, they must have a basic love for people. When one doesn't have a basic love for people, they seldom can be taught to do so.

Fourthly, we are looking for people who seem to have the call of God on their lives for this work. The responsibility of childcare is tedious, yes, but enjoyable when a good prayer life and Bible study is a daily incorporation in one's personal time. We believe that this resource is vital to Christian childcare.

The boys we help and train during whatever time they are here need a clear look at their options in this life. Many children grow into adulthood and hardly ever (even in the good 'ole USA) are engaged in a clear presentation of the gospel of Christ.

Yes, we have had boys to live here and not adhere to a profession of faith in Christ. After all – it is their decision. Our responsibility is to love them, train them, and let them know they have a "forever home." Some of the boys don't figure out things spiritually until later and we are glad that they do.

So, (1) we tell 'em, (2) we tell 'em again, (3) and then tell 'em what we told 'em. When we get tired of that, we are out of the Christian childcare business.

Children are a heritage of the Lord. Let's not forget that as we help them with all the other things about growing into a good person. Your financial help makes our work more of a pleasure than a chore. Thank you from our hearts.   Ken Johnson

RBR's First Alumni Reunion

On January 16, 2016 the Rodeheaver Boys Ranch staff and boys enjoyed hosting 18 ranch alumni and their families. They spent most of the day eating lunch in the cafeteria and receiving a tour of the ranch. Everyone enjoyed the experience and the alumni expressed their appreciation for those who were in the administration during the years they were at the ranch. Lots of memories!

Also in January of 2016, The Inaugural Rodeheaver Boys Ranch Skeet Shoot occurred with the Azalea City Kiwanis Club cooking the food and Jeff King, accompanied by Greg Bacon, Bobby Cothren, Sidney Hobbs and others, did a great job in spite of the chilly weather.

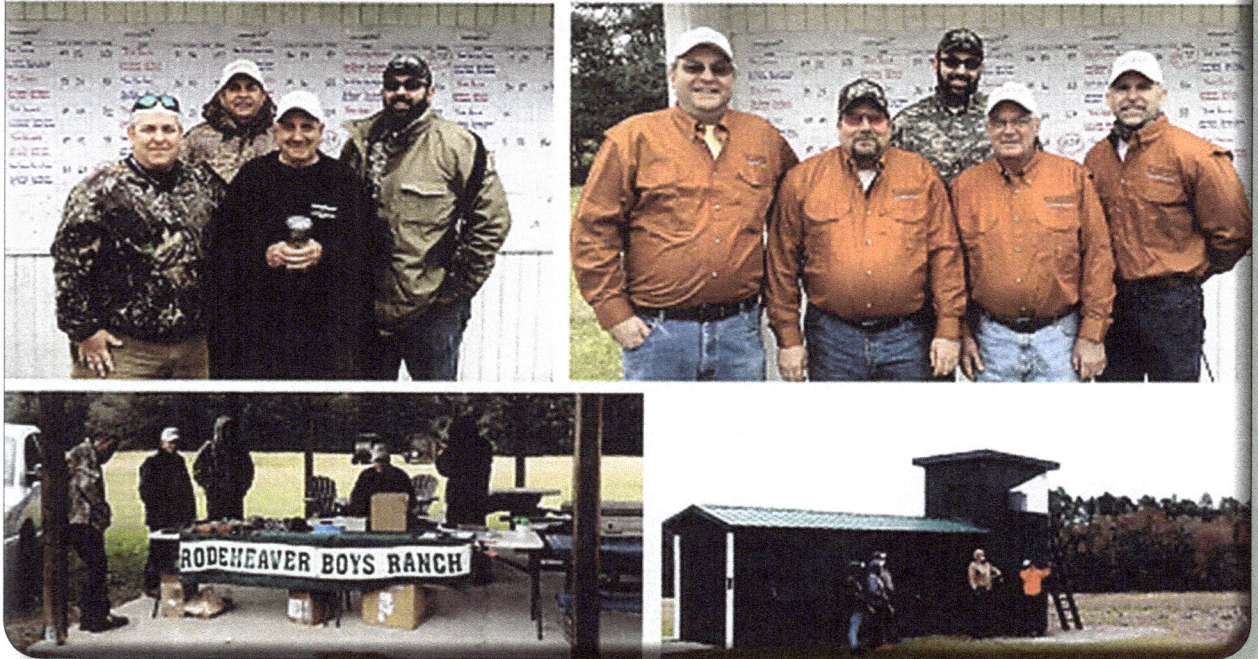

On January 23, 2016 the **Palatka Skeet Club** hosted the 1st Annual Rodeheaver Skeet Shoot. The weather was cold and windy, but a full slate of teams showed up and contributed to a very successful fundraiser to help the boys. We owe a great debt of thanks to board members Greg Bacon, Sidney Hobbs and Bobby Cothren for organizing the event.

In February of 2016, Jeff King had to get a pacemaker for his heart challenges and Patti McClure had a hip replacement which caused some concern from the staff not only for her health but for the lack of delicious meals she generally cooked for the Bluegrass Festival attendees in November. Patti sat down and gave the staff directions during the festival. Sadly, Amanda Morgan's mother passed away and the Ranch boys and staff helped with the memorial service. Soon after that, Amanda reported to her new job with the State of Florida in Alachua County.

On March 5, 2016, the Ranch received a check for $11,570.00 as a result of the 1st Annual Rodeheaver Benefit Bass Tournament, facilitated by Krista

Purcell and Becky Williams. Board members Marc Spalding and Don Holmes were there to accept the check, along with Mark Warren, Ken Johnson and Jeff King. Ranch Wrangler pics tell it all:

March 5, 2016 Crystal Cove Marina in Palatka hosted the **1st Annual Rodeheaver Benefit Bass Tournament.** The weather was great and the fish were biting. The big fish weighed in at 10.9 lbs. There were 68 boats entered in the tournament and the ranch received several thousand dollars to help the boys. The 2nd Annual tournament is already in the works for 2017.

Volunteers Al and Nancy Mathies celebrated their 50th wedding anniversary at the Ranch and Al and Roy Rowland helped staff and boys and an alumni group of boys begin construction of the Westbury/Boeing Cottage Alumni Bridge.

Krista Purcell made an impressive presentation to a Quad Club Rotary Grant Decision Panel and the grant was awarded. Lois and Ken Johnson were in attendance and applauded the work done by Krista on behalf of the Rodeheaver Foundation.

On April 30, Patti and Rick McClure resigned from their positions at the Ranch so that Rick could become a full-time pastor at New Beginnings Baptist Church in Palatka. Patti continued to have issues from hip and knee surgery. Her wonderful cooking was sorely missed by all.

Cathy Watkins' mother, Margaret Scheid, passed away in May. She was one of the special mentors to Ranch boys and to all who knew her. In April, former Executive Director Ashley Jeter passed away in Pace, Florida, where he had retired. His wife, Melba, noted he had requested that his ashes be scattered at Rodeheaver Boys Ranch someday.

Lois Johnson hosted two ladies from the Audubon Society of Gainesville who asked to document the birds on the Ranch and were able to list at least thirty types. They told Lois they were not bird watchers but bird listeners and bird whisperers and they appreciated the many varieties of birds on the Ranch that could be easily approached without having to camp in the woods.

Ring Power, as always, contributed to the Ranch with monstrous equipment including an Off Road Yuke Type Dump Truck Hauler and a huge Track-Hoe to do the work that was furnished by Ernie Cremer including the leveling for the planted pasture lands for grazing.

The Ranch Cookbook came out after many long hours of typing and compiling by Lois Johnson, and to this day, she states that this one was her favorite. The title of the 2016 Cookbook is "Recipes from the Heart – You Ain't Getting this Recipe!"

Rodeheaver Boys Ranch's Recipes from the Heart

Volume VI - You Ain't Getting This Recipe

EASY CASSEROLE

Sharon Terjung
Retired Volunteer at R B R
Sharon listens to the boys read &
helps wherever needed on the
ranch.

1 lb. Ground Beef (your choice)
(I sometimes use shredded
cooked chicken.)
1 envelope of dry Lipton Onion
Soup
1 pkg. of frozen French-style
Green Beans

Tater Tots to cover the top of
the casserole
1 can of Cream of Mushroom
Soup, thinned with ½ cup Milk
(You can use Cheese Soup
instead.)

1.) Preheat oven to 350°. 2. Place in layers the ground beef, Lipton
Onion Soup, green beans, mushroom soup in a 9 X9 pan. (I love to
double & use a 9 X 13 pan.) When done layering, cover the top with
the tater tots. Bake at 350° for 45 to 50 minutes. NOTE: This is great
with a salad. Company will request this recipe when they taste it the
first time.

BUTTER BRICKLE BREAD

Lillian Miller
Murfreesboro, Tennessee
Lois Johnson's Mom

(Lois' favorite dessert that her mom makes.)

1 box Yellow Cake Mix
1 box Instant Vanilla Pudding.
4 large Eggs
¾ c. Water
½ c. Oil

½ tsp. Butter Flavoring or
Vanilla Flavoring
1 c. Almond Brickle Chips (can
alternate Toffee Chips)
1 c. Pecans.

Preheat oven to 350°. Combine cake mix with instant vanilla pudding,
eggs, water, oil, & flavoring. Mix at MEDIUM speed for 5 min. Stir in
chips. Spray 2 med. loaf pans with cooking spray & pour batter evenly.
Bake at 350° for 50 to 55 min. or until tooth pick comes out clean. Cool
on rack for 10 min. NOTE: This is absolutely delicious with a cup of
coffee & having good friends all around you enjoying it too. Makes
perfect Christmas gifts. NOTE from daughter Lois: Years ago, Mama
made this Butter Brickle Bread from flour & not cake mix. I remember
this because it was in those days that flour came in cloth bags. Good
cloth. And when the flour was gone, Mama made clothes for us (four
daughters) from those flour bags. They wore good & lasted forever.
Mama never wasted anything. Most importantly, the cakes were so
delicious.

Fourteen Ranch boys went deer hunting with Jeff King, Roy Rowland, Don Inman, Greg Bacon, Ken Johnson, Bobby Cothren, Mike Perry, Paul Hudson, Jonathan Harper and Don Holmes at Carlton Spence's Bitter End Plantation. It was a four-day, three-night hunt and fourteen deer were harvested by the boys, ages 12 to 17. They presented Mr. Spence with a rustic game table, a Springfield 1911 45-caliber pistol, and nine ranch-made bat houses.

Officer Mike Florence of the Florida Fish and Wildlife Commission retired at the Ranch. He had been bringing staff to the Ranch for thirteen years and he brought Lt. Dan Dickson to be the new Ranch Liaison for the Commission. "Mike Florence was one of the best spokesmen we ever had," said Ken Johnson.

Hurricane Matthew hit with a vengeance in October of 2016, leaving the Ranch without power for two days while Ken and Lois vacationed on a cruise to Australia and the Fiji Islands as a gift from their children for twenty years at the Ranch. In Australia, they met their new granddaughter, Geneva, for the first time. They chose a good time to be away. Upon their return to the Ranch from Australia, Ken Johnson found a new blue leather office chair from the staff – a 20th Anniversary gift. Ken always felt bad that he was on a cruise ship while his "ship" at the Ranch was facing a hurricane at the same time.

Steve and Serena Logue

Stephen and Serena Logue visited the Ranch in November, 2016 and as they were making their way home to gather their belongings, Steve's father passed away in Colorado. They were surprised to see flowers from the Ranch. Soon, thereafter, they joined as cottage parents, bringing with them their three sons, Charlie, Max and Reagan Logue, who had no trouble assimilating comfortably into the Ranch life.

Once again, Ranch Boy Landon Madden was a main character in Charles Dickens' Christmas Carol at Palatka High School, playing Christmas Present.

President Don Holmes appropriated a large Three Diesel Generator to enhance the Ranch's Emergency Storm preparedness – a welcome addition after Hurricane Matthew.

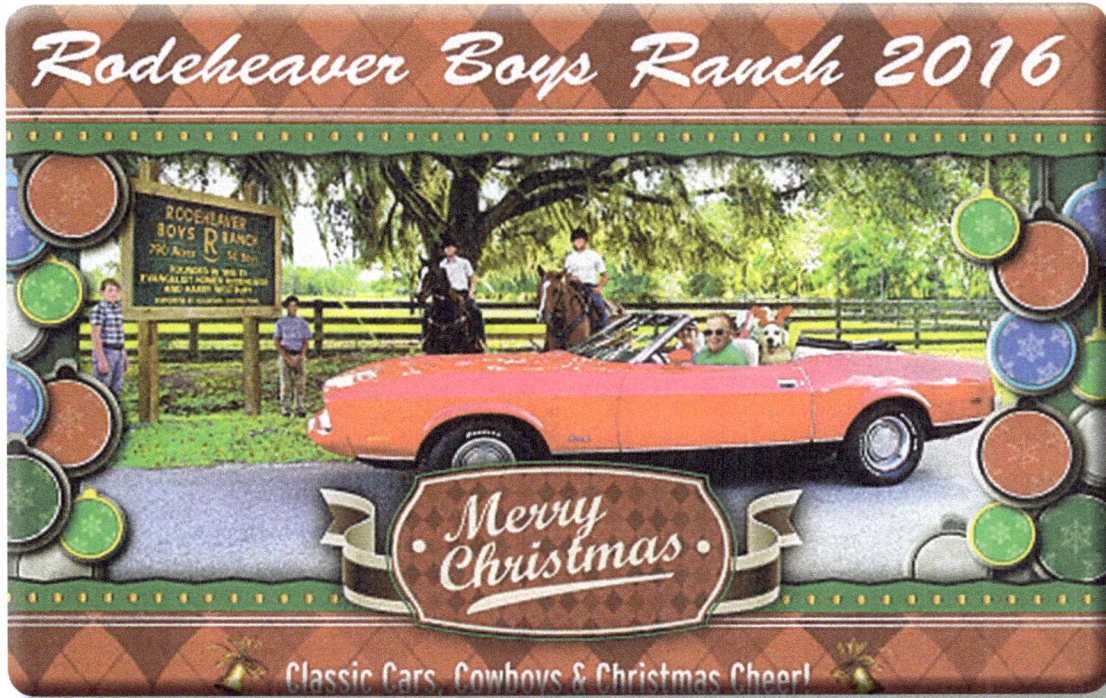

2016 Christmas card

The 2016 Christmas Card featured the Robisons with Bella, the RULON Mascot – a white retriever – sitting in a classic convertible coming through the Ranch Gate. The Ranch boys love that dog. Bella is the first to greet you at Rulon International in St. Augustine.

In January 2017, Joe and Erin Marsee and their family joined the Ranch as volunteers and were trained by volunteers Jerry and Joyce Flannery.

On February 11, 2017, the second annual skeet shoot for Rodeheaver Boys ranch was facilitated by Dwight Scifries, the event having been moved to this date

Joe and Erin Marsee

because it is between deer season and turkey season and this would satisfy the big deer and turkey hunters who participate. The Ranch boys edged out 17 other teams and came out in third place on the Palatka Skeet Club Range. Dwight also engineered, fabricated and installed new brace poles for the wildlife feeders so that the bears could not get to them, renting a high-rise forklift to stay safe. The boys helped and Dr. Mitchem footed the bill.

President Don Holmes introduced Karl Flagg to the Ranch, announcing Karl's appointment as a new member of the RBR Board.

Drs. Steve Chapman and Richard Perallon, having taken care of the boys' teeth for years, were joined on the RBR Board by Dr. Derek Morris.

Malynda Scifries ordered new computer equipment for the learning center at the Chapel and Krista Purcell documented the installation with photographs in order to make a grant report.

Clyde Barnes of Elkton, Florida, passed away on February 20th, leaving his wife Nancy, a second generation supporter of the Ranch. And speaking of supporters of the Ranch, Lois Johnson and Ken Johnson were asked to speak at the ADK Teachers Group hosted by Tim and Melanie Parker at their home. That teachers' group provides great help to the Ranch Store during the Bluegrass Festivals.

Tim and Melanie Parker

A 1949 Oldsmobile Rocket donated by Larry Higbee was used as a raffle item, and Richard Wilson sponsored the restoration paint job on the Museum's 1950 Ford 8-M Classic Farm tractor, sheltering in place behind the Museum right next to the green 1950 Chevrolet truck.

The Ranch Fair booth took first place overall at the Putnam County Fair. It was Donna King's doing as it featured the 1973 Red Mustang used in our Christmas Card. It was the longest, biggest booth at the Fair!

Pastor Bob Pugh, First Baptist Church of Crescent City, brought the church's annual Easter gift of socks and underwear to the boys, although some of the boys told the ladies they didn't wear "tightie-whities." Pastor Pugh noted this and promised to put store receipts in the bags, adding that "old people only buy one kind."

Greg and Lisa Buchanan resigned from the ranch to go to the Hershey Home for Children in Pennsylvania, thus Don Inman became the new VIP Director.

Meeko, the gentle horse that was ridden by Ken Johnson and many visitors to the Ranch who needed a friendly ride, passed away due to facial and eye cancer. Meeko was loved by all and was mourned at his passing. Ernie Cremer, Scott Brahman and Jason Pippin took care of his burial.

The 67th Annual Meeting went well, with President Don Holmes being re-elected. Barry Walsh, the second boy to come to the Ranch in 1950, spoke at the meeting, as well as former Executive Director Ed MacClellan and former Tutor Ted Callahan.

Once again, Ranch boy Landon Madden landed a main role in Les Miserables at Palatka High School. Landon also graduated in 2017, along with Jessid Herrin, Frank Carifi and Tristan Siegmund.

Bobby and Cheryl Cothren treated the Ranch staff and boys to a day at the Jacksonville Zoo on May 13, and also sprang for lunch with a $10 voucher to be used within the park. Later that month, Carlton and Ruby Spence treated the Ranch Staff and boys to an afternoon at the Shrine Circus in Jacksonville, followed by dinner after the show.

Greg Bacon won the 2017 Wagon Master Award, having risen to the top and distinguished himself with service above and beyond.

WAGON MASTER AWARD – THE HONORABLE GREG BACON
For your unselfish devotion in serving as a friend, provider and protector.
For unselfish devotion to our Creator and our God.
For making a distinction where you knew God had made a difference.
From the Staff and Boys at Rodeheaver Boys' Ranch.
2017
"ONE MAN CAN MAKE A DIFFERENCE"

On hand to present the Wagon Master Award were Ben Bates, Dr. Steve Chapman, Robert Mitchem, Karen Hughes, Judge Hedstrom, Don Holmes and Dr. Richard Perallon. Greg was accompanied by his wife, Debbie, his two children, his mother and good friends Paul Hudson and Taylor Douglas. Letters from Carlton Spence and Dan Martinez were read and were quite moving. Each Wagon Master Awards Ceremony is a special one, and this was no exception.

Ken Johnson participated in a Sunday evening community welcome to Brad Hall, the new Pastor at First Baptist Church of Palatka. Other speakers were County Commissioner Larry Harvey, Mayor Terrell Hill, Central Putnam Ministerial President Karl Flagg, Francis Baptist Pastor Jason Sharp and St. Johns River Baptist Association Director Asa Greer. Ben Bates was the moderator.

A June reception was planned by Krista Purcell and Malynda Scifries for the Quad Rotary Clubs who contributed to the computer lab at the Chapel's Learning Center. Dan Martinez and Krista Purcell were the official hosts of the reception and the Ranch boys greeted visitors as they came in.

The Ranch boys and staff had a great summer, traveling to Georgia and North Carolina, enjoying Sliding Rock, and then on to Pisgah National Forest in North Carolina, walking the hiking trails, enjoying a simulated helicopter ride reenacting putting out forest fires, and then on to white water rafting on the Nantahala River. They also enjoyed the water park in Helen, Georgia, where they camped out and cooked S'Mores over a campfire. The boys also had a great day at the Kennedy Space Center in Titusville, thanks to Larry Higbee, who paid for the entire outing.

Pauline Pellicer passed away in July of 2017, after a sixty-year journey of supporting the Boys Ranch along with her late husband, Sheriff Walt Pellicer. Their son, Walton Pellicer has been on the RBR Board and is now running for a Putnam County Commission Seat.

Walton Pellicer

Jeff King's Dad, Jerry King, was laid to rest in Tennessee with full military honors by the U.S. Air Force Color Guard Squad. Ken Johnson officiated at the graveside service.

It was a summer of newborns. Gabriel Marsee was born to Relief Cottage parents Erin and Joe Marsee, and Huntley Cottage Parents Ethan and Brianna Bullock welcomed their baby daughter, Addison into the world.

Mark and Barbara Brewer transferred to the Kitchen and food service management – a central position at the Ranch with so many hungry boys! They are especially talented in preparing and serving food.

Mark and Barbara Brewer

In August, Ken and Lois Johnson traveled to Eglin Air Force Base in Florida to help officiate at the memorial service for Carlos Branch who died at 90 years of age. Carlos is the pilot who taught Ken to fly and advised Timothy Officer to join the Air Force. He invested a lot of time, money and work on the Ranch over the years, and his wife, Carolyn, was helpful in redecorating the Lodge twice. Carlos Branch spent twenty years on the Ranch Advisory Board.

Scot and Terrie Collins

Scot and Terrie Collins came from Indiana and joined the Ranch family as farm managers and equine experts. Scot is also a counselor, musician and guitar player who soon became an integral part of the Chapel Service on Wednesday evenings. Scot and Terrie traveled to Marion, North Carolina, for training and certification as equine counselors and therapists.

Ranch boys Frank Carifi and J. D. Herrin joined the RULON International Company as employees that summer, and sadly, former ranch cook Janet Wrisner passed away in August. Her memorial service was hosted in the Ranch Cafeteria.

In September 2017, Hurricane Irma pummeled the Ranch causing the loss of one-third of the main horse barn roof and partial loss of the shingles on the Watkins' and Collins' houses. Electrical power was out for two days and the VIP fence was flattened in several places. Several trees were down on the Ranch Road and flood waters washed over Martinez Circle. The Boeing Cottage driveway was completely washed out and the Bluegrass Festival RV Park was a temporary lake. The roof on the Lodge was damaged. The Hurricane caused the cancellation of the annual hunting trip to Carlton Spence's Bitter End Plantation, but a later fall hunt was arranged. Twelve boys gathered to

dedicate Carlton Spence's Chapel in the Woods. They sang Amazing Grace, read John 3:16 and 17 and Jonathan Harper (former Ranch boy and now hunting guide) did a meaningful dedication prayer. It was a moving service, one that the boys and men who attended will always remember.

Ranch boys Brandon Matthews, John Bedgood and Bobby Wilson made the football team at Palatka High School.

At the FACCCA Meeting in Tallahassee in October, the huge damage to children's homes across the State of Florida was realized. Hit especially hard were Safe Harbor in Jacksonville, Gator Wilderness School in Punta Gorda, Oak Christian Home in Tampa, Edgewood Ranch in Orlando and Lighthouse Girls Home in Tallahassee. Prayers were said for swift recovery of all these damaged homes.

Dwight and Malynda Scifries resigned and moved back to their hometown in Indiana. They remain close friends of the Ranch.

The Bluegrass Festival in November was a great success. Alpha Delta Kappa sorority helped Lois Johnson and Cathy Watkins stock the Ranch Store for the Bluegrass Festival.

Bud and Johanna John joined the Ranch family in November, bringing with them their beautiful family, Isaiah, Sarah, Jonah and Noah. They became Boeing Cottage Parents.

The Year 2018 began with an important event on January 13th – the Dedication of the USAF Tech Sgt. Timothy

Bud & Johanna John – Boeing Cottage

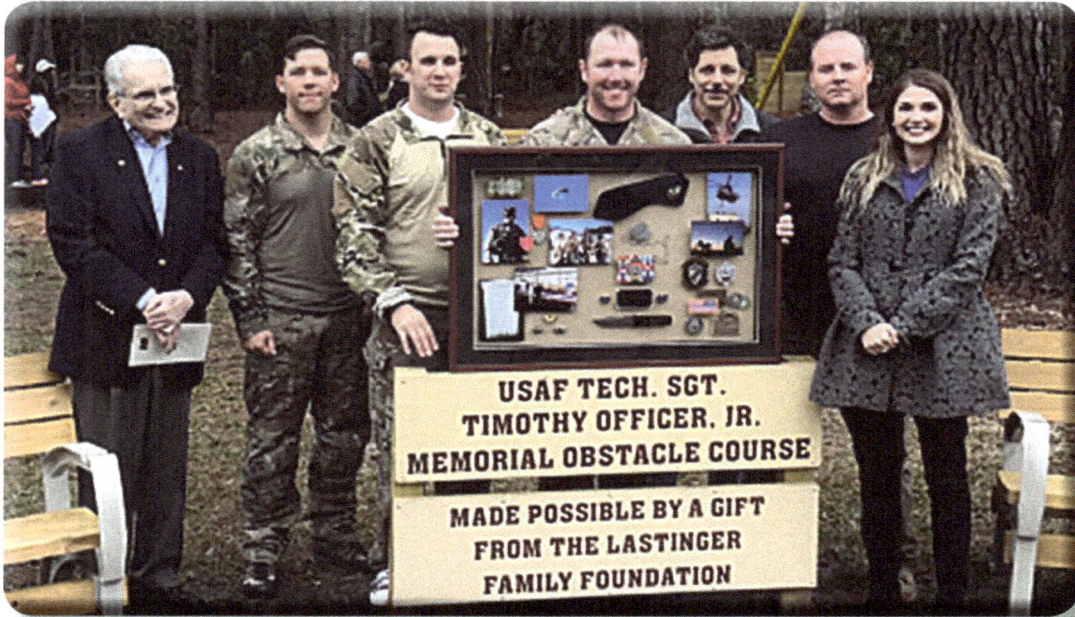

Board Members Dan Martinez and Dr. Richard Perallon, with members of Timothy Officer's unit and Krista Purcell - January 13, 2018

Officer Jr. Memorial Obstacle Course. Timothy's father, retired Master Sgt. Tim Officer, and several Airmen from Timothy's Unit attended, as well as several RBR Board Members. The Chapel Service was touching and memorable, and the boys immediately began to challenge their abilities on the new obstacle course.

On February 2, Steve and Cathy Watkins retired after 21 years of service to the Ranch. As with most of the long-time Ranch staff, they continue to be close friends of the Ranch.

There were 24 teams at the Annual Skeet Shoot in 2018, and the 15th Bluegrass Festival had 436 motor homes and campers. Jeff and Donna King's daughter, Marcia Trull, helped in the Museum and sold huge numbers of raffle tickets for the 1949 Oldsmobile Rocket and the Martin Guitar.

Carlton and Ruby Spence donated a Clave Nova Instrument System for the Chapel and Bobby and Cheryl Cothren paid for 25 tons of asphalt for the road and RV Park.

Mark and Bonnie Warren

Mark and Bonnie Warren came back to the Ranch after several years away. Mark reported as Director of Ranch Life. They were welcomed back to the Ranch with open arms.

Long-time Ranch doctor, Norman Archambeau, passed away in April and both Ken Johnson and Dr. Steve Chapman assisted at the memorial service.

Carlton Spence and his sons, Jeff and Donald, spent a day at the Ranch with Dr. Robert Mitchem checking out the Osceola Turkey population. It was a productive day.

The Fourth Annual Gospel Music Festival was held on the 20th and 21st of April in 2018, featuring The Isaacs, Jeff and Sherry Easter, The Harper Brothers, Chosen Road and the Duncans, along with the Trinity River Band. Pastor Brad Hall was the speaker on one of those evenings.

The 68th Annual Meeting was held in late April and Dr. Richard Perallon handled the nominations, with Karen Hughes chairing the meeting.

Becky Williams and Mark Roberts headed up the Boys Fishing Tournament on May 5th and it was a successful one, with good weather, many fish caught, and 40 boats!

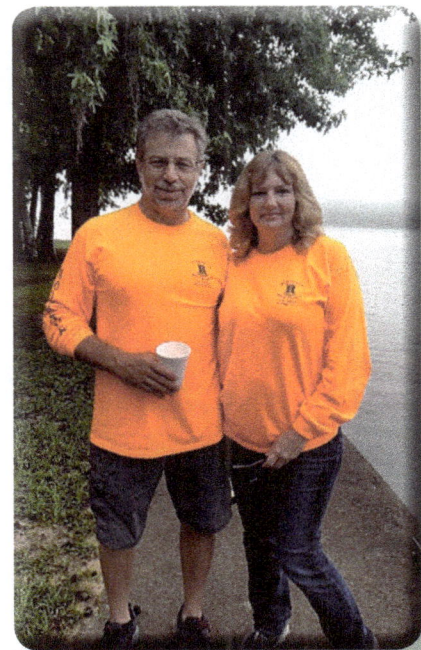

**Mark Roberts
and Becky Williams**

Dr. Mike Hudson served as the Emcee and Promoter of the Rodeheaver Golf Tournament in May of 2018, with twenty-two teams playing. Sheriff Gator DeLoach came to tee off and presented Ken Johnson with a generous check from the Sheriff's Department.

Steve and Hannah Matthews came to Rodeheaver Boys Ranch in May of 2018 as Relief Parents. They are now Cottage Parents for Huntley Cottage.

Christopher Mathews, Stephen & Hannah Matthews – Huntley Cottage Parents, & Malachi Coker

Jeff King on Tomorrow's Magic with Donna holding the reins

Sadly, after a long battle with breast cancer, Donna King passed away on June 2, 2018. Her smiling presence at the Ranch is still greatly missed to this day and her kind, loving spirit can be felt in the Ranch Museum, where she spent so much of her time and talent in her last years. A portion of her obituary follows:

Donna Jean King

Donna Jean King 62, of Palatka Florida went home to be with her Lord and Savior Jesus Christ at Flagler Hospital in St Augustine, Florida on June 2, 2018.

Donna was preceded in death by her parents, Don and Billie Clement. Donna is survived by her husband of 42 years Jeffery King, Son Chandler King, Daughter Marcia Trull and her Husband John Trull. Donna is also survived by her Brother Joey Clement, his Wife Serene Clement, their children Rachel Reed and her Husband Nate Reed, Joe Clement and his Wife Jill Clement, Hannah Burnham and her Husband Tahan Burnham. Donna is also survived by two special Grandsons William King and Samuel King and Great Nieces Evelyn Reed and Savannah Clement.

Donna loved serving the Lord with her husband Jeff at Rodeheaver Boys Ranch for the last 18 years. Donna was the curator of the ranch museum and managed the ranch donor base. Donna will be sorely missed by her immediate family and her extended family at Rodeheaver Boys Ranch.

Visitation will be held at the Johnson – Overturf Funeral Home, 307 S Palm Ave. Palatka, FL 32177 at 9:00 am Wednesday, June 6th. After visitation the funeral service will begin at 11:00 am followed by a graveside service at Oak Hill Cemetery. Dr. Ken Johnson and Pastor Slade Rickels will be officiating the service.

In lieu of flowers Donna's family requests that donations be made to the Rodeheaver Boys Ranch, 380 Boys Ranch Rd., Palatka, FL 32177.

Donna saw everyone through the eyes of God. Her list of Ten Ways to Love was shared at her funeral:

TEN WAYS TO LOVE (Donna King)
1. **Listen without interrupting. (Proverbs 18)**
2. **Speak without accusing. (James 1:19)**
3. **Give without sparing. (Proverbs 21:26)**
4. **Pray without ceasing. (Colossians 1:9)**
5. **Answer without arguing. (Proverbs 17:1)**
6. **Share without pretending. (Ephesians 4:15)**
7. **Enjoy without complaint. (Philippians 2:14)**
8. **Trust without wavering. (Corinthians 13:7)**
9. **Forgive without punishing. (Colossians 3;13)**
10. **Promise without forgetting. (Proverbs 13:12)**

Donna King was a woman of great faith, humor and compassion. She was also quite inventive. When she was diagnosed with breast cancer and went through chemotherapy and radiation, she lost her hair, but instead of lamenting, she turned her loss into a gain, becoming a major fashion statement with her imaginative hats. Her smile was irresistible and her demeanor was always positive. She created beautiful crafts from pieces of old jewelry and her devotion to the Ranch Museum and the boys and staff at the Ranch was limitless.

Ken Johnson remembers that after Donna's funeral, he was trying to be there for his good friend, Jeff, who insisted on

**Marcia Joyce King and Donna King –
Together in Heaven Now**

traveling on to Cherokee, North Carolina for the Bluegrass Festival, as he and Donna had planned prior to her death. "Jeff needed to hear from all those people," says Ken, "and I went with him just to be there with him." The following Saturday, Jeff got a call from Palatka that his mother had been taken to the hospital. She had made the decision that she was not going to fight her cancer any longer – no more chemo, no more radiation – and that she was going to Haven Hospice. On June 12, less than two weeks following the death of his beloved wife, Jeff's mother, Marcia Joyce King, 83, went home to be with Donna and the Lord.

On July 4th the Ranch staff and boys had a low country shrimp boil with hot dogs after Chapel and spent the day on tubes out on the river. Charlie Logue and his crew set up a fantastic fireworks display to celebrate our Nation's Independence Day.

Work began on the new Lodge Phase 2 Building that fall and Ken and Lois Johnson traveled to Australia to meet their new grandson, Lincoln Hanby.

Sidney Hobbs of St. Augustine received the 2018 Wagon Master Award. An unselfish person who is always there for the boys, Sidney is what Ken Johnson calls "a sparkplug" at board meetings – a man who is supportive of whatever needs to be done. Sidney's wife, Brenda, was on hand to celebrate her husband's award and daughter, Madison, was given a Crystal Level Award. Bobby Cothren, Greg Bacon, Ben Bates, Dr. Richard Perallon, Judge Ed Hedstrom and Dr. Robert Mitchem were there to honor Sidney Hobbs.

Fourteen boys went to the Bitter End for the annual hunting trip and ten of them harvested a deer. The Christmas Card in 2018 featured a photo of the boys and their guides at Carlton Spence's Chapel in the Woods.

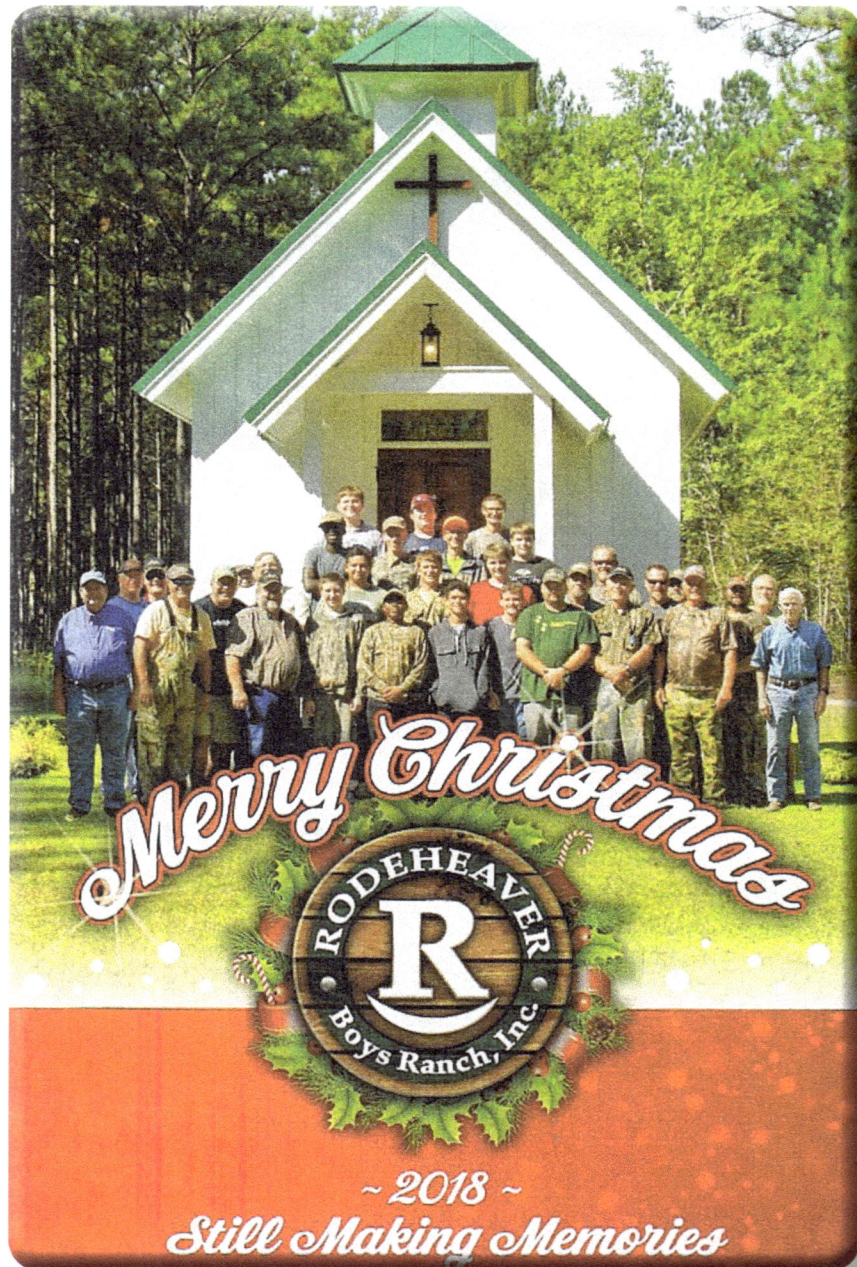

Ken Johnson announced that he would be retiring in August of 2019 and the Board of Directors began searching for a new Executive Director.

In the meantime, President Don Holmes negotiated a financial and legal settlement for a permanent natural gas line to be run on the Ranch property – Etoniah Forest – a favorable deal for the Ranch.

Evangelist, entertainer and magician Bobby McGilliard of Milton, Florida came to the Ranch as he had done for the past twenty-two years, and as always, the boys enjoyed the presentation.

The 15th Annual Bluegrass Festival went off without a hitch in February with 400 plus motor homes and campers and huge crowds. The new Lodge Building, decorated by the Spence family, was full and highly appreciated – particularly the front porch with its rocking chairs.

The 7th Annual Rodeheaver Car, Truck, and Motorcycle Show was on March 9th, as was the professional fishing tournament in Palatka. There was a great Elvis impersonator at the Car Show while there were 185 boats at the City Dock for the fishing tournament, which was run by Becky Williams and Mark Roberts with the help of Krista Purcell and Jeff King.

It was the 69th year for the Putnam County Fair as well as for Rodeheaver Boys Ranch. The Ranch's 1950 Green Truck greeted people at the entry, along with the 1950 Ford Tractor. Eight of the thirteen pigs entered by the Ranch boys placed.

Jerry and Joyce Flannery, along with several Ranch boys, assembled new picnic tables designated for the Timothy Officer Obstacle Course, Scout Camp and Ranch Pavilion.

Ken and Lois Johnson went to the FACCCA Meeting in Punta Gorda hosted by Gator Wilderness Camp School's Greg Kanagy, and were honored for their more than 30 years of membership and leadership in the organization.

The 69th RBR Annual Meeting happened in April with entertainment by the Trinity River Band. Don Holmes accepted the nomination for another year as President of the Board of Directors.

The Rodeheaver Boys Ranch Fishing Tournament was a huge success with Becky Williams and Mark Roberts facilitating it again. One of the boys at the weigh-in microphone stated, "A bad day on the river is better than a good day inside the cottage. I'd rather be fishing than anything else in life."

Mark Roberts and Former Ranch Boy Robert Siemiatkoski – Weighing In!

In May 2019, shortly after attending the Rodeheaver Boys Ranch Fishing Tournament, Lois Johnson shared gardening tips in the Ranch's beautiful Butterfly Garden with Jan Thorsen and Becky Williams. Jan is the widow of Bryce Thorsen, for whom the 2019 tournament was named in memory of his lifetime as a fishing guide and member of the Bass Anglers Sportsman Society, American Bass Anglers and National Rifle Association, as well as his support of Rodeheaver Boys Ranch. Jan is also a master gardener who thoroughly enjoyed learning about Lois's creation of Butterfly Island.

Butterfly Island – Lois Johnson, Becky Williams and Jan Thorsen – May 4, 2019

A woman of God who loves all of His creations, from butterflies to boys, Lois Johnson wrote a farewell message to the ladies of the Ranch on May 13th, knowing that Ken was retiring soon and that she would be traveling prior to his retirement. Her heartfelt message was one filled with memories and lessons as well as abundant love for the Ranch that she had long-ago come to with great reluctance. Her message follows:

May 13, 2019

Ranch Ladies,

May 7th, last Tuesday, was and will be my last Ladies' Bible Study/Prayer Meeting Time at Rodeheaver Boys Ranch. The next 2 Tuesdays, (the 14th and 21st), I will be very tied up with appointments that I need to keep. The last week of May, I will be flying to Tenn. to be with my mom to give my sister a much-needed break. But I want to plan a time that we ladies can have either a luncheon or dinner all together one more time before my departure in August 2019 from this mission field that I have called home for the last 23 years.

I want to thank those dear ladies that have been so faithful each Tuesday morning to gather with me as we shared the Word of God or heard each others' prayer requests and then took them to the Throne of God. I also shall never forget those ladies who always stayed behind just to help me clean up to the very end and then maybe shared a lunch and her heart with me.

Every time I have gone over to prepare the lodge room for our meetings, I could not help from looking around at that big table and seeing the past 23 years of the most incredible, saintly, beautiful, God-fearing women who took up those seats (I noticed that most every lady had her own special chair where she always sat; some near me and some near the door; so cute to me). When I look at a chair over there, I think with a smile, "That's where so and so always sat." There were many times, we had every seat filled, but then there were times when only one or two was present, but we would still have a time of sweet fellowship. I think of Kay Whitley on that one.

Oh, I have witnessed miraculous answered prayers, such as a school bus that was desperately needed for the boys to be able to get to school; we prayed; it came the next day. In the beginning of my time here at RBR, it seemed that the ranch was always in

financial need; bills needed to be paid; paychecks needed to go out so staff could pay their bills; the ladies would meet to pray and money would come in-- in the strangest ways. We knew God had moved His face toward us. And I have seen ladies weep over their unsaved family and friends, and especially a poor little boy that came to the ranch scared and lost and needed to be loved; we would stop everything right there and call out those names and then later on hear the great news of salvation or restoration. I now think of a great prayer warrior -- Sharon Terjung. She would wrap her arms around us all and we felt her prayers. Oh, how I miss hearing that sweet voice!

And at the end of each prayer meeting, do you remember how the ladies gathered in a circle, taking a ranch sister's arm with one lady calling out to our Heavenly Father, and you could feel His presence moving all around us? I shall hold this time dear to my heart.

To all of you ladies that were here in my 23 years , know that I loved each and every one of you and I thank God for allowing our paths to cross for a moment in time. To those who gave her time and heart here in trying to make a difference in a boy's life; God bless you. Thank you for taking time out of your busy schedule on Tuesday mornings to be a blessing.

And then those precious ladies who met with us and are now present with the Lord; we'll see you again. My darling friend, Donna, you left us too soon.

All my love to each of you; it has been my honor to have served in the trenches with you.

Lois Johnson
Eph. 2:8-9 To God be the Glory!

Always remember: GOD IS ON THE THRONE; THE REINS ARE IN HIS HANDS: HE NEVER MAKES A MISTAKE; AND HE WAS, IS, AND ALWAYS WILL BE ON TIME!!

Charlotte Brown, Lois Johnson and Daisy Mae Brown

On September 10, the ladies of the Ranch did hold a farewell luncheon for Lois Johnson at Corky Belle's Restaurant in Palatka. Many lovely tributes were paid to Lois, none sweeter and more meaningful than that of Joan Inman, former Cottage Mother and forever friend, whose husband, Don Inman, and daughter, Deanna, continue to be in charge of the Ranch's VIP Program. Joan talked at length of the many who have been touched by Lois's deep faith in God over the years and how that reliance on God is integral to each and every woman who chooses to work with the boys at the Ranch. Among those present at the luncheon for Lois were Relief Cottage Parent Charlotte Brown and her daughter, Daisy Mae, two shining examples of Godly women.

Ranch boy Zach Johnson graduated from Palatka High School at the end of May and Sidney and Brenda Hobbs gave him a vehicle for graduation.

Mark Warren and Dr. Robert Mitchem worked hard building a new Bayhead Walk Bridge to Lois Johnson's Butterfly Island.

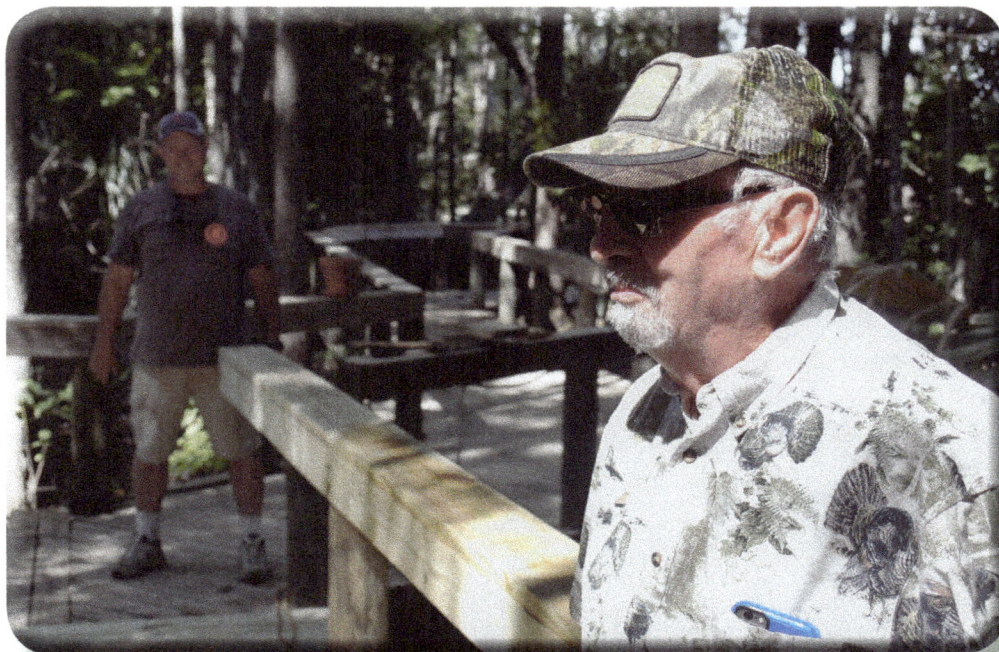

Mark Warren and Dr. Robert Mitchem – Bridge Builders

Building the bridge with Dr. Mitchem was one of Mark Warren's last acts as Director of Ranch Life. Mark resigned in the summer of 2019, moving to his new home in Levy County where he is now the Agricultural Extension Agent. As with all former Ranch staff members, Mark continues to be connected to the Ranch.

The summer of 2019 was marked by a fantastic trip to the Creation Museum of Natural History and the Ark Encounter in Williamstown, Kentucky by the entire staff and all the boys. They had an opportunity to tour the life-size replica of Noah's Ark and personally meet Dr. Ken Ham, founder of the Ark Encounter and author of several books.

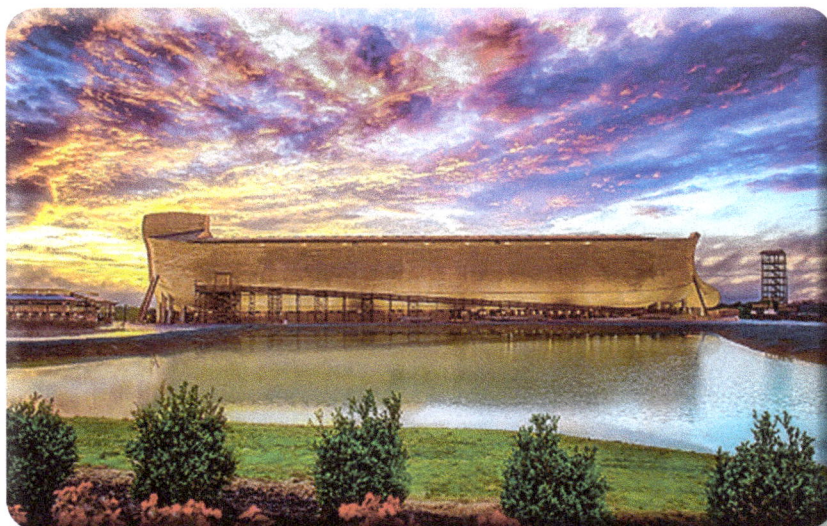

Ark Encounter – Williamstown, Kentucky

Mark Johnson & Family

In early August, Ken and Lois Johnson were treated to a Ranch Staff Retirement Dinner with several special guests in attendance. Ken was especially touched that Jonathan Harper and his wife, Mandy, were present, as well as his son, Mark and his family.

Lois and Ken Johnson enjoying the festive farewell at the Ranch

Soon after the staff party at the Ranch, another farewell party was held for the Johnsons at the First Baptist Church of Palatka – and this one was a complete surprise! All of their children and grandchildren were there, including their daughter Brooke and her husband, Justin Hanby, and their children, Geneva and Lincoln, from Australia. Most of the Board Members attended, as well as members of the Rodeheaver Foundation (past presidents of the board), and a number of Ranch alumni. Ken commented to Lois later on that it had been as much a reunion as a retirement

Sharon Terjung, Ken and Lois Johnson

party. It was a great evening for the Johnsons and their retirement was scheduled for the end of August 2019, however, God had not yet provided a replacement for Ken Johnson and so he agreed to extend his retirement date to the end of September. God and the Rodeheaver Foundation were working overtime to find the perfect new Executive Director, and this was accomplished when Brad Hall accepted the call on September 30th which necessitated Ken Johnson's extension to go until October 2019.

In late August of 2019, Jacob and Kayla Taylor from Dalton, Georgia, joined the Ranch Family as Relief Cottage Parents.

As always, the main "Pardners" (Board of Directors and Rodeheaver Foundation, made up of all living Past Presidents) actively provided support throughout the transition process. At the time of the transition of leadership from Ken Johnson to Brad Hall, the Board of Directors were as follows:

Jacob and Kayla Taylor – Relief Cottage Parents

OFFICERS:

Don Holmes, President

Greg Bacon, Vice President

Karen Hughes, Secretary

Matt Reynolds, Treasurer

Dr. Robert Mitchem, Treasurer Emeritus

LIVING PAST PRESIDENTS:

Ben Bates, Jr.

John Browning, Jr.

Dr. Steve Chapman

Bobby Cothren

Judge Ed Hedstrom

Dan Martinez

Marc Spalding

Dr. Richard Perallon

Carlton Spence

DIRECTORS GROUP I (2017-2020)

Gator Deloach

Karl Flagg

Robert Mills

Tim Parker

Walton Pellicer

DIRECTORS GROUP II (2018-2021)

Chance Clay

Sidney Hobbs

Paul Hudson

Main Ocean LLC – Jeff Spence

Jeb S. Smith

Steve Overturf

Sun Supply – Larry Soncrant

DIRECTORS GROUP III (2019-2022)

Dale Barnes

Ernie Cremer

Mark Brown

Ring Power – Randy Ringhaver

Mark Dooley

Wayne H. Robison

Julie Masters

Brad Hall came on as Executive Director of Rodeheaver Boys Ranch on November 1, 2019, and Ken Johnson, although officially retired, stayed on to help Brad Hall and the staff with the November Bluegrass Festival.

A new era had begun.

CHAPTER TEN:
2020 — FORGING AHEAD INTO THE FUTURE

The Brad Hall Family

Brad Hall is now the Executive Director of Rodeheaver Boys Ranch. He and his family, wife Karen and children, Hannah and Micah, moved into the Executive Directors House on the Ranch on November 1 and made themselves at home. After all, since first driving down Boys Ranch Road, Brad had known this was home. It was where God wanted him and he had answered the call.

The first big event happened almost immediately as the 12th Annual Fall Bluegrass Festival occurred on November 7, 8, and 9th, 2019, and was attended by thousands of fans as always. Brad handled it wisely and well, instinctively delegating a few responsibilities to Ranch boys who had never been entrusted with them before. Christopher Mathews, for instance, acted as a tour guide of the Ranch for two first-time visitors, elegant elderly ladies. Not only did he take care of them with delicacy and tact, but he gave them a beautiful tour of the Chapel, the Obstacle Course and the Dock at the River. It was a spectacular day

for Bessie Turk and her sister Jenny Guth of Jacksonville, Florida, both of whom were quite impressed by the outstanding courtesy shown them by their host, Ranch Boy Christopher Mathews.

A big announcement was made at the November Bluegrass Festival when Norm and Judy Adams, longtime promoters of the Adams Bluegrass Festivals (including the Palatka-Rodeheaver Boys Ranch

Christopher Mathews, Jenny Guth and Bessie Turk at the Ranch

Festivals), announced that Ernie and Debi Evans of Evans Media Source, were taking over the festivals. Evans Media Source online published the following article and photograph.

Evans Media Source acquires Adams Bluegrass Festivals

Posted on November 12, 2019 by John Lawless

Evans Media Source, one of the largest promoters of bluegrass events in the southeastern United States, has acquired Adams Bluegrass Festivals, who have been dominant in this business for four decades. This makes Evans Media Source, managed by Ernie and Debi Evans, the big player in the Carolinas and Florida.

Norman and Judy Adams have been running festivals for the past 45 years, and certainly deserve to enjoy their retirement. Many thousands

Ernie Evans, Norman Adams, Judy Adams, and Debi Evans at the 2019 Palatka Bluegrass Festival

of festival lovers have attended their top-rated events over that time, enjoying music and fellowship at weekend shows like the Cherokee Bluegrass Festival, and the New Years Festival in Jekyll Island.

The Evans have made a business specialty of assuming management of bluegrass festivals, either when their proprietors are ready to leave it behind, or when an event has fallen on hard times and needs to be turned around. The Adams festivals, of course, have been tremendously successful, with several running well over 40 years.

The announcement of the acquisition was made this past weekend at the 15th annual Palatka Bluegrass Festival in Florida.

As a result of this new agreement, Evans Media will now manage the following long-running Adams Bluegrass events:

- January 2-4, 2020 – 44th Annual New Year's Bluegrass Festival – Jekyll Island, SC
- February 13-15, 2020 – 16th Annual Palatka Bluegrass Festival – Palatka, FL
- June 11-13, 2020 – Cherokee Bluegrass Festival – Cherokee, NC
- August 13-15, 2020 – 46th Annual North Carolina State Bluegrass Festival – Marion, NC
- October 24-26, 2020 – Anderson Bluegrass Festival – Anderson, SC
- November 12-14, 2020 – Fall Palatka Bluegrass Festival – Palatka, FL
- November 26-28, 2020 – 51st Annual South Carolina Bluegrass Festival – Myrtle Beach, SC

These are in addition to the festivals currently run by Ernie and Debi.

- *January 14-19, 2020 – Yee Haw Music Festival – Okeechobee, FL*
- *February 18-23, 2020 – Florida Bluegrass Classic – Brooksville, FL*
- *February 28-29, 2020 – Winter String Summit – Kissimmee, FL*
- *March 26-29, 2020 – EMS Spring Bluegrass Festival – Brooksville, FL*

In acknowledging their new role in maintaining these iconic festivals, the Evans said that they feel a bit humbled.

"It is both an honor and challenge to step into the shoes of someone you consider a pioneer and a legend. Getting the initial phone call ranks high with the most exciting things that have happened in our careers, but working alongside Norman and Judy Adams for the next year will be like earning a masters degree in festival promotion. We are so grateful and still in shock."It is wonderful news that these terrific bluegrass events have a future assured into a new generation.

*Sadly, after March 2020, most large gatherings were cancelled due to COVID-19.

After a successful Bluegrass Festival, the Hall family got settled in, Hannah returning to finish out the semester at Florida State University where she was a Junior in the College of Social Work, with the goal of working in child advocacy, Micah returning to Palatka High School where he was in his Junior Year, Karen returning to her work as a preschool teacher at Peniel Baptist Academy and Brad answering God's call to lead the staff and boys at Rodeheaver Boys Ranch. Then it was Thanksgiving Break!

In keeping with the ongoing stream of communication that was established over the years by Ken Johnson and other executive directors, Brad began sending out a regular Ranch Record to the Rodeheaver Board of Directors and Staff, his first one being:

Ranch Record – 11/26/2019
Oh, give thanks to the Lord, for He is good!
For His mercy endures forever. -Psalm 136:1
Dear Board Members,

What a beautiful time to live in Florida ... at least that's my perspective from the end of Boys Ranch Road! It has been a really nice week of weather and the staff and boys have been taking advantage of the good weather by getting the grass cut and outside chores caught up. The horses have been in the pasture enjoying the grass and cooler temperatures. And the nightly sight and sound of boys playing football under the streetlights brings a smile to my face and lifts my spirits.

Thanksgiving is in the air as well. We had a chapel service Sunday night where we were reminded of "Forgiveness before Thanksgiving" from The Parable of the Unforgiving Servant in Matthew 18. Then last night we were treated to a huge Thanksgiving feast of turkey, dressing, and all the trimmings prepared by Mark, Barbara, and our kitchen staff. 58 people squeezed around one big table and we ate then shared what we were thankful for from A-Z! (See attached picture)

The boys have a half day of school today, then many of them will be picked up by family to spend Thanksgiving at their homes. Some of the boys will be staying here (this is home) and the staff will be enjoying activities and time with them. Then they will return, and we will be in full Christmas season with planned parties and dinners with groups like Jaycees, Kiwanis, Horsemen's Club, Seminole Electric, and various church groups. We even have the blessing from Firehouse

Breaking Bread and Giving Thanks at Rodeheaver Boys Ranch – November 2019

Subs again this year for a trip to Universal Studios in Orlando on December 14th! The staff and boys are looking forward to this special trip before Christmas break.

As I have gotten time, I have begun reading through each boy's file and am more thankful than ever that RBR exists! This Ranch is needed! We are making a difference! I know we can impact even more lives. We have got to do a better job of getting the word out. Scot Collins had the opportunity to speak this past week to a large group of child social workers in Jacksonville who represented agencies in our area. Out of 40 in the room, only 2 had ever heard of Rodeheaver Boys' Ranch. We can do better. We need you all to help us spread the word. We will continue to get our cottages remodeled, our staff trained, and our program ready for increasing numbers in 2020. Pray for us in this.

I'll be speaking today at the Rotary Club of Palatka. I'm enjoying getting out in the community and sharing how God is blessing our Ranch. I've been visiting supporting churches and meeting lots of people who support the Ranch. Last month, our auto auction was a huge success. We are low on units right now, so please pray and help us get more here before our next auction on December 9th. Also, Krista Purcell, with the Rodeheaver Foundation has been a huge help picking up some of Jeff's responsibilities as he is retiring. She also helped us secure a $10,000 grant for kitchen upgrades. We are thankful for this because, as you know, the dining hall is a big part of our Ranch!

Serving Christ,
Brad Hall
Executive Director

As Brad Hall so eloquently gave praise to God and those who were helping in his new ministry at the Ranch, he was also unapologetically letting board members and staff know both his concerns and his triumphs. A powerful man of God and yet a man with a servant's heart, Brad Hall consistently gave an accurate "weather report" on the physical, emotional and spiritual climate at the Ranch. Ken Johnson had shepherded the Ranch through lean times and triumphant times, and now Brad was making the changes necessary, introducing new ideas and reaching out humbly and hopefully through his Ranch Record to all of the Ranch family (past and present) for strong support going forward.

Ranch Record – 12/5/2019

"It's not hard to make decisions when you know what your values are." - Roy E. Disney

   This week has been an eventful one at RBR. We came back from Thanksgiving break and jumped right back into school, school activities, and ranch life. Several of the staff and boys have been busy decorating for Christmas around their cottages and some of the Ranch buildings. Mark and Barbara have been busy repainting the dining hall and putting in some new decor that has brought a fresh look to our central gathering place. Meals have been great. Fellowship has been strong. Morale is good.

   While the nights have been chilly, the days have been nice. We have continued to work on the grounds and have kept busy with repairs to the cottages. Our staff meeting Wednesday was focused on "values" and we talked a lot about the values of the Ranch listed in our handbook along with ways to be accountable to one another. This is important right now as I am learning the gifts and abilities of the staff. It was also necessary because we had a secretary and a relief cottage couple released in the past week. These employees were still in their introductory period and had personal issues that caused these departures. While we pray for them, we know, like Roy E. Disney, that our mission and values drive our decisions.

   I am getting ready to head into the dining hall for the Kiwanis Club of Palatka's Christmas dinner with the boys. The Jacksonville Jaycee's will be here Saturday morning for more holiday fun. We are grateful for the support of our community. Thank you all for all your support in this Christmas season. I have learned that one big way that Bro. Ken has always rewarded the staff and their families for all of their work through the year is with the annual Christmas party. This will be on December 20th this year. I could use your help with providing a nice evening and special gifts for the staff. If you would like to give toward the Christmas party or make your own individual Christmas gift to the staff, please contact the office and let me know. Some of you have already given - so thank you.

   Until next week...

Grace and Peace,
Brad Hall
Executive Director

PS: Don't forget to mark your calendars for our next Board of Director's Monthly Meeting on Monday, December 16th at 6:00 PM.

Ranch Record – 12/13/2019

What a blessed week we have had. Here are some Highlights:

- *Last Saturday, the Jacksonville Jaycees came and shared a fun day of outdoor games, lunch, and gifts with us.*
- *Sunday was a great day of worship with Christmas programs and messages preparing us for the true meaning of Christmas.*
- *Monday was our auto auction. It was a good day and we shared a great lunch and a small gift with our dealers in appreciation for their part in supporting our work.*
- *Tuesday was a "normal" day. Of course, that means lots of activities and lots of help with homework after dinner. *It was also a good day for my family as we closed the sale of our home in Palatka. Praise the Lord!*
- *Wednesday, we had staff meeting and talked about several important issues. We also met with the Foundation and volunteers on the upcoming 2020 Benefit Fishing Tournament. This will be held on Saturday, March 14th.*
- *Thursday evening was the Seminole Electric Christmas party for our Ranch at their facility off West River Rd. It was a great time. Good pizza, cake, ice cream, them a special visit from Santa, who shared a gift with each boy.*
- *Today has been filled with preparations for a trip to Universal Studios in Orlando tomorrow. Once again this year, we have been gifted free tickets from Firehouse Subs Corporation complete with a free dinner at Firehouse Subs on our way home tomorrow. We are taking a group of about 45 tomorrow and looking forward to a great day. This is a special Christmas treat for all of the boys.*

We also continued to interview boys this week. We have interviewed a total of 6 boys in the past month and we have 4 boys ready to start our program in January. This will increase our number to 22 boys in program. I will be sharing with you at our next meeting our plan to open the other 2 cottages in 2020 and continue to increase the number of boys we serve. I would like to express special thanks to Scot Collins for all of his work in this area.

I hope you all can be with us for dinner Monday, December 16th at 6:00 pm. We are looking forward to a good meal and having you here to spend some time with our boys and staff. Dinner will be followed by our Board of Directors meeting. There are several very important matters that will be brought up and discussed. I hope you can make it.

Also, one last thing. We got our final report from FACCCA and are in full compliance and a registration has been issued. I will continue to work with Serena and our other staff to update our Ranch Binder to the new FACCCA

minimum standards. Also, we will continue to work to improve our facilities and keep them safe and within standards.
Grace & Peace,
Brad Hall
Executive Director

A Happy Ranch Family at Universal Studios– Dec. 14, 2019

Two Ranch Christmas parties were held in 2019 – one on the 16th and one on the 20th. Here are a few photos from both parties:

Hunter Rabb

Christian Brannen

Davian Bonet
Boy of The Week

Dalton Price

Gabriel Marsee
Santa's Little Elf!

The Rosamond Family

Scot & Terrie Collins

Joyce & Jerry Flannery

In his first few Ranch Records, Brad Hall honestly shared his observation that life at the Ranch always has its challenges and rewards, and God is in control. The 2019 Christmas Card described what was in Brad's heart as he and the staff, the board and the volunteers forged ahead to train boys in the way they should go.

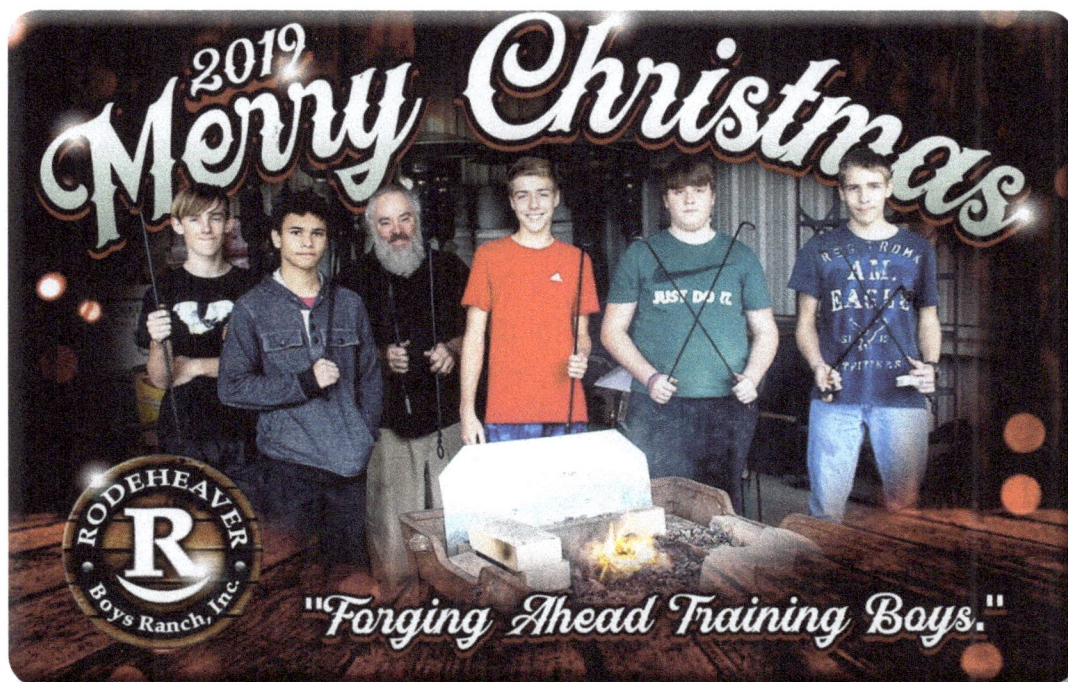

Zack Marsee, Seth Kersey-DiPaula, Blacksmith Michael Delnero, Max Logue, Christopher Mathews and Charlie Logue

Blacksmith Mike Delnero, shown with the boys on the 2019 Christmas Card, has been coming out to the Ranch for the last few years sharing his skills as a blacksmith, musician and woodworker with the boys. Mike and his wife, Mary, were devoted foster parents to more than 30 children until recent years, most of whom they remain in close

Proudly displaying blacksmith items made for sale at the Bluegrass Festival

contact with. They knew that God had prepared them, leading them to the Boys Ranch to continue their ministry. Their love of Bluegrass Music initially brought them to Rodeheaver Boys Ranch and it was their love of God and boys that kept bringing them back. Since they first came to the Ranch, the Delneros have ministered to the boys through playing worship music - teaching guitar, blacksmithing and, most recently, woodworking, all with the wholehearted blessing and support of their church, Coastal Bible Fellowship in Palm Coast. The ministry of the Delneros and their friends from Coastal Bible Fellowship, Scott and Judy Adie, was destined to expand immensely as the year 2020 progressed.

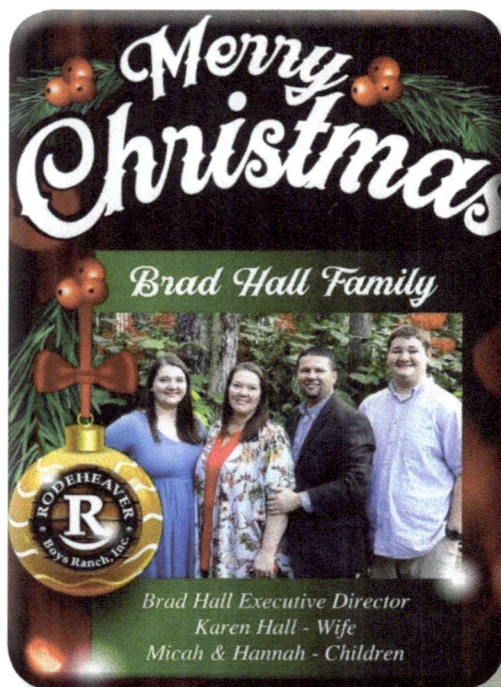

Merry *Christmas*

Brad Hall Family

Brad Hall Executive Director
Karen Hall - Wife
Micah & Hannah - Children

In a Facebook post on January 1, 2020, Brad humbly wrote, "Starting a new year for the first time in 20 years as something other than a church pastor. 2020 is going to be a big year at Rodeheaver Boys Ranch. Although I don't understand why God chose us for this task, I'm grateful to be here. Our self-absorbed gender-confused society needs a ministry that builds boys in the pattern of Christian men. I'm praying the Lord continues to sustain us."

The 70th anniversary year of 2020 was here. Change was in the air. In addition to the important transition in leadership from Ken Johnson to Brad Hall, there were more than the ordinary number of staff changes necessary, fewer than the usual number of boys (despite the obvious societal need for loving foster care), and some rudimentary and challenging changes in the rules governing FACCCA (Florida Association of Christian Child Care Agencies). Sadly, the year 2020 also brought an overwhelming sense of confusion and malaise across the globe regarding the basic Christian principles and values on which Homer Rodeheaver had founded the Ranch 70 years ago. Into this morass stepped Brad Hall, the new Executive Director of Rodeheaver Boys Ranch, armed with his strong faith in God, a loving and supportive family, and the knowledge that he had been chosen at this time and in this place to do God's work.

On January 10, 2020, Executive Director Brad Hall sent out his first Ranch Record of the new year. His reference to Mark Twain's famous quote was timely, as the transition of leadership and the ongoing repairs needed at the Ranch were challenges that, at times, seemed insurmountable, but were doable. It was a matter of prayer and positive attitude, both of which Brad employed in abundance, as evidenced by the upbeat tone of his communication.

Ranch Record - 1/10/20
"The reports of my death are greatly exaggerated." - Samuel Clemens "Mark Twain"

In 1897, Mark Twain scheduled a speaking tour in London to raise money to pay off some of his debt. While in London, Twain got sick and a rumor circulated that he was seriously ill with one American newspaper printing his obituary. When a reporter saw him and asked him about the confusion, Twain responded, "The reports of my death are greatly exaggerated."

This week, I would say the same thing about Rodeheaver Boys' Ranch. After a year of transition and some turmoil, 2020 is starting on a different note. Four new boys have arrived and started school this week. This brings our number in the program up to 22 (plus 15 staff children). We have another interview today with a prospective boy and several applications being considered. We have interviewed a married couple for a cottage parent position (to replace the ones who left the end of November) and we have also interviewed and are offering a position to a young woman to work in our administrative office assisting in development and family connections (you will receive more information at our next board meeting).

Today, I will be meeting with Riverside Builders to begin the remodel of Rodeheaver Cottage, which is going to be needed sooner than later with the rise in our boy numbers. We will be continuing maintenance projects on Westbury and Phillips Cottages as well to get them up to standards. Another exciting project is the beginning of the pool project approved at our last board meeting. A generous donor has made it possible for us to design and build an enclosure that will make the pool usable year round! In addition, another grant was received for ball field improvements and I have discussed with Mr. Bobby Cothren that the basketball court playing surface could really use a coating or resurfacing. The boys love to play basketball in the evenings.

With all of these things going on and improvements being made by our staff on the barn and in the pavilion area (in preparation for the bluegrass festival), one boy said this week, "Wow, things are really happening around here!"

Please keep in mind some upcoming dates. January 20th will be our monthly board meeting at the Ranch. It begins with dinner at 6:00 PM with a board meeting to follow. February 8th will be the 5th Annual Rodeheaver Boys' Ranch Clay Target Shoot fundraising event at the Palatka Skeet Club. February 13-15 is the Spring Bluegrass Festival hosted by Rodeheaver Boys' Ranch. Also, the bass fishing season is upon us and our Rodeheaver Boys' Ranch fishing tournament on the St. Johns River is scheduled for Saturday, March 14th on the Riverfront in Palatka. This will be followed by Spring Break then the Putnam County Fair. The 4-H pigs the boys will be showing at the fair are doing great and growing fast! The boys are having a lot of fun working them and seeing them grow.

I want to thank you all for your continued support, prayers, and involvement in our ministry. We continue to build boys in the pattern of Christian men in the legacy of those who dreamed and built this Ranch. You are a part of the story as we begin 2020 and celebrate 70 years of Rodeheaver Boys' Ranch on the banks of the St. Johns River in Putnam County. And if anyone asks, the reports of our death were greatly exaggerated!
Brad Hall
Executive Director

In Brad's January 17 Ranch Record, he announced the hiring of Zach and LeeAnn Bonds as new Cottage Parents and of Hannah Silcox as Development Assistant in the office, these newest staff members being an answer to prayer. He shared a photograph of the boys working with the pigs in preparation for the Putnam County Fair.

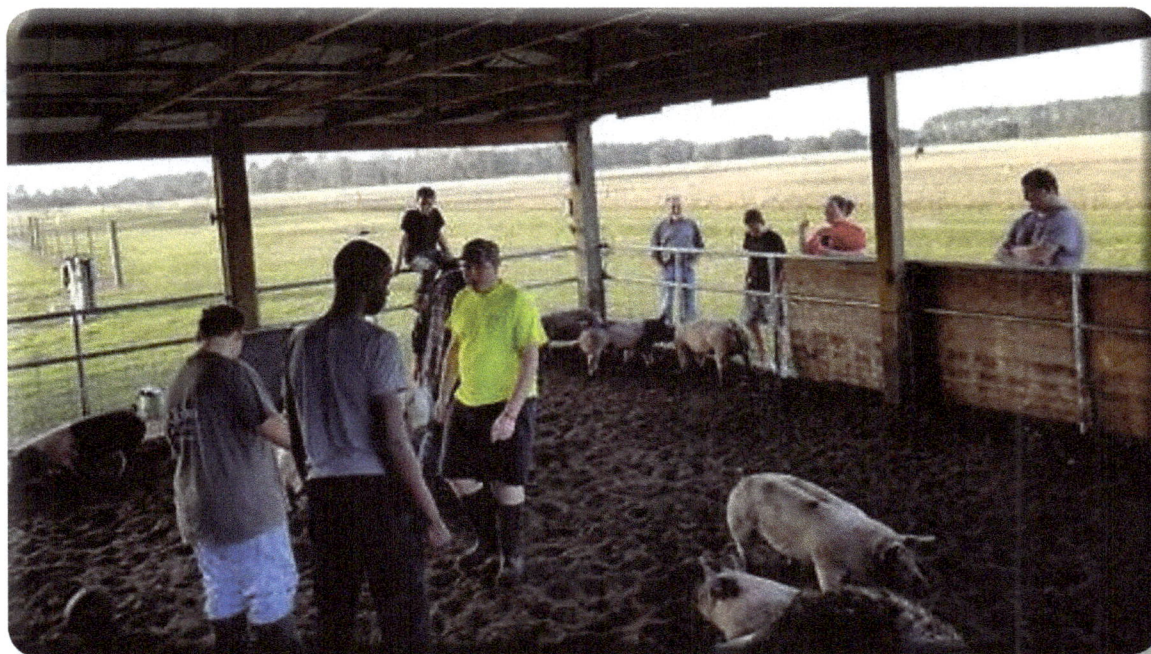

Ranch Boys tending their pigs

Rodeheaver Boys Ranch Skeet Shooting Team - 5th Annual Skeet Shooting Fundraiser - 2/8/20

On February 13 through 15, the Spring Bluegrass Festival went on without a hitch. Norm and Judy Adams were there to work with Ernie and Debi Evans for a smooth transition ... it was definitely a time of transitions! Carlton Spence, the original catalyst, with his brother-in-law Donald "Duck" Harper behind him all the way, was on hand to smooth the transition, posing with his old friends, the Adams, and his new friend, Ernie Evans.

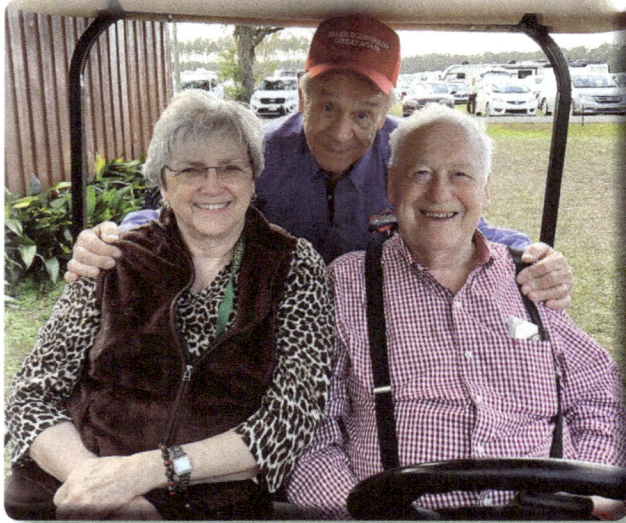

**Carlton Spence with
Judy and Norman Adams
February 2020**

**Carlton Spence and Ernie Evans
Bluegrass Festival - February 2020**

Again, Brad Hall went out of his way to delegate the tour of the Ranch to one of the boys who had been there for a while and knew it like the back of his hand. Brandon Mathews, the brother of Christopher Mathews, did the honors this time of taking another first-time visitor around the Ranch. Pat MacKenzie had heard about Rodeheaver Boys Ranch for years, but had never had the

Visitor Pat MacKenzie, Ranch Boy Brandon Mathews, and Pigs

opportunity to visit. Brandon gave her an "insiders" view of several areas, her favorite being a visit to the Pig area, where the boys' pigs receive royal treatment right up until time to go to the Putnam County Fair.

A visit to the Chapel, of course, is a given when being taken on a tour of the Ranch. When Pat and Brandon got to the Chapel, who should they run into but the new Administrative Assistant at Rodeheaver Boys Ranch, Hannah Silcox, and her husband, Bubba Silcox (a teacher at Palatka High School who, coincidentally, has had Brandon in his class!)

Hannah and Bubba Silcox

New friends to the Ranch and old friends, board members and boys, all gathering at the Bluegrass Festival and having a wonderful time. For Ken Johnson and Steve Watkins, it was reminiscent of days gone by when both of them were working instead of watching, but today, on February 15, 2020, the two were totally enjoying retirement. Also enjoying retirement were Norman and Judy Adams, posing in front of the Ranch Museum with longtime Board Member Larry Soncrant.

Norm Adams, Board Member
Larry Soncrant, and Judy Adams

Ernie and Debi Evans did a great job in publicizing the Bluegrass Festival – both before and after the event. Excerpts of their report on the Festival follow:

Palatka Bluegrass Festival – Spring 2020

Posted on February 17, 2020 by Bill Warren

Carl Jackson, Larry Cordle, and Jerry Salley at the 2020 Palatka Bluegrass Festival
photo © Bill Warren

Ernie and Debi Evans are now the promoters of the Spring Palatka Bluegrass Festival held at the Rodeheaver Boys Ranch in Palatka, Florida. Norman and Judy Adams have retired, but are mentoring Ernie and Debi through this year.

MC Sherry Boyd opened the show with an open mic session Thursday.

Carl Jackson, Larry Cordle, and Jerry Salley then brought their great show to the Palatka stage. They not only sing many of the wonderful songs they have written, but also provide the backstories of the songs. These stories make the songs even more meaningful.

The Little Roy and Lizzy show blasted onto the stage as they always do. Andy Stinnett is the new guitar player for the show. Roy still has more energy than most young men.

The Lonesome River Band put on a top flight show. Barry Reed had the tin roof of the pavilion rattling with his bass! There are few adjectives left to describe the excellence of LRB.

Norman and Judy Adams were honored by the staff of the Ranch with a commemorative brick in front of the Ranch Cafeteria and a

handmade lap quilt. Ernie Evans thanked everyone for their support and thanked Norman and Judy for their mentorship.

Rhonda Vincent closed out the festival in her wonderful way. She introduced a young man from Oklahoma, Vernon Lee Johnson, who had gone on a country cruise that she was on. He sang a couple vintage country numbers with her and did a super job. Rhonda spent all of the supper break greeting fans, signing autographs, and posing for pictures. She is very generous with her time!

Judy Adie & Mary Delnero running the Blacksmith Booth at the Bluegrass Festival

President Don Holmes & Grandsons

Don Holmes, Rodeheaver's longest serving President of the Board, was there on February 15th with his family, standing up close to the stage and enjoying the great talent of the musical lineup.

The Bluegrass Festival was over. It was time to get back in the Spring swing of things. Brad's Ranch Record of February 21 had "considerable" meaning behind it:

Ranch Record - 2/21/20
"The most decisive actions of our lives - I mean those that are most likely to decide the whole course of our future - are, more often than not, unconsidered."
- Andre Gide
 Well, I am going to start this ranch record off a little differently than I had intended. My schedule changed this morning when I got a call from a cottage parent who was responsible for one of our younger boys. He is suspended from school and giving our cottage parents a hard time. I brought him in and talked to him about his future here. I didn't know what I was going to say. The boy wouldn't talk. He just stared at the floor. Then I picked up a children's book on my counseling shelf that I hadn't thought about in a long time about a boy who was always in trouble and how he started making better decisions. I read it to him. He softened up and started to talk. I prayed with him. Then he smiled. We talked about consequences for his actions and changes we would be making to try one more time to get him on the right track. I don't know if my words and actions will be the turning point in this boy's life. Maybe it will be a cottage parent, a director, or a teacher who will finally get through to him how much we love and value him. All I know is these unplanned, unscheduled moments at Rodeheaver Boys' Ranch are what really decide the course of our future. While

all the planned meetings, engagements, and events are important, the most decisive actions are unconsidered.

Let me change gears here and share some updates with you all. I just received the final report from our Benefit Skeet Shoot that was held on February 8th. We made $10,459.78 on this one-day event. Thank you to Greg Bacon who helped organize this and to all who helped spread the word, signed up teams, cooked, showed up, and gave so generously. We are already making plans for next year and look forward to this event.

The 16th Annual Palatka Bluegrass Festival was held this past weekend (that's why you didn't get a Ranch Record last week!). It was a good event with thousands of fans and thousands of dollars raised. I will be sending you the final numbers when we finalize them, but from the early reports, we will at least match what we did last February. Once again, thank you all for the support. It was good to see many of you at this year's festival and I hope you will be making plans to join us in November.

I also want to invite you to join us on Sunday, March 1st at 6:00 pm for a special chapel service under the pavilion. Chosen Road, a young Gospel Bluegrass group from West Virginia, will be here leading us in "Appalachian Worship" and Pastor Shaun Thomas from Southside Baptist Church in Palatka will be sharing a message. I've invited our supporting churches and community to join us that night as well.

Please keep us in your thoughts and prayers as we continue to make improvements at RBR. A group from First Baptist Palatka came out and helped this week with some demo work in Rodeheaver Cottage and Riverside builders is working on the new kitchen. Phillips Cottage is getting some needed TLC as well. These are 2 of our oldest houses (at least 60 years old) and they are going to continue to need some updates as we go. We will begin some general updates in our office areas soon as well. 2020 is going to be a pivotal year as we build on the foundation at RBR and look ahead.

All things considered (and unconsidered) it has been a good week.

Brad Hall
Executive Director

A couple of days after Brad wrote the above Ranch Record, he received a letter in the mail from Wally and Teresa Summers, members of his former congregation at First Baptist Church of Palatka, filled with praise about some Ranch boys who went above and beyond to help. Having volunteered to work the concession stand during the Bluegrass Festival, Wally and Teresa already had their hearts softened toward the Ranch, but it was the boys who cemented their dedication to helping the Ranch go forward. Excerpts from the letter, signed by Teresa Summers at dated February 21, 2020, follow:

"I couldn't let another week go by without commending three boys Wally and I worked with last week during the Bluegrass Festival at the concession stand. These boys were always ready to help. They made hot chocolate in large pots and delivered them so we could sell without running out. They also warmed up large pots of soup several times in the dark delivering it with ease. (Those pots were full, heavy and HOT!) William, Dalton and Brandon even sat with us while Wally and I were taking a break and talked to us about school, their future plans and life at the ranch. These boys epitomize what I'm sure you want to convey to outsiders about the ranch. William & Dalton helped Brandon cook burgers and wrap and sell all the food. They even delivered sandwiches and coffee when a customer couldn't carry all their purchases. One man's hands were shaking so much he couldn't carry his coffee. William ran after him with a fresh cup. Although he was unable to find the man, he jumped at the challenge.

"Every night the boys hugged us goodbye and said they looked forward to seeing us again the next day. I have to say that I have tears in my eyes now just thinking about the love these boys have.

"I was sad when you left FBC, but I understand now the calling you have working and managing the ranch. Blessings to you and your family and blessings to these boys!"

Ranch Record - 2/28/20 (excerpted)

"It may be hard on some fathers not to have a son, but it is much harder on a boy not to have a father." S.D. Gilbert

The absence of fathers may be the greatest need and flaw in American society today. Much of what we do at RBR is to become surrogate fathers who fill this gaping hole in a boy's life. Mentoring and equipping sons to become men who will assume leadership for the next generation is imperative to maintaining the very fabric of our society. Please think of us and pray for us as we try to provide the best example and blessings we can to these boys.

Around the Ranch this week, we have continued work on Rodeheaver and Phillips Cottages. Even in the midst of the work, we have gone ahead and reopened Phillips Cottage. Zack and Lee Ann Bonds are cottage parents there and have started with 2 boys. We will be adding new boys during the next month. Also, on Wednesday we had Daryl Hickman with KidsFlyCubs.org to speak to our staff. I'm excited about our partnership with this organization. He will be providing free flight training here at the ranch as a reward activity for some of our boys. Daryl plans to bring his Cub training plane here for our Annual Meeting on April 26th so you can all see it and talk to him.

I got to share at San Mateo Presbyterian Church about the ministry of RBR. Special thanks to Dr. Robert Mills and the congregation for their hospitality during my visit. I was also able to share on HOPE FM and with various groups about our work this week. I am so thankful for the generosity I see and how God continues to provide for this ministry.

Brad Hall
Executive Director

On March 1, 2020, as the sun set over Rodeheaver Boys Ranch, the gospel group, Chosen Road, performed under the Pavilion for the boys and several folks who had come out to join in their music ministry. Among those enjoying the evening were Phillips Cottage Parents Zach and LeeAnn Bonds, who had come to the Ranch on January 7, 2020. Parents of three and grandparents of five, the Bondses came to the Ranch

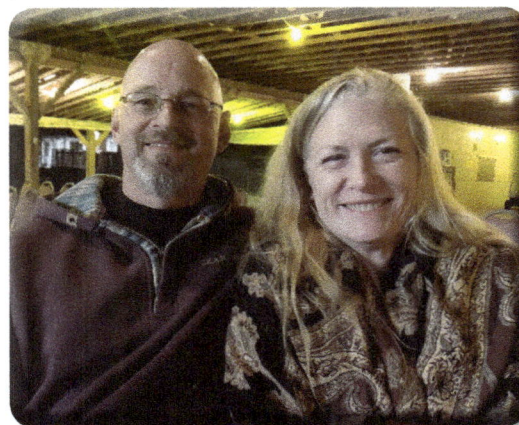

Zach and LeeAnn Bonds
Phillips Cottage Parents

on what LeeAnn calls a "long and circuitous journey, full of blessings and adventures." From life in the military to life "off the grid" (no electricity) and homeschooling their children in Idaho to life as missionaries on the tiny island of Saipan, where they shared Jesus and helped in recovery efforts after Super-typhoon Yutu in 2018, LeeAnn and Zach traveled 8,000 miles to Rodeheaver Boys Ranch. Their life experiences and their deep faith in God have more than prepared them for the blessings of building boys in challenging times.

Ranch Boys and Chosen Road – March 1, 2020 – Awesome evening of worship!

Ken Johnson and Brad Hall enjoyed the powerful worship music of Chosen Road with Board Member Greg Bacon and his wife, Debbie.

Ken, Greg and Brad

Debbie and Greg Bacon

In Brad's March 6th Ranch Record, he wrote about the busy month ahead, which included the filming of a promotional video sponsored by the Rodeheaver Foundation and arranged by Foundation Development Director Krista Purcell, the upcoming Professional Bass Tournament to benefit Rodeheaver Boys Ranch on the 14th of March and the Putnam County Fair coming up March 20 through 28th (time for the boys to show off their swine!)

Brandon Mathews holds a big bass, with Gavin DeRouen by his side, Micah Hall in the background, and Former Ranch Boy Robert Siemiatkoski volunteering (as always)

The 5th Annual Rodeheaver Boys Ranch Benefit Bass Tournament happened on a beautiful sunny Saturday, March 14th on the St. Johns River at Palatka's City Dock with 167 teams fishing in support of the Ranch. There to cheer on the anglers were several of the Ranch boys as well as cottage parents and board members, including Brad Hall, the new Executive Director of the Ranch and Ken Johnson, the Ranch's recently retired Executive Director. Austin Black of San Mateo and

Kyle Setree (holding a bag of fish)

Wyatt Kinney of Bunnell won the event's top prize of $7,500 with a 5-fish limit – official total weight of 23.78 pounds. The tournament raised around $29,000 for the Boys Ranch and a great time was had by all.

Within six days of the successful March 14, 2020 fishing tournament, the world as we know it had changed dramatically due to the rapid spread of the Novel Coronavirus – Covid-19, which began in Wuhan, China in December of 2019. The evolution of this pandemic was frightening. A global pandemic had been declared in February and by February 29, 2020, the first Covid-19 death in the United States was reported in the State of Washington. Travel restrictions to and from foreign countries were halted and cruise ships were quarantined at sea due to breakouts of the coronavirus. Suddenly, in March of 2020, hospitals across the country and around the globe began to be jammed with patients and the medical community became the heroic first-responders against an encroaching enemy of illness. Even when, on March 13, 2020, the President declared a state of national emergency and the CDC (Centers for Disease Control) warned against holding gatherings of more than 50 people, our Rodeheaver Boys Ranch Benefit Bass Fishing Tournament was held and enjoyed by all. Daily, after March 14th, conferences, festivals, parades, concerts, sporting events and even weddings and funerals were postponed or canceled altogether. New phrases such as "social distancing" and "sheltering in place" and "masking" and "bumping elbows instead of shaking hands" and "virtual classrooms" became the norm. By March 17, 2020, the Coronavirus was present in all 50 states and more cases were being diagnosed daily. Countries around the world reported virus-related deaths and on March 19th, Italy's death-toll of 4,000 people topped that of China, with New York City becoming the epicenter of the deadly Coronavirus in the United States. The President and major health experts began appearing daily on television to keep the nation informed of progress in addressing the health crisis.

Brad Hall's March 20th Ranch Record reflects the immense challenges suddenly facing him in his new role as Executive Director of Rodeheaver Boys Ranch.

Ranch Record - 3/20/20

These are indeed trying times. The present COVID-19 crisis is impacting us on a global scale. As we are all reacting to daily news, Rodeheaver Boys' Ranch is taking necessary precautions. While daily work here carries on without interruption, our staff has become more careful in the areas of cleaning, hygiene, and teaching boys the meaning of "social distancing." We are monitoring the school situation and preparing our learning center for online classes. Our main concern is the limited and slow internet capabilities here on the Ranch. We are hoping it is sufficient for online learning.

This present situation has caused us to reschedule our upcoming Benefit Golf Tournament from April 4th until May 23rd. Also, our Annual Meeting and BBQ scheduled for Sunday, April 26th, is being postponed. We will monitor the current crisis and decide later about when we might reschedule the BBQ at the Ranch. I would love for us to celebrate our 70th year together!

The Board of Directors will continue to communicate by email and other methods in the continued work of RBR. One thing I need to communicate with you all is that we will be limiting visitors at RBR until the state of emergency in Putnam County is lifted. If you would like to come out, please call first so we can maintain a safe campus for our boys. Tours for guests will not be offered at this time.

I want to take a moment to say thank you to Don Holmes and Greg Bacon for their leadership in this time as we deal with changing schedules and programs. I also could not lead in this time without the great staff at RBR. Our directors and office staff have all been working overtime this past week to keep everything running smoothly. Cottage parents and workers have been busy with ranch work and remodeling projects. I also know that Susan Brandenburg is working hard to put together the finishing touches on the next edition of our historical book.

Let's all pray for this virus to subside and the Lord to be merciful to us in this time.

Brad Hall
Executive Director

On March 24th, Japan postponed the 2020 Summer Olympics original slated to be held in Tokyo, Japan until the summer of 2021, and India announced a 21-day stay-at-home lockdown on all 1.3 billion citizens.

As of March 26, 2020, the United States led the world in Covid-19 cases, with 82,000 cases and more than 1,000 deaths. The President signed a $2 trillion Coronavirus relief bill into law on March 27th, guaranteeing loans to small businesses and providing aid to overcrowded hospitals on the frontlines of the crisis. This was the same day that UK Prime Minister Boris Johnson tested positive for COVID-19.

In his March 27th Ranch Record, Brad calmly and steadfastly reassured all readers that God was still in control.

Ranch Record - 3/27/20
"Relying on God has to begin all over again every day as if nothing had yet been done." - C.S. Lewis

Today is another day. As the world continues to move ahead slowly due to a threatening virus called COVID-19, things here at Rodeheaver Boys Ranch continue on without much change. While we don't have a county fair to attend this week, we still have finished our pig books, turned them in, and taken all the hogs to Braddocks in Seville for processing. I want to say thank you to some very generous board members who responded to my appeal last week and covered the cost of the swine for this year. This not only helped our boys but also other kids in our community by allowing the bids on the online auction to support their swine and cattle projects.

We are also working hard to get things ready for online classes starting next week through the Putnam County School District. We will be using our Learning Lab next to the chapel and scheduling the boys for computer time to complete assignments. I believe this will be a good time for the boys to receive one-on-one instruction from our Ranch Tutor and cottage parents. As long as our internet works, we will be able to make this work. We have also planned vocational, spiritual, and recreational activities every day to go along with the educational time.

Please keep in mind that we are still full steam ahead on our mission of building boys. We have a couple of boys who will be transitioning home over the next few months and we will be bringing in new boys. I want everyone to know that the Ranch is fully functioning. Horses are being ridden. Fences are being mended. The grass is greening up. The lawn mowers are tuned up. Car donations are arriving daily. The fish are biting. The swimming pool is open. The pontoon is in the water. The computer lab is ready. The freezer and pantry are full of good food. The staff are working. We are blessed and grateful.

... but we take nothing for granted. We are relying on God today as if nothing had yet been done.
Brad Hall
Executive Director
    PS: I want to share one more piece of good news: One of our boys entrusted his life to Christ a few weeks ago and was baptized at Trinity Baptist Church last Sunday in an outdoor service. We have seen such a change in his life. He is an example of the difference this program makes through a sane practical application of Christian principles. Glory to God.

In addition to his appeal to cover the cost of the boys' pigs that didn't get to go to the fair, Brad was busy at work reaching out to appeal for practical help from Michael Delnero, the blacksmith/woodworker/guitar player who had come out regularly to work with the boys until Covid-19 shut the Ranch down to outside visitors.

Brad told Mike that nobody was coming out to the Ranch and nobody at the Ranch had any symptoms of the Coronavirus. He went on to say that the boys would normally be in school but now they had more time on their hands and they needed some productive things to do. He asked, "Would you and some of your friends from the church be willing to come out and work with the boys on blacksmithing, woodworking and music?" Knowing that there were risks involved, Brad asked Mike to pray about coming and then make a decision. They did pray about Brad's request and decided to come. In the previous year before Covid-19 and during the past couple of Bluegrass Festivals, Delnero, his wife Mary, and friends from church, Scott and Judy Adie, had volunteered, working with some of the Ranch boys to teach them blacksmithing as well as guitar playing, all with the blessing and financial support of his church in Palm Coast, Coastal Bible Fellowship. Another friend from church, Alan Frieburg, played in a band called "Old Guys Rule;" he had come out to teach the boys how to play bass. Some of the blacksmithing items made by the boys had sold for a profit at the last Bluegrass festival in February, 2020.

After prayer and discussing Brad's request with his wife, Mary, who has

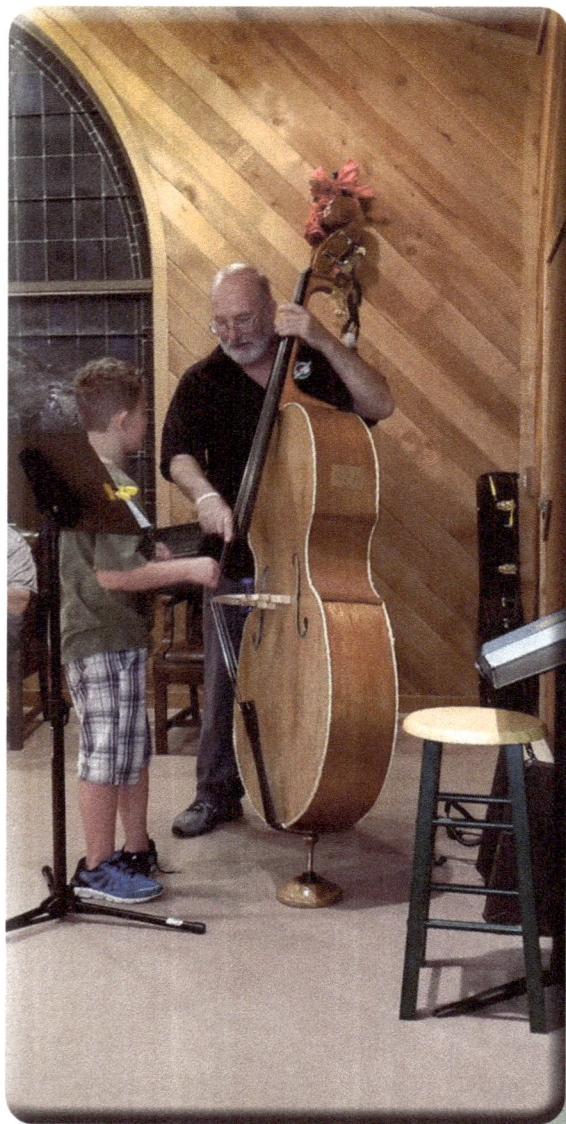
Al Frieburg teaching Bass

diabetes and might be at risk, Mike decided to go to the Ranch. That was in mid-March and it wasn't long before he and Mary and other friends from their church were coming out regularly to work with the boys. Although he had taught them blacksmithing in the past, Mike is a professional woodworker and loves praise music as well. Al Frieburg came back to the Ranch, too, and worked with the boys not only in music, but in woodworking. Al considers it an answer to prayer, as he had always dreamed of being a shop teacher someday, but it hadn't worked out ... until now.

As one million people around the world became victims of the Coronavirus, with no sign of the spread of it slowing down, the Boys Ranch began to adjust to each new challenge and Brad Hall maintained his thoughtful and decisive role as leader of the Ranch, bringing in God's helpers and trusting in Him to do the rest.

Ranch Record - 4/3/20
"It's not the tragedies that kill us, it's the messes." - Dorothy Parker
    Mentoring through a time of national crisis is not easy, but it is critically important. As we adjust to a "socially distanced" lifestyle at Rodeheaver Boys' Ranch, I remind people daily that we are used to it. After all, we are socially distanced geographically. If we didn't have media like TV and phones, most of our children wouldn't even realize there is anything going on related to a worldwide pandemic. I often note as I travel to town to run errands and get supplies how stressed everyone is, then I drive back down Boys Ranch Road and

it's like I'm transported to a place of safety and peace. That feeling doesn't last long for me because I'm the one who has to think big picture and deal with harsh realities. Yet, I want our boys to feel that safety and peace throughout this time.

The program of Rodeheaver Boys Ranch was custom made by the founders for times like this. Education is continuing in our learning center through online learning with our staff working with boys on schoolwork. We have an entire block of time now for vocational instruction and chores where the boys have been instructed this week in lawn mowing, maintenance, wood shop, blacksmithing, automotive and more. We've also scheduled daily recreation including swimming, boating, canoeing, kickball, games, basketball, and even a camping trip on our own land. The boys are happier now than I've ever seen them. I know they miss their friends and teachers at school, but they seem to do better when things slow down and they don't have to run up and down the road so often.

We've taught the boys this week the Bible verse from James 1:2-3, "count it all joy when you fall into various trials, knowing that the testing of your faith produces patience." We all need to practice endurance and perseverance within the context of faith in order to grow and mature during this time. If we allow patience to finish its work, we are less likely to make messes.
Brad Hall
Executive Director

In preparation for Good Friday and Easter Sunday, Easter coming up on April 12th, Mike Delnero and his friends began teaching the boys the hymn, "The Cross Has the Final Word." That led to the idea for creating a cross in woodworking class, which ultimately led to the most meaningful Good Friday ever.

Having shown the boys a powerful video of the hymn, "The Cross Has the Final Word" sung by the Newsboys, depicting an old woodworker making a cross and placing it in the ground, Mike was inspired to do the same thing at the Rodeheaver Boys Ranch woodshop.

Mike's search for the perfect piece of wood for the cross was the next step. "I went to a salvage yard," recalls Mike. "I needed a good-sized beam of wood and most of the ones I found were rotting. Then I saw one that was different at the bottom of a pile. It was an old pressure-treated telephone pole and

I bought it for $20!" Mike and the boys spent a few days in the woodshop making the cross and then took it to the blacksmith shop to forge words into it – words like shame, pain, sorrow, sin, etc., with the main word forged into the central beam being "LOVE."

"The Cross Has the Final Word"

There's nothing stronger, nothing higher,
There's nothing greater than the name of Jesus
All the honor, all the power, all the glory
To the name of Jesus

Sorrow may come in the darkest night
but The Cross Has the Final Word

Evil may put up its strongest fight
but The Cross Has the Final Word

He traded death for eternal Life
The Cross has the Final Word

The Savior has the come with the morning light
The Cross Has the Final Word

Cutting the notch for one of the Cross members

Branding words into the Cross

Ranch Boys learning guitar from Mike and Mary Delnero and Scott Adie

At the Good Friday service in the pavilion, the boys played "The Cross Has the Final Word" just as they had practiced, and then they put down their guitars and took up the cross for a long and meaningful walk down to the river.

Ranch boys and Mary Delnero tuning up for Good Friday Service to Perform Hymn, "The Cross Has the Final Word."

Carrying the Cross to the River

Lift Up the Cross ...

The Cross has the Final Word — LOVE

Ranch Record - 4/10/20

It's been another busy week at RBR with the modified schedule for school, chores, vocation, and recreation in full swing. School assignments have been a little tougher this week but most of the boys are doing well. A few are lagging and getting frustrated, but our cottage moms and staff have hung in there with them and are keeping them caught up. Special thanks to Putnam County Schools for sending snacks and lunches.

Some excitement happened this week when the boys saw 2 pygmy rattlesnakes near the learning center. The oak leaves have fallen and with the dry conditions, it creates a perfect environment for snakes. We've since raked the leaves and got things cleaned up to prevent more snakes.

More work continued this week on Rodeheaver Cottage with counters and plumbing for the remodeled kitchen. We've also got Phillips Cottage ready to install new cabinets thanks to some donations. New flooring was also installed in a couple of rooms. We will begin painting projects and finishing touches soon. The new wooden fence around VIP was also completed by Lowman Fence Company.

We've interviewed a couple this week for a relief cottage parent position that is coming open. The Brown family will be moving back to Tennessee the first of May and it seems like we have already found a good couple to replace them. We are hopeful the timing all works out.

Activities have continued. We've had games and something outdoors almost daily. The boys went camping last weekend and we did an outdoor movie and popcorn night last night. The dining hall is back in full swing this week and

Mrs. Barbara continues to feed us excellent meals every night. We had a full Easter Dinner last night with ham, potatoes, casseroles, salad, and homemade cheesecake for dessert!

The highlight of the week was yesterday when we had a Cross service. The boys built a cross in wood shop class out of some old treated timbers. They then had our volunteer blacksmith help them burn words like sin, guilt, shame, anger, hate, and fear into the beam. Then they burned the word LOVE into the cross beam to signify what Jesus did on the Cross. The guitar class prepared songs like "Amazing Grace," "Amazing Love," and a special song "The Cross Has the Final Word." We sang and had a time of Scripture and Prayer in the big pavilion, then the boys took turns carrying the cross all the way to the river where we set it in a special place for all to see. This will be a Good Friday these boys will always remember because that Cross will be there for years to come. They built it, carried it, and set it there. One boy, Bryce, led us in a prayer of dedication to thank the LORD Jesus for all He has done for us. We plan to celebrate the Resurrection this Sunday with a Sunrise Service at the riverfront.

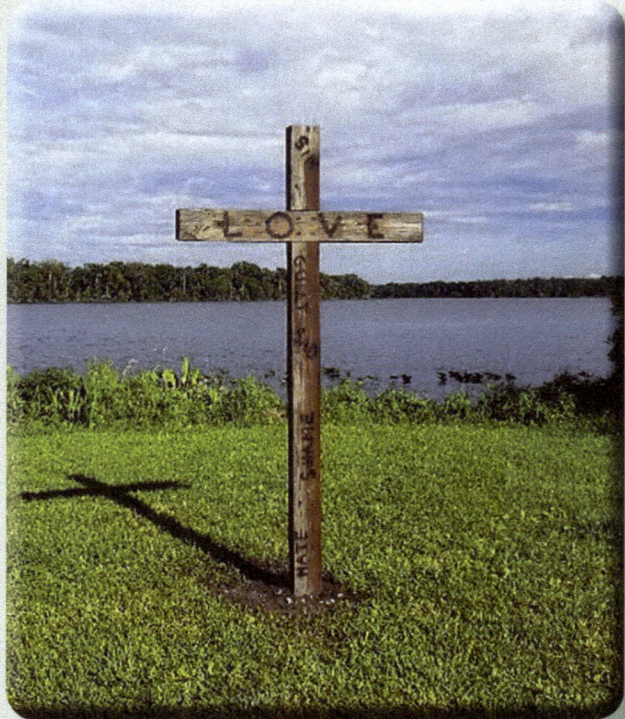

We hope you all have a blessed and happy Easter!

Brad Hall
Executive Director

As the Coronavirus continued to require sheltering in place and online schooling for all including the boys and staff at the Ranch, Brad Hall reached out to many of the Board Members, "Pardners" and former staff for suggestions about how to handle various challenges as well as support for the many repairs and replacements in both dwellings and staff. A truckload of ice cream arrived one day from Carlton Spence. A few dozen facemasks arrived one day, lovingly handsewn for the Ranch by Ken and Lois Johnson's neighbor, Linda Wagner.

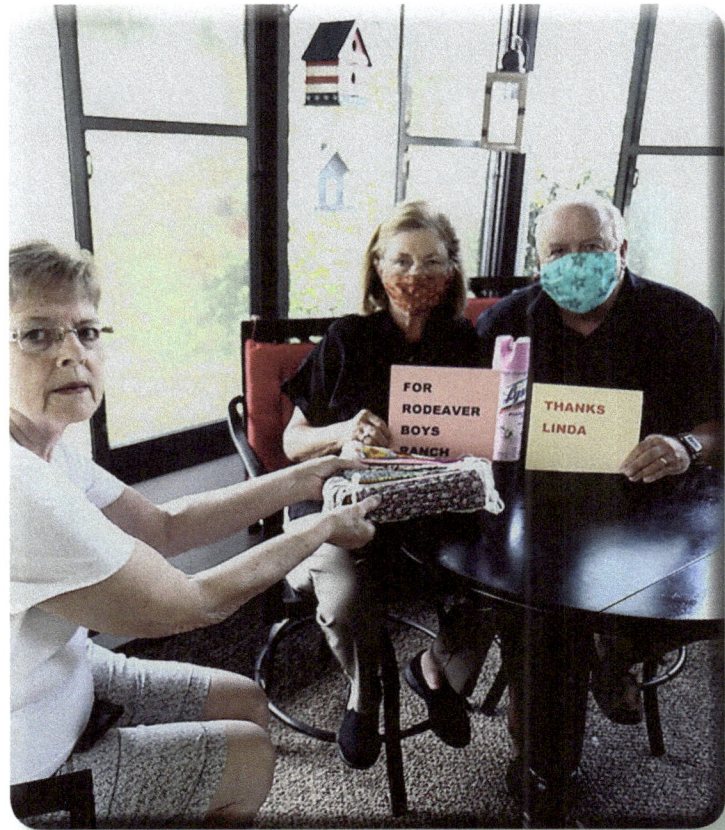

Linda, Lois and Ken – Handsewn Face Masks for Rodeheaver Boys Ranch

Ken Johnson and Jeff King visited regularly to provide support and advice as Brad Hall rose to each new challenge. Dr. Robert Mitchem continued to come out to do work on the deer feeders and Doug Webb, the "Coyote Man" continued to patrol the woods at night for varmints who were not daunted in any way by the Coronavirus. The skies continued to be blue and the grass green, and despite of the pandemic, avid golfers continued to golf at local courses. The Rodeheaver Boys Ranch golf tournament was scheduled for May 23, and Jeff King was fully committed to make it a successful tournament. But, in the meantime, the boys at the Ranch were in for a nice Spring Surprise!

Ranch Record - 5/2/20

This week we continued on-site education with the boys. Our staff is working extra to ensure that every student is staying on track. We have one boy graduating this year and we are currently helping him prepare to start at St Johns River State College in August.

This week ended with a special treat. After the morning learning center time, we treated the boys to Papa John's Pizza for lunch and introduced them to Daryl Hickman from KidsFlyCubs.org. Daryl brought his plane named "Tweety" over to the Ranch to give the boys an introduction to aviation. One of our boys even got to go up for a ride! It was a great experience on a beautiful day. We are looking forward to working with Daryl and his organization as a special vocational program for boys who have earned it.

At the Ranch and throughout the nation and the world, people were becoming more aware that this pandemic was not going to disappear right away. It was a time for reflection on our history, our relationships, our expectations, and the unexpected occurrences that change the trajectory of our lives. It was also a time to reflect on what plans God had for our future.

Brad Hall
Executive Director

Ranch Record - 5/8/20

Fifty years ago, on April 11, 1970, Jim Lovell, Fred Hayes, and Jack Swaggart strapped themselves into the cockpit of the Apollo 13 for lift-off into space. They had prepared themselves for their mission. Years of study and hours of grueling, mind-numbing simulator training prepared them, they thought, to walk on the surface of the moon. They had no idea that they would never fulfill their mission. History tells us they barely ever walked the surface of planet earth again. Yet it was their training and preparation that turned out to be the difference between life and death.

We don't know where life is going to take us. We prepare for one thing only to find ourselves facing something else altogether after lift-off. But prepare we must! The boys we care for here at Rodeheaver Boys Ranch need to prepare for life. They need to know that God has a plan - a mission - for each of them. We have to teach them that they may never make it where they envision the way they think it will go. God may have a detour planned. Prepare they must!

Three months ago, we had a plan, a calendar, and a budget. Life had a different plan. I'm thankful today that Rodeheaver Boys Ranch was prepared for such a time as this. Our mission is still building boys. Our plans and calendars have been adjusted. Faithful giving from God's people continues to sustain us. Even this week we have been blessed by several gifts and grants from supporters like you. I have also been encouraged by the continued diligent work from our staff and childcare team who get up every day and keep everything going here.

On another encouraging note, I met with Ernie and Debbie Evans from Evans Media Source, the new promoters of our Bluegrass Festivals. Despite having to cancel many of their shows, they are committed to RBR and are making preparations for November. They have contingency plans in place in case COVID-19 is still an issue. They also presented a plan for promoting and fundraising for RBR at all of their festivals. They have purchased a new Blueridge guitar to raffle along with several other ideas to benefit the Ranch. Before they left, they gave me a check for $8,000 as an additional gift from the February Bluegrass Festival.

Looking ahead, we have several things happening here that I look forward to sharing with you. Our auto auction resumes this Monday. Our Golf Tournament is coming soon. Our boys are preparing for their annual Memorial Day 5K and Pinewood Derby. Oh, and we have five new boys to interview this month who could be joining us at the Ranch this Summer.

Brad Hall
Executive Director

Ranch Record - 5/15/20

We have been blessed this week. We started the week with a good car auction that produced over $83,000 in sales. This really helps us make up for missing the April auction. Special thanks to our Vehicle Improvement Program staff, our Ranch staff, and the area dealers who made this day a good one.

We have also continued to receive donations from our annual partnership appeal. Thousands in donations have come in this week. One person sent in a $1200 "stimulus" donation that said "the government sent me this and I want to give it to a place where I know it will make an impact!" That is inspiring and a reminder of just how valuable our ministry of building boys is. Just think about the impact just one of these boys can make in our community and nation if their life is established upon good morals, biblical values, and a solid work ethic!

To say I am overjoyed with our donations this week would be an understatement. It is a testament to the faith of our present and past leadership (all the way back to our founders) that God continues to provide for the operation of this Ranch through the donations of God's people. For more than 70 years now, Rodeheaver Boys Ranch has operated by faith and without government funding or loans. I firmly believe that the Lord wants us to depend on Him completely so that He can continue to show His glory in preservation of this ministry. To know how much money and manpower it takes to run this Ranch is to recognize how big of a deal it is to be able to maintain such a position of faith and trust.

As we wind down the school year, we are making plans for summer home visits, the annual camping trip to the mountains of North Carolina, and other important summer activities and vocational opportunities. As we interview several boys over the next week, we are hopeful to introduce some new faces to our summer. Krista and the Rodeheaver Foundation have secured several grants for us to use for our summer programs. Thank you all for the continued support. I hope to see some of you at our Golf Tournament on Saturday, May 23rd.
Brad Hall
Executive Director

Ranch Record - 5/29/20

The past week has been a blessed time and worth celebrating in this newsletter. So please allow me the next few moments to boast a little...

Thursday night we celebrated the high school graduation of Brandon Mathews. Brandon has been with RBR for several years and has spent time in every cottage. He has made an impact on every staff member

and all those he has come in contact with. Most of you know Brandon and his brother Chris well. We celebrated this milestone last night with a "Fiesta" themed diner. Barbara and Mark prepared a fabulous mexican dinner and the dining hall was decorated. Brandon's grandparents were able to come and they sat with Brandon. This was especially meaningful since they have been in poor health. Brandon opened cards and gifts from staff, other children, and many cards that you sent. He was so excited. It was indeed a happy time. We look forward to Brandon's next steps as he has been accepted into the ARC nursing program with St Johns River State College beginning in July.

On Wednesday night of this week, the boys under the direction of Serena Logue, put together a staff appreciation dinner. They prepared the meal, decorated the dining hall, prepared a program of entertainment, served us, and finished the night with a moving time of sharing where each boy came up and shared special thoughts about a particular staff member. Lots of tears were shed and laughter was shared. What a great night!

This week also marked the end of the school year. Erin Marsee, our tutor, has done such a great job leading us in this time. She reported that all of our boys had worked hard and improved their grades this semester. There were no D's or F's on the final grades. This is definitely worth celebrating! Our cottage parents and entire staff are to be commended for putting in extra effort to complete online education for all of our students.

This past Monday was a special Memorial Day at RBR. We started the day with a fun run 5K race down Ranch Road. This was our salute to those who gave all. This race takes on a whole new meaning now because as we approach the finish line at the

river, we run past the Tech Sgt. Timothy Officer Memorial Obstacle Course. We are all so grateful for the sacrifice of those like Tim and his family.

Memorial Day festivities continued with a lunch together before we all gathered in the Activities Center for the Pinewood Derby. The boys (and some staff) have been working on their cars for the past month. They raced in different age brackets, earned trophies, and also competed for best in show. Our very own office assistant, Sara Josephson, earned the overall fastest car trophy! It was so much fun and the boys were all good sports about the competition.

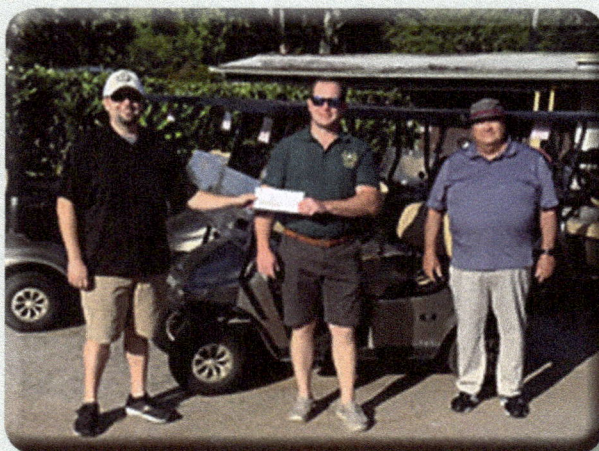

Last Saturday, the annual Golf Tournament was held. We had 19 teams and raised over $6,100 so far. Special thanks to the Palatka Golf Club and the St. Johns River Christian Golf Fellowship for sponsoring this event. I'd also like to mention Jeff King and Ken Johnson played an important role in organizing everything and the membership of Christ Independent Methodist Church provided several volunteers along with great desserts to go with the lunches the Ranch prepared.

The boys continued flying lessons this week with kidsflycubs.org. I hope you can follow this great organization on Facebook and see the absolutely beautiful pictures of RBR boys flying for the first time! We are thankful for this partnership and also would like to thank the Palatka Municipal Airport for being the base for this exciting program.

I also want to brag on a special group of volunteers who have just completed a building project on Ranch. John and Marsha Holley along with volunteers from First Baptist Church of Palatka built a nice new deck

for the entrance to the Lodge under the big pavilion. This was a needed project to construct a deck that no longer has to be moved for bluegrass events. It also now meets regulations for safety with a nice sturdy railing. If you see the Holley's or members from First Baptist Palatka, please tell them thanks. This deck, which would have cost thousands of dollars of labor to construct, was built at material cost for less than $800.

Lastly, I want to let you know that we are working hard in the office to bring in new boys and begin to grow our numbers through the summer. While we have seen some boys leave or complete our program this month, we have also interviewed several boys & families for admittance in the next month. I expect four or five new boys in June and July followed by a larger group beginning in August before school starts. Serena Logue has worked diligently to get all of this arranged while also preparing us for our next annual FACCCA inspection on July 31st.

Thank you all for your continued support of the Ranch (and to me personally)!

Brad Hall
Executive Director

In conjunction with her role as Director of Training, Serena Logue stepped up to help the Ranch staff and boys in so many ways, including putting her excellent organizational and study skills into informative power point presentations during the weekly staff meetings. One such presentation featured warm, caring encouragement as well as professional training tips to cottage parents, some of which follow (excerpted):

Support: Please utilize relief cottage parents, Scot, myself, etc. if you are feeling burnt out, stressed, feeling like you need some with your kids, etc., and need a couple of hours to yourselves! Someone can hang out and shoot hoops or something with the boys one afternoon after school, or a weekend night, especially if for some reason you are on duty for longer than typically scheduled. Self-care is vital to giving the boys our best, so please, please communicate if you need some extra support.

> *Love Covers a Multitude of Sins: Another key to success is our demeanor. People who are perceived as warm, energetic, considerate, positive, concerned and genuine are usually highly effective in any interaction because they are enjoyable to be with. [Loving] traits are learned through life experiences and can be hard to describe in objective, teachable terms. There are, however, a few observable behaviors ... pleasant facial expressions, gestures or statements of affection, humor, body positions, etc.. The degree to which staff members incorporate these behaviors into their teaching determines to a large extent how well a youth will respond to the content of what is being taught.*
>
> *Direct Teaching Approach:*
> 1. *Initial Praise, Empathy or Affection*
> 2. *Description/Demonstration of Inappropriate Behavior*
> 3. *Consequences: Loss of Privilege or Natural Consequence, then a Positive Correctional Statement*
> 4. *Description/Demonstration of Appropriate Behavior*
> 5. *Rationale*
> 6. *Requests for Acknowledgment*
> 7. *Practice*
> 8. *Feedback (Praise, Specific Description/Demonstration, Positive Consequence)*
> 9. *Praise Throughout the Interaction*
>
> *Roleplays follow, including all of the 9 Teaching Approaches*

Having researched studies into the adolescent brain, Serena presented a video about Brain Science and the fact that scientific neuroimaging demonstrates a period of continued brain growth and change during and after puberty. She quoted studies and articles, giving handouts to the staff for study and reference, and then got down to the basics of "Choosing Appropriate Words to Say." Serena wrote:

> • *The Ranch boys (and all kids ... adults too!) will undoubtedly say things that are impulsive, unkind, inappropriate, offensive, etc. etc. etc.! (of course, in addition to all of the funny, charming, kind words they often use). These are our opportunities to teach!*
> • *There are differing views on whether the teenage brain is not fully developed, thus has a deficiency that prevents a teen from thinking*

before he speaks or acts, or if it is simply part of the "normal" teenage development and experience to be "risk takers" and impulsive, both with words and actions.

- Researchers agree that either way, teenagers are still responsible for their own actions. While the adolescent brain is different from both a child's and an adult's brain, teenagers do not automatically have a loss of control, and are quite capable of making rational decisions. (Galatians 5:22-23 But the fruit of the Spirit is love, joy, peace, longsuffering, gentleness, goodness, faith, 23 Meekness, temperance: against such there is no law.(KJV)

How to choose appropriate words:
1. Look at the situation and the people around you.
2. Know the meaning of words you are about to say.
3. Refrain from using words that will offend people around you, or that they will not understand.
4. Avoid using slang, profanity or words that could have a sexual meaning.
5. Decide what thought you want to put into words and then say the words.

Suggestions for teaching ...

- New boys who come from a household and environment where using inappropriate words is commonplace will need steady, consistent teaching so he can "relearn" what appropriate words and conversations look like.
- Boys who struggle with name-calling, such as "gay," "retard," "fag," etc., should be reminded about this skill. These words and offensive words like them should not be tolerated on the Ranch. Even words like "moron," "dumb/stupid," "idiot," are not edifying and should be discouraged as the boys interact with one another.
- The best thing we can do is model this skill, and all conversation skills, around the boys. Staff should not be using inappropriate language or slang that could be viewed as offensive.
- This skill has some great steps to it, so it can be utilized during a "structured work" time when a boy has been given an assignment to think about some choices he's made. He could write out the steps to it, or give examples of positive words that he could have said in place of the negative ones, etc.
- There are many other skills and principles that have to do with our speech, conversation, etc. Words are a huge part of life, society and relationships (Ex: Initiating a Conversation, Disagreeing Appropriately, Expressing Empathy for Others).

God said it First!
- **Ephesians 4:29: Do not let any unwholesome talk come out of your mouths, but only what is helpful for building others up according to their needs, that it may benefit those who listen.**
- **Proverbs 17: 27-28: He who has knowledge restrains and is careful with his words, and a man of understanding and wisdom has a cool spirit (self-control, an even temper). Even a [callous, ignorant] fool, when he keeps silent, is considered wise; when he closes his lips he is regarded as sensible [prudent, discreet] and a man of understanding.**
- **James 3:9-12: With the tongue we praise our Lord and Father, and with it we curse human beings, who have been made in God's likeness. Out of the same mouth come praise and cursing. My brothers and sisters, this should not be. Can both fresh water and salt water flow from the same spring? My brothers and sisters, can a fig tree bear olives, or a grapefruit bear figs? Neither can a salt spring produce fresh water.**

On June 19th, Brad wrote an unusual Ranch Record, describing a severe storm the night before that began with hail and then heavy rain and wind. It felled some trees, caused tree limbs and metal debris to be strewn from pillar to post as well a loss of power until the next day. The roof of the Lodge and the door of the VIP building were damaged and the little Bluegrass Ticket building was thrown through the fence into the RV Park, with pieces of it scattered all the way to the horse paddocks. No living beings at the Ranch were injured and Brad thanked the Lord for His protection. On a more positive note, two new Ranch boys were welcomed that week, Tristan and Jamaar, both energetic and happy to be there. Each grew up in foster care, were eventually adopted and endured emotional and behavioral issues toward their adoptive parents. Different ages and from different places, each of the boys was placed at the Ranch in order to find their God-given identity and purpose. "We have a goal of working with them and their families to gain maturity and stability in their life through our program of spiritual, educational and vocational training," wrote Brad.

On another positive note, June 20th was the 14th anniversary of Sara Josephson's excellent work at Rodeheaver Boys Ranch as the Executive Administrative Assistant who is very often the first voice a person hears when they call the Ranch. Sara's loyalty to the Ranch and her active participation in Ranch activities like the Pinewood Derby, the bluegrass festivals, the holiday parties, etc. is appreciated by all of the staff and boys. Her 14th anniversary was celebrated by all who work with her.

**Sara Josephson
14 Years at the Ranch!**

Marie Watts

Bookkeeper Marie Watts recently celebrated her fifth anniversary of serving the Ranch. Her work is exemplary and she, like Sara, is devoted to the wellbeing of the Ranch.

When considering long-term commitment and loyalty, Brad holds a staff meeting, once weekly, with teaching lessons such as Serena Logue's presentation previously outlined. At a recent staff meeting, Pastor Ted Stackpole, a U.S. Missionary on assignment with Compact Family Services of the Assembly of God. Ted and his wife, Angie, have eleven children, several of whom were previously their foster children and are now adopted. The Stackpoles are well known and loved in Putnam County as U.S. Missionary Chaplains who specialize in supporting the foster care community at home and across the United States. Ted spoke to the Rodeheaver Boys Ranch staff about the challenges that come with RBR's ministry of teaching and nurturing boys, many of whom have experienced trauma. He was a great encourager to the staff.

Zach and LeeAnn Bonds, Phillips Cottage Parents, were among those staff members who received encouragement from Ted Stackpole, and when asked to give an update on how their ministry as cottage parents has progressed since they arrived in January 2020, LeeAnn wrote the following:

"Our lives have changed immensely since coming to Rodeheaver. We had already survived several plunges into the deep end of the pool as Relief Parents. These four-day stints in different cottages scared us a bit, taught us a lot, and gave us ideas about what our own Cottage Parent style might look like. Starting off slowly in Phillips Cottage, we cared for just two boys for a while. Then the Ranch rearranged the cottage populations, and overnight we were full-blown Cottage Parents caring for eight boys, ages 11 to 17.

We've learned more than we ever thought possible about the many ways a boy can wriggle around a rule and into your heart. About the plethora of uses for couch cushions beyond product concept. About fads that blaze through the ranch, like modifying bikes, wearing crocs with jibbets on them, or currently, in our cottage, poking holes in the lid of a box and catching lizards and grasshoppers to keep as pets. We've learned about the endless necessary paperwork and regulations, about critical relationships with the various schools in town, doctors' and dentists' offices, donors, and many other local folks who support the work we do here.

We are still learning how to love these brokenhearted boys and teach them how to make their way in this big, scary world. And we're learning how to introduce them to the Source of peace, strength, love and comfort who can carry them through life's joys and sorrows long after they leave us behind."

Ranch Record - 7/3/20

Happy Independence Day! It's a blessing to live in the USA and to experience the freedoms that our forefathers envisioned. I know they didn't envision things like Coronavirus, wearing face masks in public, or stay-at-home orders, but in spite of this inconvenience, we still are blessed like few people in the world to live in this constitutional republic.

The hot "dog days" of summer have officially arrived at the Ranch. It's a real challenge to keep up with all the mowing and trimming. Many boys are going on home visits today to see their families for the 4th. They will stay a week and be back in time to catch up on mowing before we leave for our annual camping trip in the mountains of North Carolina. We are grateful for the grant we received through the Rodeheaver Foundation for this trip and our other Summer activities.

Our next car auction will be on Monday, July 13th. We have been getting lots of donations this month. We also are happy to see our vocational programs get up and running consistently. New this summer are welding and art classes. These are in addition to woodworking, automotive, and equestrian. It's great to see how the boys love to work with their hands. Many of them have never done more than push buttons on a video game controller. When they realize they can create, build, and repair things, you see many of their insecurities start to disappear.

Thank you all for your continued support during these times. We are seeing the need for RBR amplified in our times. Boys are struggling and families are reaching out to us for help! It is so good to know that because of you, we can continue to offer our services without charge. While many families agree to give what they can afford, most would never be able to pay the full cost for a program like this. I pray we will continue to receive support so we can stay an option for all boys regardless of where they come from.

Brad Hall
Executive Director

Brad observed that the boys lose many of their insecurities when they realize they can create, build and repair things with their hands; he has seen this happen often, especially since he initiated his RBR Jobs Program a few months ago.

RBR JOBS PROGRAM

The purpose of the RBR Jobs Program is to provide real training in applying, interviewing, training and holding a part-time job in preparation for gainful employment as an adult.

Jobs

While staff and volunteers can fulfill many roles, there are specific jobs that are good vocational learning opportunities for teenage boys. Jobs in janitorial, food service, landscaping, lawn care, auto service & detailing, painting, animal care, clerical, etc. are examples of some jobs our boys can do. These are hourly jobs, but school and church/chapel will always have priority. Household chores will still be assigned and carried out even if the boy has a job.

Applications

Boys will be able to pick up applications for posted jobs in the office and will work with cottage parents to learn how to fill out an application and in some cases prepare and present a resume.

Interviews

After applying for a job, boys will be called in to interview for the position with the Ranch Life Director and a designated staff supervisor.

Training

Boys who earn jobs will be trained and supervised by a designated staff member to successfully carry out the job description. Performance evaluations will be given at regular intervals.

Rewards

The jobs program will seek to teach the boys how to earn and manage money. Boys will keep track of their earnings through a savings account and as they get older through a checking account. The jobs will start at minimum wage, and give raises based on performance and consistency. For example, a boy who starts at $8.56 per hour can be raised to $9.00 per hour if he shows responsibility and is not late for work over a period of several months. We want the boys to learn the value of working their way up instead of expecting something for nothing.

Funding

The budget for the vocational program will come from a combination of general funds and designated donations. Sponsors will also be sought who see value in such a program. Their pay will be added to their allowance, so they will not be "employees" of the Ranch.

It's better to build a boy who knows how to work
than to provide social welfare for a man who doesn't.

On July 4, 2020 – America's Independence Day – Brad's message on Facebook pulsed with meaning and passion:

God and Country. I was told that you shouldn't put those two things together. But without God we wouldn't have this country. I don't think it's wrong to acknowledge that - even as we assemble in our houses of worship on Sunday. Decorating a church in Red, White, and Blue and singing patriotic hymns may be interpreted as idolatry if the object of our adoration becomes skewed toward a nation over God. But if it's one nation under God, and the object of our thanksgiving and praise is the LORD, then God is glorified by our prayers, our songs, and our proclamation of His Providence and Sovereignty - of His evidenced mercies and abundant grace.

Randy Moore - God Bless America!

Also, on July 4, 2020, a young mentee of Brad's, Dakota Breed, produced a fabulous video featuring the Ranch's Wrangler, Randy Moore, singing God Bless America and a group of Rodeheaver Boys Ranch horse riders, with Randy in the lead proudly carrying the American Flag. It was a great tribute to our country and our Ranch, and beautifully produced.

Morning Horseback Riding before the heat of the day

Ranch Record - 7/27/20

All work and no play makes a dull boy. We are in the midst of a busy season at Rodeheaver Boys Ranch. While there's always work to do, we took a week and went to North Carolina for a great time of hiking and rafting in the Smoky Mountains. Our staff worked hard to put this trip together and pull it off while staying safe and socially distanced. Then we came back to the Ranch and spent several days catching up on mowing and trimming. Everything is looking good.

This week we are preparing for our annual FACCCA licensing inspection. Our paperwork, policy manuals, records, houses, and property have to be in top shape so we can continue our great reputation of operating a safe and secure program. This has been a little more challenging this year as we made many adjustments to stay in compliance with the changing child care regulations and COVID-19 suggestions.

Rodeheaver Boys Ranch is 😌 feeling blessed in **Scaly Mountain, North Carolina**.
July 18 · 🌐

Greetings from the pinnacle of Scaly Mountain, North Carolina! Today the boys hiked a little over four miles to the summit and back down Scaly Mountain.
Following the hike and a quick lunch in the parking area, the group cooled off with a swim in the cool waterfalls of the Cullassja River.

All of us at Rodeheaver Boys Ranch and Rodeheaver Foundation would like to thank our generous donors for their gracious support towards our Summer Activities Program. The boys are having a BLAST!! 😊

👍❤️ 55   4 Comments 7 Shares

👍 Like   💬 Comment   ➤ Share

We are now interviewing to hire a new set of house parents. There is nothing we do more important than making sure we have good, service-minded couples in our houses. I've also interviewed a state Licensed Mental Health Counselor (LMHC) from Melrose who wants to come to work for us. If this works out, we will be well equipped to minister to the needs of these boys and their families. I am a trained Biblical Counselor (spiritual), Scot Collins is an experienced Guidance Counselor (vocational/ educational), and if we add a LMHC who can help us with the specific social and emotional issues these boys are dealing with, we will be able to provide counseling in three different areas of development. Please keep us in prayer at this time and ask the Lord to give us great wisdom and grace in these decisions.

Brad Hall
Executive Director

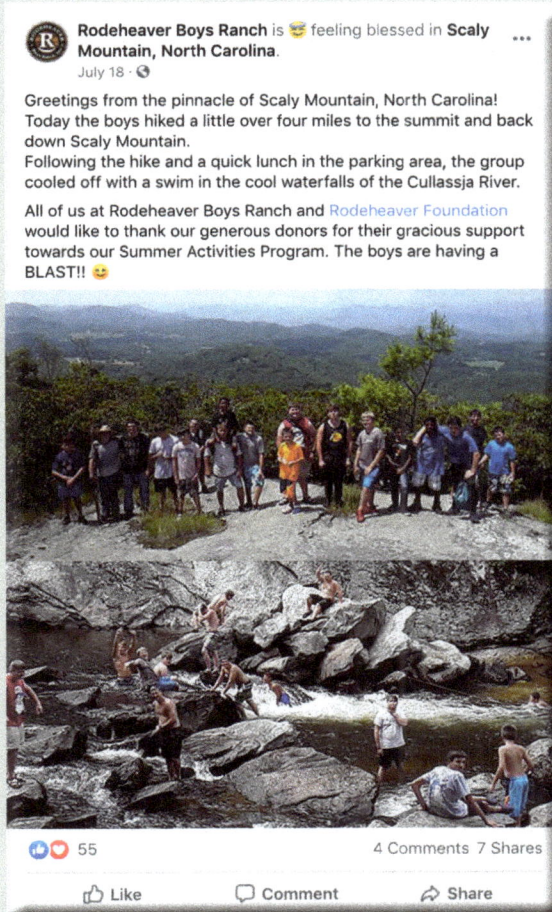

During the writing of this 70th Anniversary Edition of the Rodeheaver Boys Ranch history, a plea went out to current Ranch boys for a few words on what the Ranch has meant in their lives. Here are some of their responses:

"This ranch helped me become a man. I also feel like the ranch helped me with public speaking and also with cleaning."

*Daniel has since returned to his family, a young man who has gained a great deal of confidence and self-discipline as a result of Rodeheaver Boys Ranch.

Daniel McNair

Brandon Mathews

"My story is when I first got here, I was 12. Now I'm 17.* I like the ranch a lot. It has helped me get through tough times. No matter how hard it got they were always there for me. I have been at the ranch for 6 years. So, since 7th grade I've been at the ranch and now I'm in 12th grade.* The ranch has helped me by teaching me how to raise pigs. It has also taught me how to save money and plan for the future. Now I'm trying to get a car so I can drive to college. I'm going to college and the ranch is trying to help me get in college so I can get my AA in nursing. Those are my plans and that is what the ranch did for me."

*Brandon is now 18 years old and has graduated from Palatka High School

"My name is William Tyndale and I live at Rodeheaver Boys Ranch and this is how the ranch has helped me. The ranch now has provided an environment where I can have my religious beliefs and pray to God. I have gotten and still am in the pig program. It's taught me hard work and to connect with animals. I have learned self-control and to get closer with the Lord. Thanks for your time."

William Tyndale

Caleb Arnold

"Hello, my name is Caleb Arnold. I have been in Rodeheaver Boys Ranch for six months. I am 15 and in the 8th grade. The greatest thing I have experienced on the ranch is getting to work with the horses. They have taught me a lot. Also, while being here I have taken care of my pig named Oliver. I am very thankful for the ranch and everything they have done for me and my brother. And lastly, I am very thankful for my cottage mom and dad."

I came to Rodeheaver Boys Ranch to improve in school and work on my relationship with my family. I enjoy the sports activities at RBR and really like playing basketball. I have learned responsibility since being here. I have also got to learn how to do blacksmithing and play the guitar. I hope to keep improving in school and my goal is to study sports medicine at Duke University. I would tell other boys thinking of coming here that it is important to get along with others. Be prepared to work but also know that jobs here can be fun.

Bryce Fisher
"Louisiana Boy"

Christian Ibanez
"One Tough Kid"

I came to Rodeheaver Boys Ranch because I had trouble getting along with my family and had been fighting. Coming to RBR was a better opportunity for me. Mrs. Terrie Collins has been like a second grandma to me. She has helped me and is my favorite part of RBR. I have been learning how to take care of and ride horses. I also have learned welding and woodshop. I now know how to do chores like making my bed and doing my own laundry, which is not that bad. I want to keep improving in school and play football. My life goal is to be a Marine. I also want to have a better relationship with my family. Being at RBR is helping me meet those goals.

The Bluegrass Festival planning is underway for February 2021. Ernie Evans is thrilled to be planning the November Bluegrass Festival at Rodeheaver Boys Ranch, and will do everything he can to make it as safe and enjoyable as it can be!

Ernie and Debi Evans of Evans Media Source – New Bluegrass Festival Owners

"Rodeheaver Boys Ranch and its staff have become much more than an event to us, said Ernie Evans. "We found out quickly that they are a partner that will allow us to develop creativity where the sky is the limit. This is not only an event producer's dream but the opportunity could not have come along at a better time in our lives. The next bluegrass festival will be proof of that. Everybody wins."

The boys always look forward to the Bluegrass Festivals. In the meantime, they are keeping busy with many activities that enhance their growth and knowledge day by day at the Ranch. One of those activities is learning the art of welding from retired professional welder, Paul Clark, another dedicated Ranch volunteer.

Paul Clark was on a Christian Men's Ride (motorcycles) and was talking with Steve Logue and Scot Collins, who were Riders and also on the Ranch

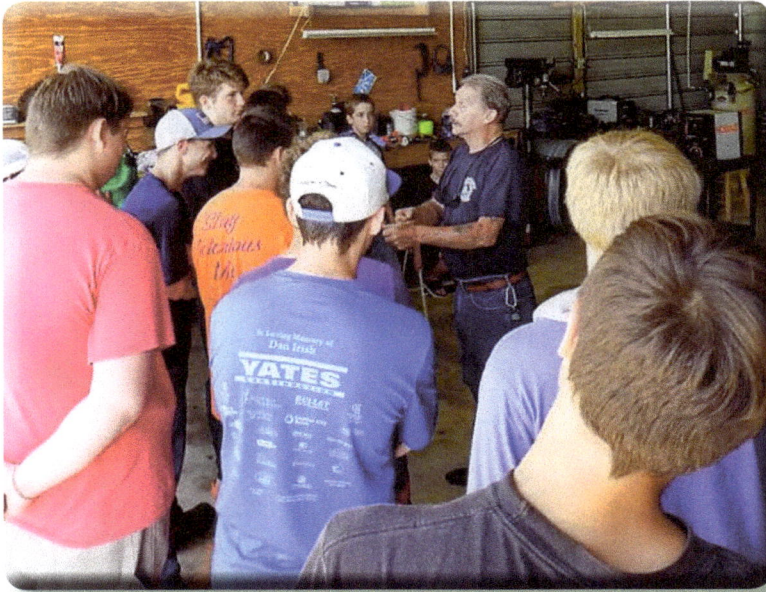

Paul Clark – Introduction to Welding Class

staff. The possibility of him teaching the boys to weld came up in conversation after Paul mentioned that he had welded all his life and was now volunteering at the Bread of Life Ministry, feeding the need twice a week. Now retired, Paul has worked all over the world as a welder and was eager to teach young men how to do what he does so well. "Even if they never become professional welders, they'll be able to weld their children's bicycles someday, and if one young man chooses to do it for a living, I'll have been part of his future," said Paul. "The staff at Rodeheaver is so appreciative, they make you feel right at home. I've got five boys in the first class and six in the second one, and I'm just being myself and doing what I love to do. God's got His Hand on my shoulder."

And, speaking of feeling right at home, Karen Hall is beginning to take on some of the activities that so endeared her predecessor, Lois Johnson, to the boys and the Ranch staff ... activities such as tending the blueberries, making jams and jellies, and being in charge of the Ranch Store. In addition, Karen is planning to help bring the Ranch Museum up to date and add features to it that were not there before. Karen is also considering taking on the job of tutoring the boys after school. Having taught pre-school for eight years as well as Sunday School and Bible School, she is eminently qualified to do this. "I'll help out wherever I'm needed," she says, as her proud husband, Brad, urges her to show off her talents at quilting and painting. A long-time quilter, Karen also enjoys painting on rustic pieces of wood, which she will place in the Ranch Store for sale to benefit the Ranch. As a get well gift, one of her painted wood

Micah, Brad, Karen (holding her art) and Hannah Hall

pieces went straight to the heart of Philip Barnes, the graphic designer for this 70th Anniversary Book, who recently underwent cancer surgery. In a message of thanks, Philip wrote: "I see love and healing powers sent my way from the Father, Son, and Holy Spirit, and I love the archway at the bottom because that's where I can go in. Karen, your art will have a special place in my home!"

On July 22, 2020, after bragging about his wife, Karen's wonderful art, Brad boasted just as happily about another new boy who recently came to the Ranch. His name is Tristan Thomas and he is 15 years old. Tristan rode his bike by the Ranch Store while Brad and Karen were sitting outside and Brad called him over to meet a visitor. Tristan was friendly and not the least bit shy about saying that Rodeheaver Boys Ranch was a dream come true for him, after memories of years in foster care. Adopted at the age of 4, Tristan remembers

Brad with Tristan Thomas

being in one foster care home where there were 24 children. He loves his adoptive parents but still has some issues to work through and the Ranch is the perfect place for him to do that. Tristan says he loves everything about the Ranch (except the chores, of course) ... but he willingly took off on his bike to finish his chores when Brad reminded him. "Tristan is adjusting well to life on the Ranch," said Brad. "He's a good boy."

Artist and teacher Bonnie Sieta is another dedicated volunteer at the Ranch who comes out and works with the boys on art projects. Bonnie described why she does what she does:

Bonnie Sieta

"My passion for sharing art with kids has developed over many years. I have learned that creating art in its various forms while meditating in some fashion on God's love for me is an incredible, therapeutic way to relax, process my thoughts, and find inner healing. I am a self-taught artist and love to work with all kinds of art mediums, and although I am not great at everything, I sure have fun with it! As a survivor of multiple childhood traumas, I understand well what many troubled youth experience. I struggled for years to find peace

and nearly lost my own life running down the wrong roads. Working with expressive arts as a teenager always helped me to find my focus and regain confidence during stressful times. Often, I would find myself sketching and before I knew it, the world would just melt away. Coming to know Jesus Christ as my personal Savior at the age of 16 was the great turning point in my life. Later, as I realized the potential to help stabilize troubled youth by combining the arts with a Christian foundation, my heart became all wrapped up in the desire to bring the art-life to troubled kids while sharing the hope found in God's love through Christ. Being a part of building in an integrated art program for the youth at the Rodeheaver Boys Ranch is an honor and a huge blessing back to my heart. I love these kids and I am thankful beyond words to be a part of their lives."

Austin masters the string trimmer

Attached is a picture of what we do at RBR. Austin is a brand new resident who came to us Monday. He will be twelve years old in a couple of weeks. He is probably the smallest boy on the ranch in terms of size and experience. One of our house parents showed him how to run a string trimmer for the first time Wednesday. After about 5 minutes of instruction, Austin pulled the rope for the first time on his own and the trimmer rumbled to life! Austin smiled as his house parent in this picture walked with him showing him how to trim along the sidewalk. It was a hot day. No one really wanted to be outside working. But this will be a day that Austin will never forget!

I can remember the first time I mowed the yard with my dad ... my first round driving the old Snapper riding mower by myself - running it into a fence - then running and crying to my dad, who helped me get it out of the fence and back in line. I remember the first time I used a string trimmer ... then years later having my own mowing business while still in high school and making enough money to take care of my needs during my senior year when my dad was out of work. I bet he remembered showing me how to mow and recognized that his time teaching me helped us both out in a time of need.

Rodeheaver Boys Ranch is more than an institution. It's more than a program. It's a place where futures are made. It's a place where God takes men and women and puts them with boys for a purpose that we don't yet see. I just want to take a moment to thank you all for your support and for giving of your time, talents, and treasure for the futures of these boys. During this trying time of pandemics and political wranglings, aren't you glad we can still make a difference in our future by investing in our children?

Just a couple of notes of importance: We have our monthly vehicle fundraiser auction this Monday, August 10th. The auction will start at 10:00 AM this month to beat the heat. Also, we have had to institute a strict set of health and safety precautions on Ranch due to a boy who may have been exposed to the COVID-19 virus last week. I am working with the Health Department and following all recommendations of isolation and separation until we can be sure he doesn't have it. Please join us in praying that we can stay healthy during this time.*
Brad Hall
Executive Director

*On August 12, 2020 – Brad Hall sent out the following message:

Just a quick update to say "Praise the Lord!" for some good things at the Ranch. Our boy who was in isolation returned a negative test for COVID-19 this week. So we are all healthy. Also, we had a great auction on Monday with $97,000 in sales.
Brad Hall
Executive Director

NEWEST MEMBERS OF OUR RANCH FAMILY

Everett and Ashley Neely

Everett and Ashley Neely are the newest cottage parents at Rodeheaver Boys Ranch, having started their employment on September 1, 2020. Both in their early 20s, the young couple met in church and have been married for just over a year. Everett, an evangelist and multi-talented musician, jokes that he was "born

in the back pew" of the First Assembly of God Church in Palatka (now the Church of the Heights), and has been groomed all of his life to do the ministry of caring for the boys at Rodeheaver Boys Ranch. "Ashley and I are training to be cottage parents full-time - working as relief parents right now - and we're looking forward to having boys of our own at Westbury Cottage."

The Neely's came highly recommended by Pastor Ted Stackpole, their former senior pastor at Palatka's First Assembly of God Church and the pastor who married them. "Pastor Stackpole knows us," said Ashley. "He knows that we love the Lord and the children."

Neither of them had ever been out to Rodeheaver Boys Ranch, even though they had grown up in Palatka, and they were thrilled with what they found when they came for the first time. "I had a preconceived notion about the Ranch - that it was like a prison camp for boys," said Everett. "It's exactly the opposite! There are so many opportunities for these boys - it's a great alternative to foster care. My first thought when I toured the Ranch was, 'This is fun!"

Everett has discovered other musicians among the staff members and they are already contemplating a Chapel Worship Team. As to their readiness to act as cottage parents, Ashley and Everett both grew up in large families and feel comfortable about acting as role models and parents of the boys. "I come from a long line of teachers and preachers," said Ashley. "Teaching is in my blood and in my heart. Even though we're only about six years older than the oldest boys here, they already see us as authority figures and we feel that they respect us. Everyone here has encouraged and welcomed us. We plan to stay here at the Ranch for as long as God wants us to be here."

Susan Wilson, LMHC, believes that God is the Ultimate Healer. She came to the Ranch as the new Child Care Counselor in September of 2020, and has been prepared to help the boys and staff at Rodeheaver Boys Ranch by both her vast and versatile experience as a counselor and her Christian faith. Susan has been a counselor and an educator in schools; homes; residential facilities; outpatient mental health facilities; substance abuse facilities, and even in the tourist industry. She notes that "Train a child up right in the way he should go and he will not stray from it when he is older" (Proverbs 22:6) is a core Biblical principal in childrearing, but many youth of today lack the role models, training, or even family involvement to help them on their journey. It truly does take a village, or in our case, a Ranch to raise a child. She looks forward to helping our youth develop their emotional

Susan Wilson

health, their relationships with others, and God; as addressing their spiritual health needs are often not afforded in secular counseling and are essential.

Susan will be on hand to listen and help in the development of core skills, such as: communication skills; coping skills; anger management; emotion regulation; responsibility; making good choices; establishing goals; learning that all choices have consequences/rewards ... Many of these basic life skills will be offered to teens individual; in small groups; with their house parents and cottage families; and with their biological families when they transition from the Ranch. "I will be an integral part of the admission and discharge processes at the Ranch, as well as helping in linking them to outside resources if needed," says Susan. "I believe that family needs to be involved in the transition planning, especially for youth who are not aging out of Ranch life but are successfully completing their stay at the Ranch."

She will be working with cottage staff and parents on conflict resolution and specific strategies to address difficult youth behaviors. Susan will also provide monthly mini trainings to staff as well as helping with their everyday concerns. "I am excited and blessed to be part of the Rodeheaver Family," says Susan, "and look forward to continuing to help serve the boys and staff."

There is a great deal more to our new Food Service Assistant Eric Bryant than meets the eye! Tall and lean, with a smile that is as wide and friendly as

Eric Bryant

it can be, Eric is a bright presence in the dining hall – where hungry boys consume wholesome food and are eager to be greeted with good cheer at the end of their day.

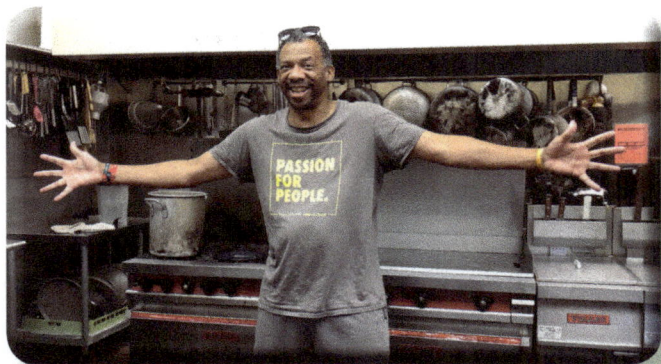

There's a twinkle in Eric's eyes, though, that indicates he has a delightful secret to share ... and that secret is now out ... Eric is an innovator who invented a game called "Mini Ball Courts," a virtual reality basketball game played on actual mini-printed NBA courts ... "coming to a Printer Near You," and available on Amazon.com. He is also an "IT Guy," and may one day expand his Ranch work beyond the kitchen and into the computer room.

Eric loves shooting hoops with the boys and enjoys playing volleyball and going to the pool with them. As with all of our newest Ranch family members, Eric Bryant is a gifted child of God.

On Sunday, August 30, 2020, Former Ranch boy Shawn Turberville returned after eight years away, having been at the Ranch from 2009 to 2012. Since leaving the Ranch at age 16, Shawn has led an extremely challenging life, often veering away from but always returning to the Christian principles he learned

Shawn Turberville

as a Ranch boy. Recently, he was dramatically reminded about the value of friendship when two old friends from the Ranch died untimely deaths. The tragic loss of two former Ranch boys under unfortunate circumstances has haunted Shawn and several other young men who remember them fondly from their days at the Ranch.

Arriving at the Ranch with his family, wife Victoria, 2-year old son, Brookston Alexander Turberville, and one-month old daughter, Freya Sawyer Turberville, Shawn was excited to return and eager to share his Christian testimony and memories of the Ranch at the Sunday evening chapel service. He was determined to convey to the boys how blessed they are to be here and how important it is to learn what the Ranch has to teach them.

Wearing his fatigues and Army boots, Shawn proudly displayed his decorated U.S. Army uniform and his official Army photograph as he reminisced about

his days at the Ranch and spoke of the two friends he will not see again. He talked of John, who was small and full of fun, and Julio who was from a tough neighborhood but was incredibly generous to others. He talked of cottage parents like Teddie and Elizabeth Betonio and Scott and Susan Phillips, and a special

mentor, the late Richard Cooper. He talked of adventures at the Ranch, hunting in South Carolina, and hiking at Philmont Boy Scout Ranch in New Mexico (one of the best times of his life!).

Shawn described coming to the Ranch at age 12 after being bounced from family member to family member because he was undisciplined and acting out. His biological mother had abandoned him and his father and step-mother didn't know what to do with him. When he came to the Ranch, he thought his depression and anxiety were at an end, but that was not to be. Over and over, his family rejected him – waiting until the last minute to inform him he was not coming for a home visit. His plight was one that many other boys experienced, and they eventually learned that the people they could depend on were right in front of them at the Ranch. "Take everything to the Lord, Shawn," Richard Cooper would tell him. Talking of memorization of Bible Verses at the Ranch, Shawn recited Romans 12:1-2 - I appeal to you therefore, brothers, by the mercies of God, to present your bodies as a living sacrifice, holy and acceptable to God, which is your spiritual worship.

Today, at age 25, a man of God, a well-traveled Army veteran, and a husband and father with a responsible job that supports his family, Shawn credits Rodeheaver Boys Ranch with teaching him the life and management

skills he employed as a soldier and now as a civilian. Through his Ranch family, he gained the insight to love his fellow man and learned the value of friendship and brotherhood. He told the boys to trust one another, adding that Faith and Trust are two keys to maturity. He also told them to "stay headstrong," demonstrating

how to walk with your head held high and always looking forward. Sadly, he noted that it took him nearly five years after leaving the Ranch to truly give himself to Christ. He was in a homeless shelter when he called his former Cottage Mom, Susan Phillips, and after talking for hours, she gave him the answer he needed to hear. "What you seem to be lacking, Shawn, is JESUS."

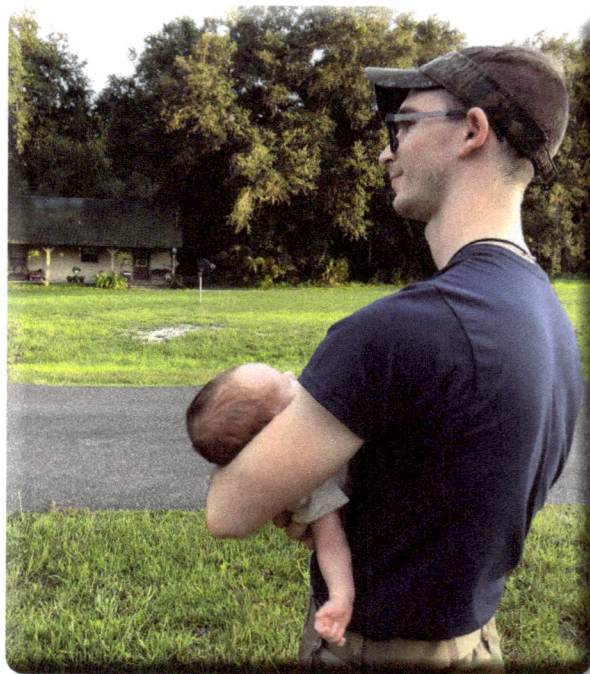

Shawn ended his testimony by telling the boys to never give up and never back down from the fight – stressing that he was talking about the internal emotional fight – the moral struggle involved in doing the right thing in the eyes of God. "I thank God on a daily basis for a place like this Ranch," he said. "Here, they truly do stick to their motto – it is better to build boys than to mend men. I'm thankful the Ranch taught me to become a man and to be a better father to my own children."

On September 29, 2020, Brad Hall penned a letter to Ranch "Pardners" and supporters inviting all to help celebrate the Ranch's 70th Harvest Year with a "Drive-Thru BBQ" on Sunday, November 1, 2020 – "a socially distanced drive through our beautiful campus and a chance to pick up a delicious pulled-pork BBQ plate!"

Brad wrote: "As we celebrate the harvest this year, we look back on 70 years of God's providence and bounty. This Ranch is a licensed child-care facility, but will always have a foundation in agriculture. Timber, cattle, horses, fruits and vegetables along with ongoing mowing and fencing will always be a part of what we do. We hope you will pray for us to prosper in our agricultural pursuits here. It takes a lot to keep all of this running. Would you take a moment and consider a contribution to help us maintain our harvest roots?"

We look forward to celebrating the Thanksgiving and Christmas Holidays in this challenging year of 2020 ... and then, on January 1, 2021, celebrating the first day of the next 70 years!!

Throughout this 70th Anniversary edition of the Rodeheaver Boys Ranch History, you have had the opportunity to take a detailed look into the long and fruitful life of the Ranch from the perspective of the founder, Homer Rodeheaver, the devoted "Pardners" over the years, and many of the boys who have benefited from their time here.

It is our hope and prayer that the Lord will continue to hold the Ranch in His loving hands for the next seventy years, or as long as there are boys who need our help in order to grow up and reach their full potential as Men of His Kingdom.

During the decades that Ken Johnson served as Executive Director of the Ranch, he often removed a small square of folded paper from his wallet, read the message to himself or to others present, and returned it to his wallet for safe-keeping. The powerful message, The Bridge Builder, by William Drum Goole, was one that always reminded Ken and others of the meaningful work they were doing for the boys. For those who read this book, Ken has once again shared his treasured, tattered, oft-folded and refolded message as follows:

THE BRIDGE BUILDER — WILLIAM DRUM GOOLE

An old man, traveling a lone highway,
Came at the evening cold and gray,
To a chasm vast and deep and wide.

The old man crossed in the twilight dim,
The sullen stream held no fears for him.
But he stopped when he reached the other side,
And built a bridge to span the tide.

"Old man," said a fellow pilgrim near,
"You are wasting your strength with building here,
Your journey will end with the ending day,
You never again will pass this way.

You have crossed the chasm deep and wide
Why build you a bridge at eventide?"
And the builder raised his old gray head:
"Good friend, on the path I have come," he said,
"There followed after me today
A youth whose feet will pass this way.

"This chasm, which has been as naught to me,
To that fair-haired boy may a pitfall be;
He, too, must cross in the twilight dim
Good friend, I am—
building this bridge for him."

WILL YOU BE A
BRIDGE BUILDER?

Rodeheaver Boys Ranch
380 Boys Ranch Road
Palatka, FL 32177
Phone: (386) 328-1281
Email: rodeheaverboys@gmail.com
Web: www.rbr.org

www.ingramcontent.com/pod-product-compliance
Lightning Source LLC
Chambersburg PA
CBHW040858100426

42813CB00015B/2844